Enterprise Resource Planning

D1560524

Enterprise Resource Planning

Mary Sumner

School of Business
Southern Illinois University Edwardsville

PEARSON
Prentice
Hall

Upper Saddle River, New Jersey 07458

Library of Congress Cataloging-in-Publication Data

Sumner, Mary.
  Enterprise resource planning / Mary Sumner.—1st ed.
    p. cm.
  Includes bibliographical references and index.
  ISBN 0-13-140343-5
  1. Business planning. 2. Management information systems. I. Title.

  HD30.28.S8925 2004
  658.4'012—dc22   2004018850

Executive Editor: Robert Horan
VP/Editorial Director: Jeff Shelstad
Project Manager: Lori Cerreto
Editorial Assistant: Robyn Goldenberg
Senior Media Project Manager: Nancy Welcher
Managing Editor: John Roberts
Production Editor: Suzanne Grappi
Production Manager, Manufacturing: Arnold Vila
Manufacturing Buyer: Indira Gutierrez
Cover Design Manager: Jayne Conte
Cover Design: Bruce Kenselaar
Composition/Full-Service Project Management: Interactive Composition Corporation
Printer/Binder:

Microsoft® and Windows® are registered trademarks of the Microsoft Corporation in the U.S.A. and other countries. Screen shots and icons reprinted with permission from the Microsoft Corporation. This book is not sponsored or endorsed by or affiliated with the Microsoft Corporation.

Pearson Education LTD.   Pearson Education Australia PTY, Limited
Pearson Education Singapore, Pte. Ltd   Pearson Education North Asia Ltd
Pearson Education, Canada, Ltd   Pearson Educación de Mexico, S.A. de C.V.
Pearson Education–Japan   Pearson Education Malaysia, Pte. Ltd

10 9 8 7 6 5 4 3 2 1
ISBN 0-13-140343-5

To my mother, Louise Roberts,
a great teacher for 67 years.

Brief Contents

Contents

Preface

Enterprise Resource Planning (ERP) systems represent a significant business investment. ERP systems can help to assure competitiveness, responsiveness to customer needs, productivity, and flexibility in doing business in a global economy. Implementing ERP enables companies to re-engineer business practices around "best practices" and to leverage integrated information resources. The success of ERP depends upon effective management, organizational change, and the use of advanced technology.

The underlying rationale for this text is that the successful implementation of ERP requires a set of skills and knowledge. To date, many ERP implementations have been less successful than planned, and noteworthy failures at companies such as FoxMeyer Drug have generated new questions about how to realize the value of ERP. Many ERP projects incur time and cost overruns. Many projects are driven by technology motivations instead of business justifications. Many companies fail to harness the full potential of ERP, and others fail to measure the business outcomes of the ERP investments they have made.

◆ WHAT THIS BOOK PROVIDES

The skills and knowledge you will gain from this text will enable you to address the challenge of successful ERP implementation. This text equips you with powerful tools that will make the difference between successful and unsuccessful projects. In a nutshell, these tools will enable you to address these issues:

- ✓ How do we make a business case for ERP?
- ✓ Should the firm re-engineer business processes to "fit" the ERP software, or customize the package?
- ✓ What are the ten ERP implementation steps?
- ✓ What are the components of ERP modules supporting sales and marketing? Accounting and finance? Production and materials management? Human resources?
- ✓ What are the risk factors associated with managing ERP projects?
- ✓ What strategies can be used to minimize these risk factors?
- ✓ What are the differences between successful and unsuccessful ERP projects?
- ✓ How does ERP facilitate supply chain management?
- ✓ How does ERP provide a foundation for eBusiness?
- ✓ How does ERP support business intelligence?
- ✓ What criteria should be used to evaluate alternative ERP delivery options, including Application Service Providers?

◆ HOW THIS BOOK IS ORGANIZED

The first three chapters provide theoretical foundations for understanding ERP and its evolution. The first chapter provides a rationale for integrated information systems by describing the business case for ERP. The second chapter describes how enterprise resource planning systems facilitate business process re-engineering and the redesign of business processes around "best practices." One of the most important issues to be addressed in ERP systems design is whether to re-engineer business processes to "fit" the software, or whether to customize the software to support existing business processes. The third chapter examines the trade-offs to be considered in deciding on re-engineering versus customizing.

The next four chapters deal with the ERP modules and their interrelationships. The discussion of ERP modules supporting functional areas includes sales and marketing (Chapter 4), accounting and finance (Chapter 5), production and materials management (Chapter 6), and human resources (Chapter 7). It is important to understand the interrelationships among these modules, and the text provides numerous examples of how integrated modules improve operational performance and provide shared information.

The final section of the book deals with the management of ERP projects and the future directions of ERP. Chapter 8 describes the unique risk factors that complicate ERP projects and how to minimize these risks. Chapter 9 describes the interrelationships between supply chain management and ERP, and between eBusiness and ERP. It also describes business intelligence and the emerging use of Application Service Providers for ERP acquisition.

◆ HOW TO USE THIS BOOK

This text is designed to give you the skills and knowledge you need to successfully plan, design, and implement ERP systems. In order to develop these capabilities you will participate in many problem-solving activities, which are provided in the end-of-chapter activities ("Questions for Discussion," "Cases," and "Featured Articles"), including:

✓ Conducting a needs assessment for ERP
✓ Conducting a re-engineering analysis
✓ Selecting an ERP vendor
✓ Analyzing ERP modules and their interrelationships
✓ Conducting a cost-benefit analysis
✓ Developing a project plan
✓ Analyzing ERP risk factors

In addition, the Integrated Case Study: Bandon Group, Inc., provides you with an opportunity to conduct a feasibility study for ERP. Based upon a business scenario, extensive management interviews, and competitive industry analysis, you will evaluate alternative ERP implementation options and recommend an appropriate

ERP strategy for a mid-market firm. The capstone case integrates material throughout the text.

ERP enables companies to align business strategy with information systems strategy. Learning how to implement and manage ERP projects is an important priority for organizations in most industries today. The skills and knowledge you will gain in this text will enable you to plan and develop ERP systems successfully.

◆ SUPPLEMENTS

This text is accompanied by a "Companion Website" www.prenhall.com/sumner where adopters can access the password-protected Instructor's Manual written by Mary Sumner. PowerPoint slides by Linda Fried, University of Colorado at Denver, are also available on this site, for students and faculty alike.

Acknowledgments

I would like to thank the following faculty for their time and efforts in providing valuable feedback as manuscript reviewers:

Behrouz Aslani, California Polytechnic University–Pomona

Susan C. Borkowski, La Salle University

Peter F. Brown, Duquesne University

Russell Fish, University of Washington

Ronald Lau, The Hong Kong University of Science and Technology

Paul J. Lazarony, California State University–Northridge

Yvonne Lederer Antonucci, Widener University

Nirup Menon, University of Texas–Dallas

Luvai Motiwalla, University of Massachusetts–Lowell

Judy Scott, University of Colorado–Denver

Mohammad Shariat, Florida A&M University

Mary Sumner
Southern Illinois University Edwardsville
May 2004

bout the Author

Mary Sumner is Professor of Computer Management and Information Systems and Associate Dean of the School of Business at Southern Illinois University Edwardsville. She directs the undergraduate CMIS program and teaches undergraduate and graduate courses in Software Systems Design, Business Systems Design, Enterprise Resource Planning, and Management Information Systems. She has over 25 years of teaching experience at New York University, Washington University, and Southern Illinois University Edwardsville.

She has authored the books *Computers: Concepts and Uses* (1985 and 1988) and *Management Information Systems* (1988, 1991, 1994, 1998). Her research and scholarship comprises over 50 referred articles in a variety of publications, including the *Journal of Information Technology, the Journal of Computer Information Systems, Information Resources Management Journal, Information and Management,* and *Database.* Her research addresses the risk factors in ERP projects, management of end-user computing, issues in managing information technology personnel, and the organizational impacts of computer-mediated communications.

She has been concerned with creating business/university partnerships, including the Technology and Commerce Roundtable, a forum of CIOs and faculty that has met over the past six years to discuss key information management issues. In her role directing executive education and professional development programs, she initiated and organized the High-Tech Bootcamp, an intensive program designed to re-skill individuals for opportunities in the information technology field. The success of this technology program led to the funding of the Technology and Management Center at Southern Illinois University Edwardsville.

She is actively involved in professional organizations, including the ACM Special Interest Group in MIS and Computer Personnel Research, the Association for Information Systems, and the Decision Sciences Institute. Her academic background includes a bachelor's degree from Syracuse University, a master's degree from the University of Chicago, a master's degree from Columbia University, and a doctorate from Rutgers University.

CHAPTER 1

A Foundation for Understanding Enterprise Resource Planning Systems

Objectives

1. Develop an understanding of how ERP systems can improve the effectiveness of information systems in organizations.
2. Understand the business benefits of enterprise resource planning (ERP) systems.
3. Understand the history and evolution of ERP.

◆ THE EMERGENCE OF ENTERPRISE RESOURCE PLANNING SYSTEMS

In the past several years, many organizations have initiated Enterprise Resource Planning (ERP) systems, using such packages as SAP, Peoplesoft, and Oracle. The ERP market is one of the fastest growing markets in the software industry. In research conducted by APICS, 34.5% of companies with revenues over $1 billion who were APICS members planned to purchase or upgrade an ERP system (Umble, Haft, and Umble, 2003). AMR Research predicts that the sales of ERP software will reach $180 billion by 2002 (Kalling, 2003). According to one study, the ERP market may reach $1 trillion by 2010 (Bingi, Sharma, and Godla, 1999).

Enterprise resource planning systems are a major investment. Companies have invested between $50,000 and hundreds of millions of dollars in ERP software, using a variety of business justifications, including the replacement of numerous legacy

1

systems, reduction in cycle times from order to delivery, and reduction in operating costs. The on-line, real-time operational data that ERP systems provide enable managers to make better decisions and improve responsiveness to customer needs (Ross, Vitale, and Willcocks, 2003). There is evidence that organizations are satisfied with ERP. Based upon a sample of 117 firms in 17 countries, the Conference Board reports that 34% of the organizations were satisfied with ERP, 58% were somewhat satisfied, 7% were somewhat unsatisfied, and only 1% were unsatisfied (McNurlin, 2001).

WHAT IS ERP?

ERP systems are the software tools used to manage enterprise data. ERP systems help organizations deal with the supply chain, receiving, inventory management, customer order management, production planning, shipping, accounting, human resource management, and other business functions (Somers and Nelson, 2003).

According to Deloitte Consulting, an ERP system is a packaged business software system that allows a company to "automate and integrate the majority of its business processes; share common data and practices across the enterprise; and produce and access information in a real-time environment." ERP systems are different from legacy systems in that organizations use ERP to integrate enterprise-wide information supporting financial, human resources, manufacturing, logistics, and sales and marketing functions (Shanks, Seddon, and Willcocks, 2003). An ERP system provides an enterprise database where all business transactions are entered, processed, monitored, and reported.

One of the most challenging issues associated with ERP systems is that the software imposes processes on the organizations that implement it. The issue of whether to make modifications or not is a significant challenge that every organization implementing ERP must face.

To be competitive, organizations must improve their business practices and share information with their suppliers, distributors, and customers. An ERP system introduces "best practices," which are defined as "simply the best way to perform a process." The biggest mistake made in implementing ERP, especially in a manufacturing environment, is to redesign the new system to work in the old environment (Honig, 1999).

THE EVOLUTION OF ERP

In the 1960s, most software packages included inventory control capability. Material Requirements Planning (MRP) systems, which were introduced in the 1970s, used a master production schedule and a bill of materials file with the list of materials needed to produce each item (see Table 1-1). Later on, MRP systems were enhanced by adding tools for sales planning, customer order processing, and rough-cut capacity planning—which provided input into production scheduling, known as closed-loop MRP (Somers and Nelson, 2003). In the 1980s, MRPII systems incorporated the financial accounting system along with manufacturing and materials management systems (Somers and Nelson, 2003).

MRPII led the way toward an integrated business system that developed the material and capacity requirements for production and translated these requirements into

Types of Systems	Time	Purpose	Systems
TABLE 1-1 Historical Evolution of ERP Systems			
Reorder point systems	1960s	Used historical data to forecast future inventory demand; when an item falls below a predetermined level, additional inventory is ordered	Designed to manage high-volume production of a few products, with constant demand; focus on cost
Materials requirement planning (MRP) systems	1970s	Offered a demand-based approach for planning manufacture of products and ordering inventory	Focus on marketing; emphasis on greater production integration and planning
Manufacturing resource planning (MRP-II) systems	1980s	Added capacity planning; could schedule and monitor the execution of production plans	Focus on quality; manufacturing strategy focused on process control, reduced overhead costs, and detailed cost reporting
MRP-II with manufacturing execution (MES) systems	1990s	Provide ability to adapt production schedules to meet customer needs; provide additional feedback with respect to shop floor activities	Focus on the ability to create and adapt new products and services on a timely basis to meet customers' specific needs
ERP (enterprise resource planning) systems	Late 1990s and onward	Integrate manufacturing with supply chain processes across the firm; designed to integrate the firm's business processes to create a seamless information flow from suppliers, through manufacturing, to distribution to the customer	Integrates supplier, manufacturing, and customer data throughout the supply chain

financial information. By the 1990s, ERP systems provided seamless integration of all information flows in the company—financial accounting, human resource, supply chain management, and customer information (Somers and Nelson, 2003).

THE "INTEGRATED" SYSTEMS APPROACH

ERP systems impose an "integrated systems" approach by establishing a common set of applications supporting business operations. In fact, successful implementation of an ERP system typically requires re-engineering business processes to better align with the ERP software (Brown and Vessey, 2003; Dahlen and Elfsson, 1999). Limited customization makes it simpler to upgrade the ERP software as new versions and add-ons emerge over time. As you can see from Table 1-2, an ERP system overcomes the inefficiencies of independent systems and non-integrated data by providing integrated data to support multiple business functions.

TABLE 1-2   Before and After ERP: Systems Standpoint

	Before ERP	*After ERP*
Information systems	Stand-alone systems	Integrated systems
Coordination	Lack of coordination among business functions (e.g., manufacturing and sales)	Supports coordination across business functions
Databases	Non-integrated data; data have different meanings (e.g., customer); inconsistent data definitions	Integrated data; data have the same meaning across multiple functions
Maintenance	Systems are maintained on a piecemeal basis; inconsistencies result; it is costly to maintain separate legacy systems	Uniform maintenance; changes affect multiple systems
Interfaces	Difficult to manage interfaces between systems	Common interfaces across systems
Information	Redundant, inconsistent information	Consistent real-time information (e.g., about customers, vendors)
System architecture	May not be state of the art	Relies on a client-server model
Processes	Incompatible processes	Consistent business processes which are based upon an information model
Applications	Disparate applications (e.g., many different purchasing systems)	Single applications (e.g., a common purchasing system)

◆ BUSINESS BENEFITS OF ERP

From an overall business standpoint, an ERP system achieves a number of important objectives, including maximizing throughput of information, minimizing response time to customers and suppliers, pushing decision making down to the lowest appropriate level, and providing timely information to decision makers. Most important, an ERP system integrates information throughout the supply chain. From a business standpoint, this means cost reduction, inventory reduction, and improved operating performance (see Table 1-3).

ERP systems are designed to provide business benefits in sales and distribution, manufacturing, costing, field service, and accounting. Surveys of U.S. and Swedish manufacturing firms show that ERP benefits include timely information, increased interaction across the enterprise, and improved order management (see Table 1-4).

In sales, increased efficiency leads to the ability to provide lower quotes, reduced lead times, and improve overall responsiveness to customers' needs. In manufacturing, concurrent engineering means faster product design and production. In field

TABLE 1-3 Before and After ERP: Business Standpoint

	Before ERP	*With ERP*
Cycle time	Costly bottlenecks	Time and cost reduction of business processes
Transactions processing	Multiple transactions use multiple data files	Faster transactions, using common data. Reduces the time and cost of multiple updates
Financial management	Increased cost of excess inventory, cost of overdue accounts receivable	Improves operational performance (e.g., less excess inventory, reduction in accounts receivable)
Business processes	Proliferation of fragmented processes with duplication of effort	Re-engineering around a business model that conforms with "best practices"
Productivity	Lack of responsiveness to customers and suppliers	Improvements in financial management and customer service
Supply chain management	Lack of integration	Linkages with suppliers and customers
eBusiness	Web-based interfaces support isolated systems and their components	Web-based interfaces are front-end to integrated systems
Information	Lack of tactical information for effective monitoring and control of organizational resources	Allows cross-functional access to the same data for planning and control. Provides widely available information
Communications	Lack of effective communications with customers and suppliers	Facilitates organizational communications with customers and suppliers

TABLE 1-4 Benefits of ERP

ERP Performance Outcomes	*Sweden Average**	*U.S. Average**
Quickened information response time	3.81	3.51
Increased interaction across the enterprise	3.55	3.49
Improved order management/order cycle	3.37	3.25
Decreased financial close cycle	3.36	3.17
Improved interaction with customers	2.87	2.92
Improved on-time delivery	2.82	2.83
Improved interaction with suppliers	2.78	2.81
Reduced direct operating costs	2.74	2.32
Lowered inventory levels	2.60	2.70

*scale: 1 (not at all) to 5 (a great extent)

Sources: Mabert, Soni, and Venkataramanan, 2000; Olhager and Selldin, 2003.

service, data on customer service histories and parts under warranty are available to show charges are accurate. Suppliers are paid more rapidly because accounts payable systems are responsive and accurate. Overall, the level of operational excellence throughout the business is optimized, from customer order through distribution and service. Case studies from organizations implementing ERP illustrate the business benefits noted in the surveys (Mabert et al., 2000; Olhager and Selldin, 2003).

Table 1-5 shows the tangible benefits of ERP are lower inventory levels, improved on-time delivery, and decreased financial closing cycles. In addition to hard-dollar savings, such as reduced procurement costs and increased manufacturing

TABLE 1-5   Business Benefits of ERP

ERP Performance Outcomes	Examples
Quickened information response time	• Responses to customer billing inquiries occurred in real-time as opposed to 15–20 minute response time at IBM Storage Products Company (Jensen and Johnson, 1999)
Increased interaction across the enterprise	• Simplification of processes at Boeing (Jensen and Johnson, 1999) • Growth in interfacility coordination at Owens Corning (Palaniswamy and Frank, 2000) • Real-time access to data across the organization at Diebold (Palaniswamy and Frank, 2000)
Improved order management/ order cycle	• 90% reduction in cycle time for quotations from 20 to 2 days at Fijitsu (Jensen and Johnson, 1999) • Faster, more accurate order processing at Valenite (Palaniswamy and Frank, 2000) • Time for checking credit upon receiving an order was reduced from 15–20 minutes to instantaneous at IBM Storage Products Company (Jensen and Johnson, 1999)
Decreased financial close cycle	• 50% reduction in financial closing time from 10 days to 5 days at Fijitsu (Jensen and Johnson, 1999)
Improved interaction with customers	• Lead times to customers were reduced from 6 weeks to 2 weeks at Par Industries (Bingi, Sharma, and Godla, 1999)
Improved on-time delivery	• On-time product delivery rate increased to 90% at Earthgrains (Bingi, Sharma, and Godla, 1999) • Delivery performance improved from 80% on-time to more than 90% on-time at Par Industries (Bingi, Sharma, and Godla, 1999)
Reduced direct operating costs	• Operating margins improved from 2.4% to 3.9% at Earthgrains (Bingi, Sharma, and Godla, 1999)
Lowered inventory levels	• Inventory levels were reduced significantly at Owens Corning (Palaniswamy and Frank, 2000) • Lower levels of inventory at Valenite (Palaniswamy and Frank, 2000) • Work-in-process inventory dropped almost 60% at Par Industries (Bingi, Sharma, and Godla, 1999)

TABLE 1-6 Company's Motivation to Implement ERP		
Company's Motivation to Implement ERP	*Swedish Average**	*U.S. Average**
Replace legacy systems	4.11	4.00
Simplify and standardize systems	3.67	3.85
Gain strategic advantage	3.18	3.46
Improve interactions with suppliers, customers	3.16	3.55
Ease of upgrading systems	2.96	2.91
Link to global activities	2.85	3.17
Restructure company organization	2.70	2.58
Solve the Y2K problem	2.48	3.08
Pressure to keep up with competitors	2.48	2.90

*scale: 1 (not important) to 5 (very important)

throughput, ERP systems provide soft-dollar benefits, including increased sales and revenues, improved margins, and improved productivity (Laughlin, 1999). ERP can speed up business processes, reduce cycle time, and reduce the cost of business processes, such as credit checking (Piturro, 1999; Davenport, 2000).

ERP systems offer many advantages from a systems standpoint. They eliminate legacy systems that maintain incompatible data and cause fragmentation. Integrated systems provide shared information across the organization, and this information can be used to monitor business performance (Davenport, 2000; Oliver, 1999). In addition, ERP systems are a foundation for eBusiness because they provide the back-office functions that enable customers to place and to track orders via the web (Davenport, 2000). Additional applications such as Customer Relationship Management (CRM) rely on the foundation of ERP (Oliver, 1999).

In surveys of the motivation to implement ERP in Sweden (Olhager and Selldin, 2003) and the United States (Mabert et al., 2000), some of the major motivations include the need to replace legacy systems, the need for standardization, the importance of gaining a competitive advantage, and the need to improve interactions with suppliers and customers (see Table 1-6).

◆ ERP MODULES

The major ERP vendors, including SAP, Oracle, and Peoplesoft, support the major functional areas of the business, including sales order processing, purchasing, production planning, financial accounting, management accounting, and human resources. Vendors addressing the mid-cap market (e.g., $50 to $400 million in sales) include Microsoft's Great Plains ERP software. In an analysis by Mabert et al., the most popular modules which are implemented by firms in the United States are the financial

Function	SAP	Oracle	PeopleSoft
Sales Order Processing	Sales and Distribution (SD)	Marketing Sales Supply Chain	Supply Chain Management
Purchasing	Materials Management (MM)	Procurement	Supplier Relationship Management
Production Planning	Production Planning (PP)	Manufacturing	
Financial Accounting	Financial Accounting (FA)	Financials	Financial Management Systems
Management Accounting	Controlling (CO)		
Human Resources	Human Resources (HR)	Human Resources	Human Capital Management

TABLE 1-7 ERP Modules Supported by Vendors

Source: Vendor Websites

and accounting modules (Mabert et al., 2000). Most firms implement a single ERP package rather than selecting different modules from different ERP vendors.

◆ ERP DESIGN ALTERNATIVES

In evaluating ERP, most organizations consider alternative design options and each of these options has its own price as well as its own advantages and disadvantages. A "vanilla" ERP implementation, which is the complete implementation of a vendor ERP system, is costly and time-consuming but offers the benefits of total integration and re-engineering of business processes. Implementation of selected ERP modules, such as the financial and accounting modules, is less costly and time-consuming but lacks the benefits of total integration of data across multiple functional areas of the business. This alternative is less costly but the benefits are not as great.

Building an in-house ERP system is the most time-consuming and expensive alternative, and it poses considerable risks. The advantage of this approach is that the organization can build a software system based upon its own unique processes, and its software will not be shared with its competitors as with the "vanilla" ERP alternative. However, management can argue that operational processes, such as financial accounting, production planning, and materials management, do not necessarily provide a competitive advantage, and the substantial investment involved in developing and implementing a customized system cannot be justified.

Finally, another alternative is to maintain current legacy systems. The problem with this approach is the organization could be putting itself into a competitive disadvantage by not having an ERP system in place when its competitors do. An ERP system is built upon the re-engineering of business processes around "best practices" and provides the advantages of data integration and standardization. By implementing an ERP, an organization can keep up with its competitors.

TABLE 1-8 Menu of ERP Alternatives

Option	Cost and Time	Advantages	Disadvantages
Vanilla ERP implementation	$150 million over 5 years	Complete standardization of business processes based upon vendor's "best practices"	Competitors have access to the same system Disruption of operations over 3–5 years
Partial ERP implementation (e.g., selected modules)	$108 million over 2–3 years	Partial changes in business processes	Disruption of operations over 2–3 years
In-house development	$240 million over 7–10 years	Custom-designed ERP system — unique from competitors	Long-term analysis and design process; high expense
Status quo	No cost but no gain	No business process change; little disruption of operations	May provide a competitive disadvantage because competitors have an ERP system

TABLE 1-9 Implementation Approach

Implementation Approach	Swedish %	U.S. %
Single ERP package	55.6	39.8
Single ERP package with other systems	30.1	50
Multiple ERP packages with other systems	6.5	4.0
Best-of-breed from several ERP packages	3.9	3.9
Totally in-house developed	2.0	0.5
In-house plus specialized packages	2.0	1.0

Based upon a number of factors, including data integration, cost-effectiveness, competitive environment, business impact, and time, most organizations conclude vanilla ERP implementation or partial ERP implementation are preferable to in-house development or maintaining the legacy system. Table 1-8 provides possible scenarios for ERP implementation in "Fortune 500" type corporations.

In two surveys of ERP implementation in the United States (Mabert et al., 2000) and Sweden (Olhager and Selldin, 2003), the authors note that implementing a single ERP package was the most common approach (see Table 1-9).

◆ THE BUSINESS CASE FOR ERP

One of the major requirements in justifying the acquisition of an ERP system involves an assessment of the tangible (e.g., hard-dollar) and intangible benefits. According to a survey of 62 Fortune 500 companies by Benchmarking Partners, Inc., for Deloitte

Consulting, the most important tangible benefit realized after the ERP system went live was inventory reduction (Fryer, 1999). The survey results in Table 1-10 showed these tangible benefits:

TABLE 1-10 Tangible Benefits with ERP	
Tangible Benefits	*% of Companies*
Inventory reduction	32
Personnel reduction	27
Productivity improvement	26
Order management improvement	20
Financial close cycle reduction	19
IT cost reduction	14
Procurement cost reduction	12
Cash management improvement	11
Revenue/profit increase	11
Transportation/logistics cost reduction	9
Maintenance reduction	7
On-line delivery improvement	6

Source: Fryer, Bronwyn, "The ROI Challenge," *CFO,* September, 1999, p. 90.

In terms of intangible benefits, information availability is a big factor (see Table 1-11). Information can enable managers to make better decisions about how to allocate resources effectively. In addition, improved customer responsiveness, process integration, and increased flexibility, though intangible, can lead to tangible benefits

TABLE 1-11 Intangible Benefits with ERP	
Intangible Benefits	*% of Companies*
Information/visibility	55
New/improved processes	24
Customer responsiveness	22
Integration	13
Standardization	12
Flexibility	9
Globalization	9
Y2K	8
Business performance	7
Supply/demand chain	5

Source: Fryer, Bronwyn, "The ROI Challenge," *CFO,* September, 1999, p. 90.

because they put the organization in a better position to win contracts and to generate increased revenues by cost reduction (Fryer, 1999).

COST-BENEFIT ANALYSIS FOR ERP

The decision to implement an ERP system is a business investment decision, similar to the decision to build a new warehouse, hire a new executive, or invest in a training program. As such, the ERP investment decision must create measurable business benefits that justify the acquisition costs and the costs of system implementation. As you have learned in this chapter, the business benefits of ERP include streamlining business processes, providing web-based access to information resources, reducing inventory and personnel, and improving overall productivity. The costs of implementing an ERP include the hardware, software, technical support, project management, internal team commitment, external consultants, and training.

In their analysis of the cost components of ERP, both surveys of ERP implementation in the U.S. (Mabert et al., 2000) and Sweden (Olhager and Selldin, 2003), indicate that software cost and consulting costs are major cost components (see Table 1-12).

One method of conducting a cost-benefit analysis of an ERP project is to use net present value. Net present value takes into consideration the time value of money. The time value of money can be understood through a simple example. If you invested $1,000,000, assuming an interest rate of 10%, you would expect to receive a return of $1,610,510 in five years. In determining the net present value of a capital budgeting decision, the time value of money is taken into account. A five-year timeframe is appropriate in evaluating an ERP project since a minimum of three years will be spent in actual implementation. In a large-scale project, the timeframe for evaluating returns on the investment in ERP might be as long as ten years.

In Table 1-13, you will see a cost-benefit analysis for an ERP project, using the net present value method of evaluating the project proposal. Costs are non-recurring, or start-up costs, and recurring costs. The start-up costs include the original investment in the ERP software. In this case, the software cost is $2,420,000. The original hardware investment is $1,850,000, which includes servers and networking capability in a client server environment. The other non-recurring costs include consultants' time in installing and configuring the software, which is an additional $3,000,400. Project management time, internal team time, and project steering committee time is estimated to be $400,000, and initial training time is $1,280,000. These figures are in line with research on ERP implementation costs conducted in the United States and Sweden (Olhager and Selldin, 2003; Mabert et al., 2000).

TABLE 1-12 ERP Cost Components		
ERP Cost Component	***Swedish %***	***U.S. %***
Software	24.2	30.2
Hardware	18.5	17.8
Consulting	30.1	24.1
Training	13.8	10.9
Implementation team	12.0	13.6

TABLE 1-13   Net Present Value of an ERP Project

	Year 0	Year 1	Year 2	Year 3	Year 4	Year 5
Software	2,420,000					
Software Licenses		220,000	220,000	220,000	220,000	220,000
Hardware	1,850,000					
Consulting	3,000,400					
Training	1,280,000					
Implementation Team	400,000	400,000	400,000	400,000		
Total Costs	8,950,400	620,000	620,000	620,000	220,000	220,000
Savings	0					
Reduced Inventory Costs		2,750,000	2,750,000	2,750,000	2,750,000	2,750,000
Reduced Administrative Costs		1,250,000	1,250,000	1,250,000	1,250,000	1,250,000
Intangible Benefits						
Total Savings	0	4,000,000	4,000,000	4,000,000	4,000,000	4,000,000
Net Balance	−8,950,400	3,380,000	3,380,000	3,380,000	3,780,000	3,780,000
DCF Factor	1.000	0.909	0.826	0.751	0.683	0.621
Discounted Bal.	−8,950,400	3,072,420	2,791,880	2,538,380	2,581,740	2,347,380
Cumulative Discounted Bal.	−8,950,400	−5,877,980	−3,086,100	−547,720	2,034,020	4,381,400

In our example, the recurring costs (i.e., costs which recur over time) include the costs of software licenses, maintenance agreements, project management time, internal team time committed to the project, and consultants' time used on a recurring basis. For example, ongoing software licenses represent 10% of the original software cost, which is $220,000 per year. The time spent by the implementation team will continue to be budgeted for $400,000 per year.

The benefits of the ERP project will not take place until the system is in operation. Assuming that project implementation takes three years at a minimum, the benefits will not accrue until the project's fourth year. In our example, the measurable, or tangible, business benefits include inventory reduction, which represents a savings of $2,750,000 per year. In addition, personnel reduction represents an additional savings of $1,250,000 per year. Intangible benefits might include improved employee morale, improved customer satisfaction, and less duplication of effort in maintaining multiple databases, but these intangible benefits are not recorded in the spreadsheet.

As you can see from Table 1.13, the proposed ERP project will have a positive discounted balance in Year 1, and the company will break even on its software investment in ERP in Year 4, when the cumulative discounted balance is $2,034,020. Based upon this analysis, the investment in an ERP system is a wise investment.

CAN ERP PROVIDE A COMPETITIVE ADVANTAGE?

Ultimately, for the return on investment in ERP systems to be realized, these systems should yield a strategic advantage. In many industries, however, all the major companies have an ERP system. If an entire industry is adopting ERP systems, as in the case of industries such as oil, chemicals, consumer products, and computers, then the basis for attaining a competitive advantage is unrelated to implementing the ERP. The basis for achieving a competitive advantage shifts to implementing the ERP system better than anyone else (Davenport, 2000). Another way to achieving a competitive advantage is to migrate to new software versions more quickly than competitors do (Kremers and Van Dissel, 2000).

Another source of gaining competitive advantage through ERP implementation is to use vanilla ERP modules to support core operations and to build customized modules to support unique processes which provide a competitive edge (Holland, Light, and Kawakek, 1999). The increased availability of operational data and the use of data for analysis may also provide companies with an advantage (Mabert, Soni, and Venkataramanan, 2001).

Even if ERP implementation may not provide a competitive advantage, companies which do not implement ERP may still find themselves at a competitive disadvantage, particularly in industries in which ERP implementation is widespread. Companies using ERP will be able to take advantage of best practices in running their businesses to reduce cycle time, to improve the speed and accuracy of information, and to attain better financial management (Davenport, 2000).

◆ THE CHALLENGE OF IMPLEMENTING AN ERP SYSTEM

ERP systems projects involve considerable time and cost, and it may take some time to realize ERP's benefits. Research by Standish Group illustrates that 90% of ERP projects are late or over budget. Meta Group survey data, based on 63 companies, showed that average implementation cost of ERP was $10.6 million and took 23 months to complete (Stein, 1999).

The successful implementation of ERP requires a multi-stage approach (Markus, Axline, Petrie, and Tanis, 2000; Parr and Shanks, 2000; Holland and Light, 2001), and the benefits of ERP may not occur until later stages. Markus et al., proposes three stages: the project phase, the shakedown phase, and the onward and upward phase. The ERP software is introduced during the project phase and is implemented into the firm's operations during the shakedown phase. It is not until the onward and upward phase, during which the ERP modules are successfully integrated with operations, that the organization can achieve the actual business results, such as inventory reduction (Markus et al., 2000).

Parr and Shanks identify four phases: a planning phase, a re-engineering phase, a design phase, and a configuration and testing phase (Parr and Shanks, 2000). They note that re-engineering business practices around the ERP software is critical to successful implementation. In their stage analysis, Holland and Light (2001) suggest the benefits of ERP occur when ERP modules are implemented successfully and when organizations can use the ERP foundation to add advanced modules such as customer relationship management (Holland and Light, 2001).

♦ SUMMARY

In summary, organizations have a business justification for implementing ERP systems. The business benefits of ERP include improved accessibility of information, real-time access to data across the organization, improved cycle time for orders, decreased financial close time, reduced operating costs, and lowered inventory levels. In addition, ERP systems provide the opportunity to re-align business processes with best practices and to integrate enterprise-wide information supporting financial, human resources, manufacturing, and sales and marketing functions.

Questions for Discussion •

1. Use on-line library databases to identify articles in trade publications that provide case studies of ERP implementations. These articles may provide some insight into each of these questions:
    a. How widespread is the use of ERP across certain industries?
    b. What are the benefits reported from implementing ERP?
    c. What are its limitations?
2. Research and learn about the implementation of ERP. Use trade publications and on-line library databases (e.g., ABI Inform, ProQuest, First Search, Wilson Select Plus, available through your library) to conduct a search for articles.
    a. Find a success story of ERP implementation. What factors contributed to the success of this implementation?
    b. Find a story of problems encountered with an ERP implementation. What factors contributed to the encountered obstacles?

♦♦♦ Case

Business Research

You are a business analyst for MPK Industries, a consulting firm that tracks worldwide trends in information technology. Using suggested on-line databases and Internet resources, provide answers to the following questions:

1. What is the expected future growth of the ERP marketplace in terms of overall sales?
    a. Break this down by sales in the United States and international sales.

    b. Break this down by Fortune 500 companies and mid-cap companies (e.g., mid-cap companies are defined as having sales between $50 and $400 million per year).
2. What is the relative market share of the major ERP vendors?
    a. Break this down by sales in the U.S. and international sales.
    b. Break this down by Fortune 500 companies and mid-cap companies.

SUGGESTED RESOURCES FOR ON-LINE RESEARCH

Web site	*What It Provides*
www.amrresearch.com	Results of vendor surveys
www.technologyevaluation.com	Market research
www.computerworld.com/softwaretopics/erp	Links to useful ERP sites, articles, publications, and chat rooms
www.erpfans.com	Links to support groups for many vendors
www.apics.org/resources/magazine/current	Link to current APICS news

References

Beard, Jon W., and M. Sumner. 2004. "Seeking strategic advantage in the post-net era: Viewing ERP systems from the resource-based perspective." *The Journal of Strategic Information Systems* 13: 129–150.

Bingi, P., M. Sharma, and J. Godla. 1999. "Critical issues affecting ERP implementation." *Information Systems Management* 16: 7–14.

Brown, C. V., and I. Vessey. 2003. "Managing the next wave of enterprise systems: Leveraging lessons from ERP." *MIS Quarterly Executive* 2: 65–77.

Dahlen, C., and J. Elfsson. 1999. "An analysis of the current and future ERP market—With a focus on Sweden." Master's Thesis. Stockholm, Sweden: The Royal Institute of Technology. http://www.pdu.se/xjobb.pdf.

Davenport, T. 2000. *Mission Critical: Recognizing the Promise of Enterprise Systems*. Cambridge: Harvard University Press.

Fryer, Bronwyn. Sept. 1999. "The ROI challenge." *CFO* 85–90.

Holland, C., B. Light, and P. Kawakek. 1999. "Beyond enterprise resource planning projects: Innovative strategies for competitive advantage." *Proceedings of the 7th European Conference on Information Systems*, J. Pries-Heje, C. Ciborra, K. Kautz, J. Valor, E. Christiaanse, D. Avison, and C. Heje (Eds.), Copenhagen Business School, 288–301.

Holland, C., and B. Light. 2001. "A stage maturity model for enterprise resource planning systems use." *Database for Advances in Information Systems* 35: 34–45.

Honig, Susan. 1999. "The changing landscape of computerized accounting systems." *CPA Journal* 69: 14–20.

Jensen, R., and R. Johnson. 1999. "The enterprise resource planning system as a strategic solution." *Information Strategy* 15: 28–33.

Kalling, T. 2003. "ERP systems and the strategic management processes that lead to competitive advantage." *Information Resources Management Journal* 16: 46–67.

Kremers, M., and H. Van Dissel. 2000. "ERP system migrations." *Communications of the ACM* 43(4): 53–56.

Laughlin, S. P. 1999. "An ERP game plan." *Journal of Business Strategy* 20: 32–37.

Mabert, V. M., A. Soni, and M. A. Venkataramanan. 2001. "Enterprise resource planning: Common myths versus evolving reality." *Business Horizons* 44: 269–276.

Mabert, V. M., A. Soni, and M. A. Venkataramanan. 2000. "Enterprise resource planning survey of U.S. manufacturing firms." *Production and Inventory Management Journal* 41: 52–88.

Markus, M. L., S. Axline, D. Petrie, and C. Tanis. 2000. "Learning from adopters' experiences with ERP: Problems encountered and success achieved." *Journal of Information Technology* 15: 245–265.

McNurlin, B. 2001. "Will users of ERP stay satisfied?" *Sloan Management Review* 42: 13.

Olhager, Jan, and Erik Selldin. 2003. "Enterprise resource planning survey of Swedish manufacturing firms." *European Journal of Operational Research* 146: 365–373.

Oliver, R. 1999. "ERP is dead. Long live ERP." *Management Review* 88: 12–13.

Palaniswamy, R., and T. Frank. 2000. "Enhancing manufacturing performance with ERP systems." *Information Systems Management* 17: 43–55.

Parr, A., and G. Shanks. 2000. "A model of ERP project implementation." *Journal of Information Technology* 15: 289–303.

Piturro, M. 1999. "How midsize companies are buying ERP." *Journal of Accountancy* 188: 41–48.

Plotkin, H. March 1999. "ERP: How to make them work." *Harvard Management Update* 3–4.

Ross, Jeanne, Michael Vitale, and Leslie Willcocks. 2003. "The continuing ERP Revolution: Sustainable lessons, new models of delivery," in *Second-Wave Enterprise Resource Planning Systems*. Graeme Shanks, Peter Seddon, and Leslie Willcocks (Eds.), Cambridge: Cambridge University Press, 2003. pp. 102–132.

Shanks, Graeme, Peter Seddon, and Leslie Willcocks. 2003. "Introduction: ERP—the quiet revolution," *Second-Wave Enterprise Resource Planning Systems*. Cambridge: Cambridge University Press, 2003. pp. 1–23.

Somers, Toni, and Klara Nelson. 2003. "The impact of strategy and integration mechanisms on enterprise system value: Empirical evidence from manufacturing firms." *European Journal of Operational Research* 146: 315–338.

Stein, T. 1999. "Making ERP add up—companies that implemented enterprise resource planning systems with little regard to return on investment are starting to look for quantifiable results." *Information Week* 24: 59.

Umble, Elisabeth, Ronald Haft, and M. Michael Umble. 2003. "Enterprise resource planning: Implementation procedures and critical success factors." *European Journal of Operational Research* 146: 241–257.

CHAPTER 2

Re-engineering and Enterprise Resource Planning Systems

Objectives

1. Recognize the factors associated with the evolution to enterprise systems, including business process re-engineering, client-server networking, and the emergence of integrated databases.
2. Understand the role of process modeling in re-designing business processes.

◆ BACKGROUND

In the twentieth century, we have seen the emergence of the "factory farm," which revolutionized American agriculture through the use of technology. Technology alone, however, was not the main reason for the tremendous productivity improvements associated with this form of organization, the factory farm. These productivity improvements were possible because of the combination of technology plus new, innovative procedures. This was one of the first instances of "re-engineering." In this chapter, you will learn how ERP has contributed to business process re-engineering, combined with the use of new information technology.

The definition of re-engineering is "the fundamental rethinking and radical redesign of business processes to achieve dramatic improvements in critical, contemporary measures of performance, such as cost, quality, service, and speed" (Hammer and Champy, 1993). To understand re-engineering, it is important to understand the concept of the value chain. The value chain consists of the primary and secondary activities of the firm. Re-engineering strives for the efficient re-design of the company's value chain.

In Table 2-1, the primary activities of the firm include inbound logistics, operations, outbound logistics, marketing, and service. These activities are essential to creating, producing, marketing, selling, and supporting a product or service. An information system supports each of these primary activities. This information system can cut the cost

TABLE 2-1   The Value Chain: Primary Activities

Primary Activities	*Inbound Logistics*	*Operations*	*Outbound Logistics*	*Marketing and Sales*	*Service*
Functions	Materials handling; delivery	Manufacturing; parts assembly	Order processing; shipping	Advertising; promotion	Service; repair
Information systems supporting primary activities	Automated warehousing systems	Manufacturing control systems	On-line order entry systems	Marketing analysis systems	Remote machine diagnostics

TABLE 2-2   The Value Chain: Secondary Activities

Support Activities	*Information Systems*
Organization	Electronic mail (facilitates communications throughout the organization)
Human resources	Skills databases
Technology	Computer-aided design and manufacturing
Purchasing	On-line links to suppliers' databases

of performing a value activity, or it can be used to provide a "value-added" feature to the product or service. For example, the value activity, called outbound logistics, deals with processing orders to customers. An on-line order entry system which enables customers to order electronically can cut the time and cost of this value activity. The value activity, called service, can be supported by remote machine diagnostics, which "adds value" by providing on-line diagnostic support.

In Table 2-2, a set of secondary activities support the primary activities of the organization. These secondary activities include organizational structure, human resources, technology, and purchasing. Information systems can support each of these secondary activities as well. For example, electronic mail can support the organizational structure by facilitating timely communications. Information systems can support purchasing by enabling purchasing agents to link into suppliers' databases to place orders, determine inventory levels, and check pricing.

Supply chain management, which is covered in greater depth in Chapter 9, involves the planning and control of all tasks along the business value chain. In this way, suppliers can link directly to manufacturers, manufacturers can link directly to retailers, and retailers can link directly to customers. These electronic linkages reduce costs, improve the timeliness of order processing and delivery, and increase service levels.

TABLE 2-3	Motivation for Business Re-engineering		
Driving Forces	*External Responses*	*Internal Changes*
Deregulation	Customer focus	Re-engineering work
Consolidation	Quality emphasis	Corporate cultural change
Changing values	Responsiveness	Teams
Customer sophistication	Strategic relationships	Empower workers
Technological advances	Downsizing	Quality management

In today's economy, some of the major motivations for streamlining and re-engineering business processes are customer sophistication, deregulation, and increasing competition on a global level. These driving forces provide a rationale for re-thinking existing business practices and using technology to create new forms of work (see Table 2-3). As with the factory farm, productivity increases require the use of technology and changes in existing work methods and procedures. ERP can introduce process improvement and process re-design.

In a work environment which has fragmented business processes, an external event, such as a competitor's price change, may trigger a whole set of fragmented business processes, which involve multiple individuals and take extra time (see Illustration 2-1). In general, responsiveness to market demands and a focus on customer needs require quick response time and the simplification and integration of processes.

◆ BUSINESS PROCESS RE-ENGINEERING

In many current systems, technology has mechanized old ways of doing work. The best way to see this is to use several case studies, explaining the situation before and after re-engineering took place. The first case study deals with the Accounts Payable System at Ford Motor Company. In the "before re-engineering" situation, independent databases were maintained by Purchasing, Receiving, and Accounts Payable. When items were purchased, a record was set up in the Purchasing database. When shipments from the Supplier were received, the Receiving Department would update its database with the amount received. If the shipments were partial shipments, then the record in the Purchasing database did not match up with the record in the Receiving database. These inconsistencies created problems in Accounts Payable, which had its own database and was responsible for providing the vendor payments

After re-engineering, an integrated database supporting Purchasing, Receiving, and Accounts Payable included "common data." You will see these re-engineered processes in Illustration 2.2. The company instituted a new "business rule" that Accounts Payable should only pay Suppliers when shipments were received (i.e., we pay for what we get). In this way, many of the inconsistencies were eliminated. The

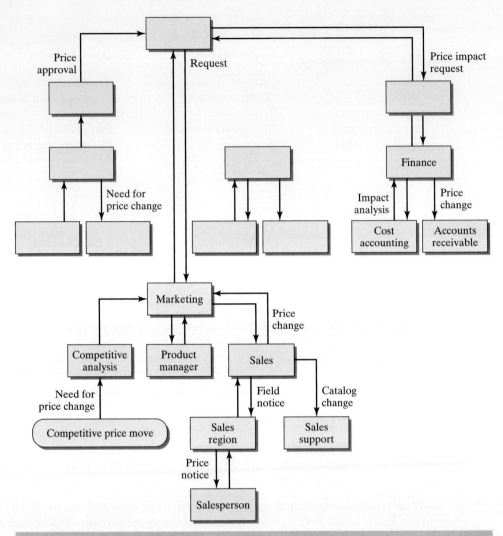

Price
approval

Request

Price impact
request

Finance

Need for
price change

Impact
analysis

Price
change

Cost
accounting

Accounts
receivable

Marketing

Price
change

Competitive
analysis

Product
manager

Sales

Need for
price change

Field
notice

Catalog
change

Competitive price move

Sales
region

Sales
support

Price
notice

Salesperson

ILLUSTRATION 2-1   Work Environment with Fragmented Business Processes

number of administrative staff in Accounts Payable was significantly reduced with
the procedures and the common database. One of the most important principles of
business re-engineering is to "break away from outdated rules." In this case, the proce-
dural change, the technological support, and the cross-functional collaboration
reduced the administrative cost. Elements of business re-engineering are summarized
in Table 2-4.

In addition to Ford Motor Company's Accounts Payable re-engineering example, many excellent case studies in re-engineering exist (see Table 2-5). At IBM
Credit Authorization, for example, the re-engineering process eliminated a multi-step

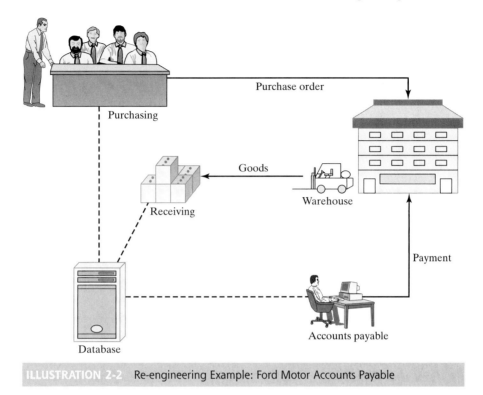

Re-engineering Example: Ford Motor Accounts Payable

authorization process involving multiple departments and led to the design of a position responsible for making the credit authorization decision. At Xerox Product Development, a concurrent engineering process, using a common integrated database, reduced product development lead times and improved responsiveness to market needs. Proctor and Gamble collaborated with Wal-Mart to manage the inventory of

TABLE 2-4   Elements of Business Re-engineering

Elements	*Activities*
Business processes	Do not automate existing business processes; break away from outdated rules
Integration	Integrate business processes
Technology	Use technology to re-design business processes
Cross-functional coordination	Re-design business processes from a cross-functional view
Timing	Improve processes continuously
Objective	Implement market-driven strategies designed to provide a competitive edge

TABLE 2-5	Re-engineering Case Studies		
	Before Re-engineering	*After Re-engineering*	*Business Impact*
Ford Motor Company Accounts Payable	Independent databases maintained by purchasing, receiving, and accounts payable	An integrated database supporting multiple functions (e.g., purchasing, receiving, accounts payable)	Fewer inconsistencies; reduction in clerical overhead; better responsiveness to customers
IBM Credit Authorization	Multi-step credit authorization process involving multiple departments and multiple individuals (e.g., a pricer, checker)	A "deal structurer" makes the credit authorization decision, using multiple databases	Timely decision making; more effective customer service; elimination of redundant tasks and bottlenecks
Xerox Product Development	Sequential product development process, which meant that workers had to wait until prior steps were completed	Concurrent engineering, using a common integrated database and a computer-assisted design system	Elimination of bottlenecks and delays; faster product development; responsiveness to market needs
Wal-Mart Inventory Management	Wal-Mart ordered its own stock of merchandise from vendors; dealt with excess inventory or insufficient inventory	Wal-Mart let its vendor, Proctor and Gamble, replenish its inventory according to market trends	Better inventory management; more effective inventory replenishment
Hewlett-Packard's Purchasing Process	Decentralized purchasing led to a loss of corporate-wide discounts	Central negotiation of corporate volume discounts and use of a shared database of negotiated prices	Cost savings through the use of centrally negotiated discounts

Wal-Mart stores. Hewlett-Packard (HP) reaped substantial cost savings by creating a shared database of centrally-negotiated prices.

You will see an illustration of Xerox Product Development's process before and after re-engineering in Illustration 2-3.

In summary, these re-engineering examples apply a number of principles, which are summarized in Table 2-6. One of these principles, "organize around outcomes," provides a rationale for creating newly designed jobs, such as Mutual Benefit Life's position of "case manager," who is responsible for coordinating all underwriting tasks. This position is possible because the case manager has access to multiple databases. In this example, as in others, the combination of a re-engineered job and information technology is the key to improved productivity and reduced costs.

The HP Purchasing database supports two different re-engineering principles. One principle, "treat geographically dispersed resources as if they were centralized," is implemented because local branch managers have access to a common database of centrally negotiated vendor prices. In addition, local managers can make their

ILLUSTRATION 2-3   Re-engineering Example: Xerox

Before

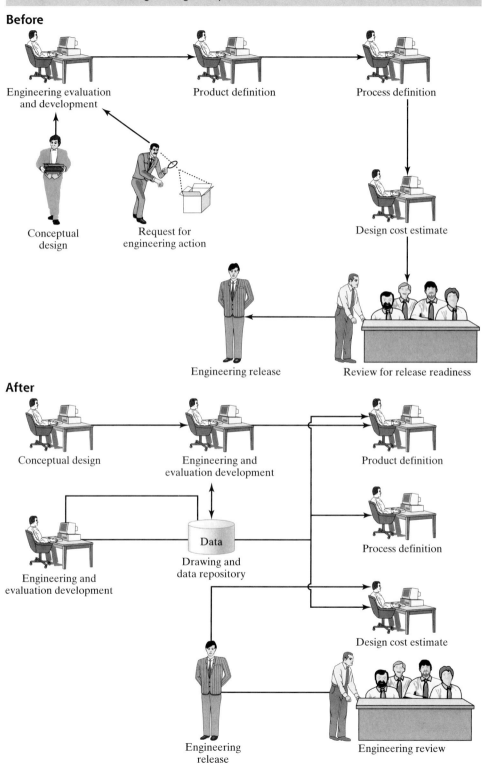

Engineering evaluation
and development

Product definition

Process definition

Conceptual
design

Request for
engineering action

Design cost estimate

Engineering release

Review for release readiness

After

Conceptual design

Engineering and
evaluation development

Product definition

Engineering and
evaluation development

Data

Drawing and
data repository

Process definition

Design cost estimate

Engineering
release

Engineering review

TABLE 2-6   Principles of Re-engineering Applied

Principle	Case Study	Example
Organize around outcomes, not tasks	Mutual Benefit Life	A case manager performs and coordinates all underwriting tasks centrally
Have those who use the output of the process perform the process	Hewlett-Packard	Department managers make their own purchases using a shared database of approved vendors
Link parallel activities during the process, rather than at the end of the process	Xerox	Concurrent engineering teams participate in new product design and engineering
Treat geographically dispersed resources as if centralized	Hewlett-Packard	Each division has access to a shared purchasing database at HP's corporate office
Capture information at the source	Mutual Benefit Life	Customer service representatives enter insurance application information into a central database
Subsume information processing work into the real work that produces the information	Mutual Benefit Life	Customer service representatives have access to information for decision making
Flatten organizational layers	Mutual Benefit Life, Hewlett-Packard, Xerox	Decision making is decentralized to the appropriate level; in many cases, this eliminates or lessens the need for mid-management

own purchases, rather than going through a central purchasing bureaucracy. This implements the principle "have those who use the output of the process perform the process."

All of these re-engineering examples support common themes. One of these themes is to decentralize decision making to the decision maker to be responsive to the customers' needs. This has the effect of flattening organizational layers because there is less need for mid-level management. Another common theme is that the use of information technology (e.g., shared databases, networking) facilitates the newly re-engineered processes. In the Mutual Benefit Life, Hewlett-Packard, Xerox, and Ford examples, access to central databases is essential to new ways of doing work. These new ways of doing work mean re-designing jobs. The positions of "customer service representative," who makes underwriting decisions at Mutual Benefit Life, and "deal structurer," who makes credit authorization decisions at IBM Credit, are examples of re-engineered jobs. With decentralized decision making, these positions entail judgment, leadership, and the ability to adapt to changing customer needs (see Table 2-7).

TABLE 2-7	Re-structuring Business Processes Means Re-structuring Jobs	
Organization	**Traditional**	**Re-engineered**
Job design	Narrow	Broad
Structure	Hierarchical	Flat
Career moves	Vertical	Horizontal
Work rules	Procedures	Judgment
Management	Supervision	Leadership
People skills needed	Structured	Adaptive

◆ PROCESS MODELING

In order to depict the changes in data and processes associated with business re-engineering, a commonly used tool in systems analysis is the process model. The process model consists of five objects:

- The business process: The process depicts the business activities which are accomplished (e.g., check credit, mail invoice).
- The data store: The store depicts data that are needed by the business processes.
- The data flow: The flow depicts data being transferred from a process to another process or between a process and a data store.
- The organizational unit: The organizational unit depicts the units of the organization in which these processes take place (e.g., Accounts Receivable, Sales).
- The event, including triggers and outcomes: A trigger is an event which "triggers" a process, and an outcome is an event which results from a process.

A short case illustrates the design of a process model. Neighborhood Food Cooperative is a rapidly expanding organization which provides its members with groceries at favorable rates, because of its ability to buy in bulk from farmers and wholesale suppliers. The Board of the Cooperative is interested in analyzing its administrative processes, including purchasing and distribution. A process model can depict the following processes.

The Cooperative functions on a weekly cycle. Members may send in or deliver a shopping list at any time during the week, either in handwritten form, or using the pre-printed form for which the Cooperative has suppliers (e.g., eggs, meat, vegetables, etc.). The list is scanned, and any items which the Board has decided will not be supplied this week (e.g., coffee) are deleted. Each Friday afternoon, all the lists are merged to get an overall demand for each item, so that the staff can survey the prices (by calling each supplier for each item) and get the best deal. By closing time on Friday, orders covering all goods needed have been placed with suppliers by phone; these are followed by written confirmations. Suppliers invoice the Cooperative, ten days net, and the invoices are held in Accounts Payable and paid weekly. On Sunday, the shipments are delivered to the Cooperative where they are checked to be certain that the

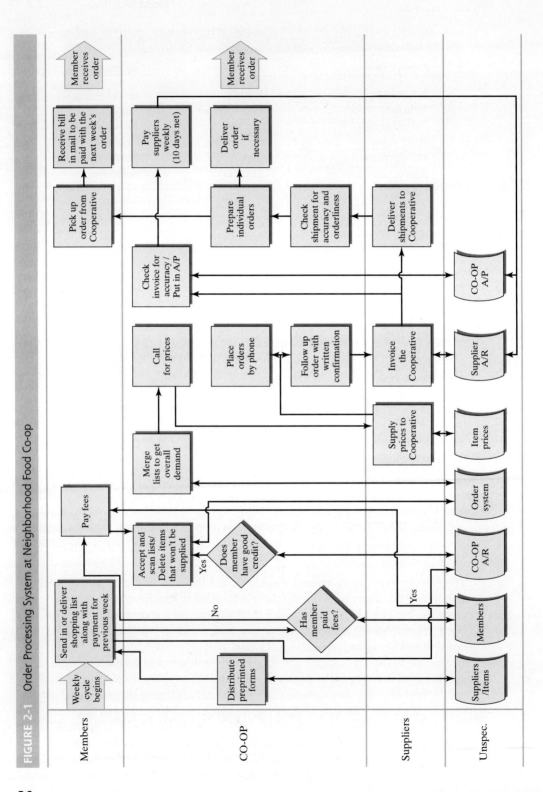

FIGURE 2-1   Order Processing System at Neighborhood Food Co-op

26

correct items were shipped. The individual shopping baskets of the members are then made up for pick-up by the customer or for delivery.

In Figure 2-1, you will see a process model depicting an order processing system at Neighborhood Food Cooperative.

The process model is useful in the re-engineering process. First, it is useful for analytical purposes because it provides a graphical representation of the activities of the current system. An analysis of the current system provides insight into changes in process, information flows, work structure, and organization which are needed to improve the productivity of the current system. Based upon these changes, a process model can be built that incorporates these changes and is based upon "best practices." A best practice is a better way of doing business; it is an improved method.

The best practices supported by modules within ERP systems are based upon the following: re-engineered process models, which depict improved process changes; integrated data, which are shared by multiple processes; and structural changes, which streamline business functions and maximize productivity. Seeing the differences between the current business process model and the new process model is useful because this gives everyone an opportunity to analyze the changes in work flow, work systems, and work structures that will occur as a result of the ERP implementation.

◆ RE-ENGINEERING AT RELIABLE FINANCE COMPANY

A case study will provide an excellent example of how a process model can be used to depict the changes in business processes and information in re-engineering.

BACKGROUND OF THE BUSINESS

The Reliable Finance Company (RFC) started in a small mid-western town in the 1890s, lending money to farmers and businessmen. RFC assumed risks that the commercial banks were unwilling to take and charged slightly higher interest rates.

Now, RFC has 178 branches, from Denver to Cleveland and from Detroit to Houston. The company is committed to making loans to individuals to assist them in making such purchases as automobiles, appliances, and home improvements.

Ed Clarkson, grandson of its founder, along with a new management team, manages the company. They have decided on a growth plan that would expand the number of RFC branches to 400 within the next three years and to 1,000 branches within another five-year period after that. The locations will be selected in growing suburbs, especially in Texas, Florida, California, and Arizona.

These expansion plans will require an enhanced information system to support transactions processing for loans, payments, and settlements. The President has asked the MIS Department to develop recommendations for the re-design of the existing consumer loan system.

ANALYSIS OF THE CURRENT LOAN APPLICATION AND SCREENING SYSTEM

The first system to be analyzed is the loan application and screening system. Some of the activities for loan application screening are handled by the branches, and some of the activities are handled by the home office, which is located at Centerville, Indiana.

Each RFC branch has a manager, several customer service advisors, and clerical staff. Applicants for loans complete a Loan Application Form with the assistance of a customer service advisor. The branch personnel check local income and bank references, and the Branch Manager gives the application a preliminary screening prior to sending the materials to the Home Office in Centerville. At the Home Office, the staff in the Screening Department check if the loan applicant has defaulted on any prior loans with RFC and check on outstanding and delinquent loans to ensure all current loans held by the applicant are in good order. Finally, the Screening staff obtain an external credit report from TRW to determine the applicant's creditworthiness based upon other external loan activities. Based upon data from the Branch and Home Office credit searches, the Loan Officer in the Home Office determines whether to accept or reject the loan application.

If the loan application is accepted, the Loan Department generates a check for the loan amount and sends a confirmation of the loan's acceptance to the branch personnel. Loan paperwork is sent to Accounting, which sets up the loan account in the Outstanding Loans File. The Accounting Department prints a Voucher Booklet, which is sent to the Branch. Once the Branch receives the letter of acceptance and the Voucher Booklet, it notifies the customer to come and collect the check and Voucher Booklet.

The branch personnel keep copies of the vouchers in a local Outstanding Loans file for each customer. These voucher copies are organized by due date. In this way, the Branch Manager can see what payments are due each day. The information systems department produces monthly management reports summarizing new loans by branch.

When a new loan is confirmed, the branch personnel set up an index card file for each customer, with details such as name, address, Loan ID, and principal amount. This information is not shown on the voucher copies, and it is often useful in identifying accounts to which payments should be applied. Figure 2-2 depicts the current loan application screening process.

CURRENT PROBLEMS

At the current time, RFC is planning to expand the number of branches from 187 to 400 in the next three years, and to a target of 1,000 branches over the next five years after that. To accommodate expansion plans, the current system will need to be streamlined, modified, and enhanced.

One problem is the various steps in the loan approval process typically take 10–13 working days. In many of the cities where RFC has branches, commercial banks approve or disapprove loan applications in 2–3 days. This means that some of the best loan candidates (e.g., those who are the best credit risk) obtain approval for their loans at least a week before RFC gets around to approving them. RFC is losing some of its best loan prospects to the commercial banks.

OBJECTIVES

Management is interested in achieving the objective of reducing the time it takes to approve a loan from 10–13 days to 2–3 days in order to be competitive with the commercial banks. In order to attain this goal, a new process model has been designed. In the new process model, a branch-level customer service representative has local access to all of the databases needed to make the loan approval decision (see Figure 2-3).

FIGURE 2-2 Process Model of the Current Loan Application Screening System

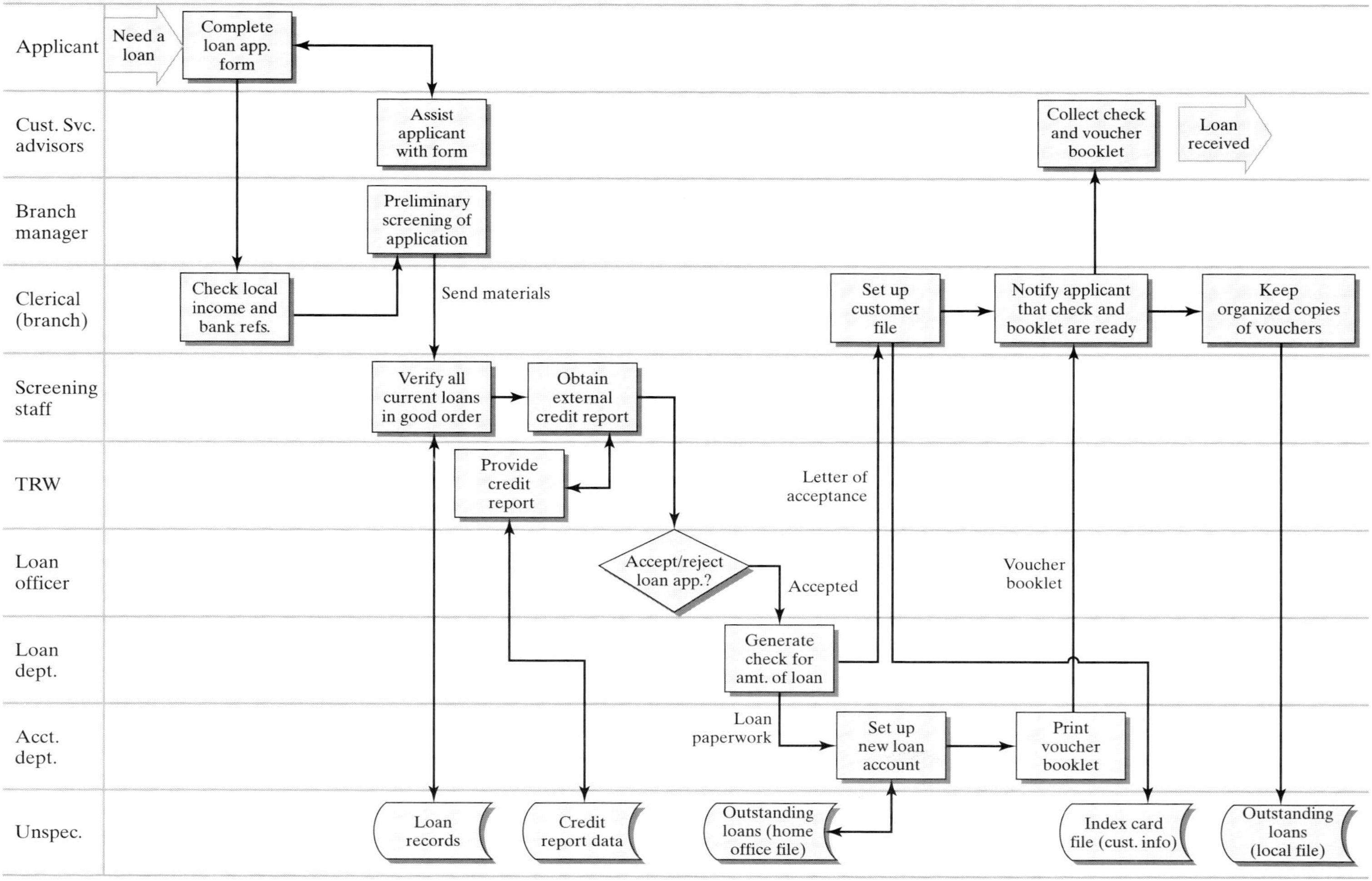

Applicant: Need a loan → Complete loan app. form → Collect check and voucher booklet → Loan received

Cust. Svc. advisors: Assist applicant with form

Branch manager: Preliminary screening of application

Clerical (branch): Check local income and bank refs. · Keep organized copies of vouchers · Notify applicant that check and booklet are ready · Set up customer file

Screening staff: Send materials · Verify all current loans in good order · Obtain external credit report

TRW: Provide credit report

Loan officer: Accept/reject loan app.? · Letter of acceptance · Accepted · Generate check for amt. of loan · Voucher booklet

Loan dept.: Set up new loan account · Loan paperwork · Print voucher booklet

Acct. dept.:

Unspec.: Loan records · Credit report data · Outstanding loans (home office file) · Index card file (cust. info) · Outstanding loans (local file)

29

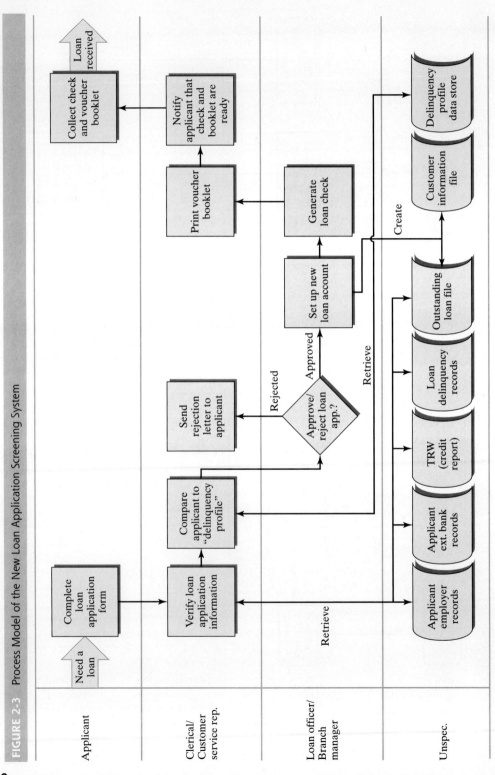

FIGURE 2-3 Process Model of the New Loan Application Screening System

In his analysis of why re-engineering efforts are a failure, Rosenthal argues that organizations need to apply a "clean slate approach" to process re-design and to move away from the status quo. Based upon an in-depth study of re-engineering projects in 20 companies, Rosenthal found that 11 of the 20 projects measured less than 5% in overall returns, through increased revenues or decreased costs, from re-engineering efforts (Rosenthal, 1993).

The reason why so many re-engineering projects fail, Rosenthal notes, is that many of these projects are too narrowly focused (e.g., they focus on a single activity within a single function, such as accounts receivable) or are too general in nature (e.g., their objective may be to create more knowledgeable reservations agents, whereas customers just want faster bookings). When a process or series of processes is re-engineered, jobs need to be re-designed and reward structures need to be in place to provide incentives to change behavior.

Re-engineering efforts at Banca di America e di Italia (BAI), AT&T, and Siemens Nixdorf illustrate re-engineering that works. At BAI, when a customer comes in to make a deposit, the teller can analyze the customer profile using on-line databases and suggest new financial services. AT&T created a project management position to coordinate PBX sales from the beginning to end, resulting in a percentage increase from 31–71% in bills paid within 30 days of installation. At Siemens Nixdorf, remote diagnostics of networking issues helped troubleshoot 80% of the possible repairs and enabled service technicians to focus on the important issues. In addition, parts were loaded into service technicians' cars so they did not need to make two trips, one to diagnose the problem and another to make the repair (see Table 2.8).

A clean slate approach to process re-design calls for continuous training for new roles so individuals do not fall back into "old behavior." There must be a way of measuring performance and tracking progress toward achieving new goals. Communications are important so people understand why their behavior should be changed. Finally, information technology should support the re-engineering of business processes (Rosenthal, 1993).

TABLE 2-8 Re-engineering that Works

Company	Re-designed Processes	Before	After
BAI	Branch customer service	64 activities, 9 forms, 14 accounts	25 activities, 2 forms, 2 accounts
AT&T	PBX sales	12 project handoffs	3 handoffs
Siemens Nixdorf	Field service	30 support centers; 1,800 headcount	5 support centers; 800 headcount

◆ HOW INFORMATION TECHNOLOGY FACILITATES ERP

ERP relies upon the use of information technology, including client-server computing and shared databases. Many of the changes in business process design, work re-engineering, and sharing of information resources are facilitated through the implementation of information technology.

EMERGENCE OF CLIENT-SERVER COMPUTING

The basic rationale for client-server computing is that application use is divided between a "client," which is usually a personal computer, and a "server," or multiple servers, which offer certain resources. The components of client-server computing include a relational database, a server or servers, workstations, a network, and client software for the workstations. In the client-server environment, desktop systems are connected via networks to dedicated background servers, including file servers, print servers, application servers, and database servers. Its advantages can be seen in Table 2-9.

INTEGRATED DATABASES

The emergence of integrated databases is a foundation for ERP systems. Prior to integrated databases, each functional unit within an organization created, maintained, and updated its own databases (e.g., customer databases, supplier databases, employee databases) (see Illustration 2-4). After the emergence of integrated databases, organizational units shared common data maintained in central databases.

The advantages of integrated databases are data sharing, reduced data redundancy, improved data consistency, data independence, and improved data integrity. Data sharing means a common data resource supports functional units across the company. This reduces redundancy and contributes to data consistency. For example, a customer number is consistent across modules, including sales and marketing, financial accounting, and customer service. If for some reason a vendor number changes, this change is made anywhere the vendor number is used across application modules.

In addition, data independence means that data can be maintained separately from the application modules, which use the data. If a data definition is changed,

TABLE 2-9 Characteristics of a Client-Server Computing Environment	
Increased power	Client workstations have access to server-based software
Increased control	Server-based software can be systematically maintained and upgraded
Increased efficiency	Multiple locations can use common information resources
Improved user interfaces	Graphical user interface (GUI) interface
Improved database control	Common access to a relational database

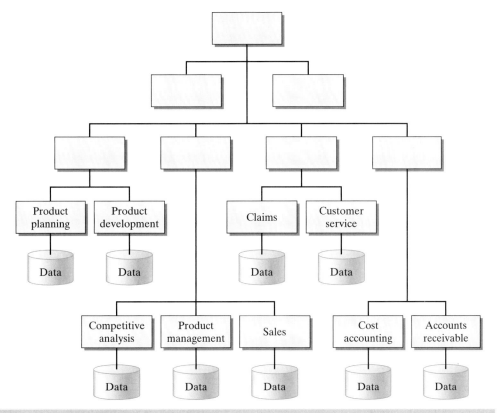

ILLUSTRATION 2-4   Before: Data Are Maintained Independently By Various Organizational Units

then changes do not need to be made to application modules, which use the data. For example, if a customer zip code is changed from a five-digit numeric field (63102) to a nine-digit numeric field (63102-1107), the data definition for the zip code is changed in the database management system, but the programs using this data element need not be changed. This substantially reduces application maintenance costs.

Finally, a database management system improves data integrity and provides central data administration. The database administrator can control access to data, updates to the database, and security. Professional data administration procedures, including backup and recovery, are assured. The security and integrity of the database are important for the management of information and the effective use of information for decision making.

ERP systems rely upon the use of an integrated database, in which data elements and their relationships are defined to support multiple applications. Integrated databases provide concurrency control, which enables multiple users to make updates to the database. In addition, the database administrator provides controls to assure that only authorized personnel can add, delete, and update data in the database. Security procedures include login identification, account codes, and passwords.

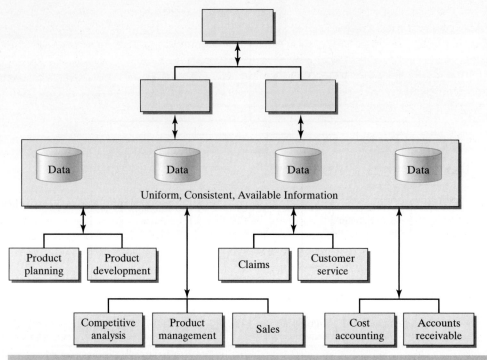

ILLUSTRATION 2-5   After: Databases Are Integrated Across Functional Lines

◆ THE EMERGENCE OF PROCESS ENTERPRISES

As organizations implement ERP, they are moving away from the "silos," or the specific units focused on products, regions, or functions. To emerge as a process enterprise, organizations need to stress teamwork over turf and hierarchy and to focus on achieving "process goals." One of the ways of making the transition to process management is to give authority over work and budgets to "process owners." (Hammer, 1999).

A case in point is Texas Instrument's calculator business in the early 1990s. TI had long product development life cycles, and they were losing business to competitors. Management wanted to re-engineer TI's calculator business, and this is what happened:

> *The first pilot teams not only failed to achieve the desired reductions in development times but also barely managed to operate at all. They were, in effect, sabotaged by the existing organization, which viewed them as interlopers. Functional departments were unwilling to cede people, space, or responsibility to the teams. The technical writers and designers charged with creating documentation got instructions from the product team and then got conflicting orders from their supervisors in the marketing department. The corporate training unit refused to relinquish control over the development of training materials, and the advertising department insisted on continuing to create product advertising. An effort that had been intended to create harmony in product development instead created discord.*

The problem was that the power still resided in the old functional departments. Management tried to superimpose an integrated process on a fragmented organization. To introduce re-engineering successfully, management created organizational units responsible for product development (e.g., of calculators) and created a process owner with budgetary authority to manage the process. The process owner had authority over designing the process, measuring its performance, and training the workers. The result was that product development time was reduced by 50% (Hammer, 1999).

At IBM, a similar transition occurred. IBM wanted to standardize its operations worldwide, by instituting common processes for order fulfillment and product development to replace the diverse processes used in different parts of the world and for different products. However, independent country and product managers provided a roadblock to rolling out the standardized processes.

What did IBM do? It changed the management structure and gave responsibility for each process to a member of the Corporate Executive Committee. This shifted power away from the country and product managers to senior management and resulted in the successful implementation of standardized processes, resulting in customer satisfaction and $9 billion in cost savings (Hammer, 1999).

ERP AND BUSINESS PROCESS CHANGE

The process changes associated with making re-engineering work are critical to the success of ERP. At Owens Corning, an ERP implementation failed because regional managers rejected the software or sought to tailor it to the needs of their own units. To overcome this resistance, Owens Corning created the role of "process owner," with the authority to design the process, measure its performance, and train front-line workers to perform it. This role had to be maintained, or the old organizational structures would have re-emerged (Hammer, 1999).

◆ SUMMARY

ERP provides an opportunity to re-design business processes. With re-engineering, business processes are simplified and business rules are improved. In addition, re-designing processes provides the foundation for new opportunities, such as eBusiness. To make process management work, all employees must "buy into" the new processes and understand their role in contributing to the success of the new system. Re-engineering with ERP enables organizations to be more responsive to changing markets and to shifts in competitors' strategies.

Questions for Discussion ●

1. Conduct a search of on-line databases to find a case in business re-engineering, similar to some of the cases mentioned in this (e.g., Ford Motor Company, Mutual Benefit Life, Hewlett-Packard).
   a. Was an ERP system associated with the business-process re-engineering?
   b. What business benefits were derived from adopting best practices?
   c. What obstacles needed to be overcome as a result of implementing changes in work flow, work methods, and work systems?

2. How does the implementation of ERP contribute to business process re-engineering?
3. How does information technology facilitate the process of business re-engineering. Without information technology, would business process change be possible?

◆◆◆ **Case**

Re-engineering the Payment Processing System at RFC

Read the following case, which describes the current payment processing system at RFC, and complete the activities at the end of the case.

DESCRIPTION OF THE CURRENT PAYMENT PROCESSING SYSTEM

Once the loan is set up, customers can pay in three different ways. First, customers can bring their payments into the branch in the form of cash, check, or money order. Second, they can mail their payments to the branch. The branch personnel verify their Loan ID, if necessary by checking the Customer card file, and update the loan Outstanding Loans File by pulling the voucher copy corresponding to the payment and stamping it "paid" and then filing it in the Paid Vouchers file in sequence by Loan ID and due date sequence.

The actual payments are then batched and deposited in the branch bank each afternoon. The Home Office is notified by means of an Advice of Payment Received (APR), which is filled out for each payment and mailed to the Home Office.

Third, customers may pay the Home Office directly. If they do so, the Home Office Payment Processing Department verifies that each payment is complete, by checking the enclosed voucher. If the voucher is missing, the payment processing clerk uses a printout of the central Outstanding Loans File to look up the Loan ID corresponding with the correct account. Then the branch personnel are notified of the payment by means of an APR, which is then mailed to the branch personnel.

The details of the payment are used to update the Outstanding Loans File in the Home Office. Each evening, a batch payment processing run is used to update all the accounts centrally, based upon payments received during that working day. In addition, the branch personnel use the APRs from the Home Office as well as its own internal records of payments that have been sent directly to the branch personnel to update its own local Outstanding Loans File.

Payments made directly to the Home Office are batched and sent directly to the Home Office bank. The payment processing system produces a payment report for the Accounting Department and a branch-by-branch payment report for each Branch Manager.

DELINQUENCY ANALYSIS SYSTEM

On a weekly basis, the delinquency analysis system is run. It checks the Outstanding Loans File in the Home Office and determines if payments are overdue. It generates an Aged Trial Balance Report, which indicates which payments are 15, 30, 45, and 60 days overdue. When a payment is 15 days overdue, a polite First Reminder is sent. When a payment is more than 30 days overdue, a second (less polite) reminder is sent. Four reminders, with increasing degrees of insistence, are sent. All of these reminders are computer-generated. After the loan becomes 60 days overdue, it is moved to the Collections Department, and collections agents follow up at that time.

SETTLEMENT ACCOUNTING SYSTEM

From time to time, customers want to finish paying a loan before it becomes due. In these cases, the customer requests a settlement figure, which is the amount required to settle the outstanding balance on the loan. If the request is urgent, the Branch Manager will phone the request to the

Home Office. The information systems department now prepares a settlement run, which is processed nightly, with the urgent request for the settlement balance. The settlement balance is sent back to the Branch Manager the next morning.

PROBLEMS WITH PAYMENT PROCESSING

At the current time, RFC is planning to expand the number of branches from 187 to 400 in the next three years and to a target of 1,000 over the next five years after that. To accommodate expansion plans, the current system will need to be streamlined, modified, and enhanced. Some of its current problems are the following:

1. About 80% of the payments are made to branch personnel, and the rest are mailed to the Home Office. Of the payments that are mailed, the payment voucher from the Voucher Booklet is missing in about half the cases. This does not matter so much at the branch location because the branch personnel maintain a local customer card file with the name and Loan ID. However, at the Home Office, it is more difficult to trace payments. At the current time, incoming payments without an accompanying voucher are identified by checking against a printout of the Outstanding Loans File. However, unidentified payments sometimes generate an APR to the wrong branch, and the entire process causes more clerical work and error correction.

2. The bottlenecks in processing payments trigger additional problems. Considerable clerical overhead is caused by situations where people do not pay until ten days after their due date, and because of various delays, their payment does not actually get posted to the Outstanding Loans File until after the Delinquency Analysis run has sent them their first reminder. When they call the branch personnel to protest receiving a reminder, the personnel have to call the Home Office and trace their payment. Forty-four people are currently tied up in the Customer Service section at the Home

Office, and much of their time is spent dealing with late and missing payment matters.

3. Throughout the system, excessive clerical overhead occurs. In 129 of the 187 branches, a full-time clerical person was engaged in maintaining the local branch loans file, in pulling voucher copies, in recording payments, and in making out APRs. In the other 58 branches, these activities take between 2–5 hours per day.

4. Since the Outstanding Loans File is always several days out of date, it is often difficult to isolate loans that are delinquent until it is too late. About 2.5% of all loans are never repaid. Last year $4,795,000 was written off as uncollectible. Although processing delays account for not flagging late payers sooner, management feels that RFC could do a much better job of weeding out potential delinquents during the initial approval process. To do this, RFC wants to build a picture of the potential delinquent, including age, occupation, income, family size, location, mobility, and a host of other criteria. A delinquency profile will aid in identifying "high potential for delinquency" accounts. This profile can be developed, maintained, and modified by Operations Research personnel on an ongoing basis.

5. Because of error and adjustment activities, it is rarely possible to balance the books for month end before the twelfth (12th) of the succeeding month. This greatly complicates planning for cash flow and frequently requires RFC to borrow more money that it needs and at higher interest charges.

CASE EXERCISE

1. Draw a current process model for the payment processing system at RFC.
2. What changes in business processes and information do you feel will improve the payment processing system at RFC?
3. Draw a new process model for a re-engineering payment processing system at RFC.

References ●

Hammer, Michael. 1990. "Re-engineering work: Don't automate, obliterate." *Harvard Business Review* 68: 104–112.

Hammer, Michael. 1999. "How process enterprises really work." *Harvard Business Review* 77: 108–118.

Hammer, Michael and Champy, James. 1993. *Re-engineering the Corporation.* Harper Business.

Rosenthal, Jim. 1993. "How to make re-engineering work." *Harvard Business Review* 71: 119.

•CHAPTER• 3

Planning, Design, and Implementation of Enterprise Resource Planning Systems

Objective

Understand the information systems development process for enterprise systems, including planning, design, and implementation.

In this chapter, you will learn about the traditional approach to information systems design and how it compares with Enterprise Resource Planning (ERP) systems design. ERP design and implementation differs from traditional systems development. In ERP design, the organization acquires a packaged software system that defines processes and practices for the business. The main challenge in implementing ERP is whether to change the organization's business processes to fit the software or whether to modify the software to fit the organization's business processes. In this chapter, you will learn about the trade-offs involved in re-engineering business processes to fit the software versus customizing the software.

◆ TRADITIONAL SYSTEMS DEVELOPMENT

The traditional systems development life cycle included the phases of problem definition, feasibility study, systems analysis, systems design, detailed design, implementation, and maintenance (see Table 3-1). In systems analysis, the analyst undertakes a detailed analysis of the current system, using tools and techniques, such as process models and data models. Using these models, the systems designer analyzes bottlenecks, duplication of effort, inconsistencies, and other problems with the current system.

The fundamental approach used in traditional systems development is to analyze the current system's shortcomings and to develop a "new" system, which builds in changes in processes and data that will support the firm's business requirements. The rationale is that automating the current system is counterproductive because the current system may have problems, including redundant processes, insufficient data,

TABLE 3-1   Information Systems Design: Traditional Approach

Step	*Activities*	*Tools and Techniques*
Problem definition	Identify problems with the current system	Interviewing and data collection
Feasibility study	Assess the need for a systems project, including technical, economic, and management feasibility	Preliminary cost analysis
Systems analysis	Undertake a detailed analysis of the current system, including processes, information flows, and work organization	Logical process models — present system; Logical data models — present system; Organization charts (functional hierarchy diagrams)
Systems design	Development of objectives for the new system; re-engineering of processes and information	Logical process models — proposed system; logical data models — proposed system; organization charts — proposed system
Detailed design	Design of specifications for the proposed system	Program design specifications output design; input design Database design; forms design
Implementation	Software implementation; training end-users; development of reporting systems; design of controls and security	Coding; testing; documentation
Maintenance	Ongoing technical support; ongoing upgrades and enhancements	

and inefficient workflow. The systems design process provides an opportunity to re-engineer or re-invent the current system prior to automating it. The systems design process seeks to assure logical database design prior to detailed design, during which the specifications for the physical system are developed (e.g., output design, input design). Once the physical design specifications are set, then the system is programmed, tested, and implemented.

The problem with the traditional systems development life cycle is that it takes too much time and costs too much. The traditional life cycle follows a "waterfall" approach, in which there is a sequence of steps, starting with planning and analysis to be followed by design, detailed design, and implementation. Since the mid-1980s, companies have been seeking faster methods of developing information systems.

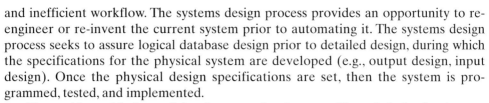

◆ NEW APPROACHES TO SYSTEMS DEVELOPMENT

Three different approaches designed to speed up the building of information systems were prototyping, end-user development, and software packages. In the late 1980s, prototyping was introduced as a methodology for obtaining user requirements more quickly and accurately. Using prototyping, systems designers could show "models" of systems documents (e.g., reports, screens) to end-users to get a better idea of their requirements. While this approach enabled end-users to specify their requirements, it did not necessarily speed up the systems implementation process, including coding, testing, and debugging.

End-user development was another approach introduced in the mid- to late-1980s and is still relevant for many applications. Equipped with spreadsheets and database packages, like Microsoft Excel and Access, end-users constructed their own information systems. While this approach worked effectively for local departmental applications, it was not appropriate for the development of large-scale production systems requiring quality assurance, security, documentation, backup, and live production.

In the late 1980s, software packages became more prevalent. They offered economies of scale in development, enhancement, and maintenance, and many companies moved toward purchasing commercial off-the-shelf software. ERP systems are large-scale, integrated commercial off-the-shelf software packages that support the entire value chain of business functions.

◆ THE ERP SYSTEMS DEVELOPMENT PROCESS

The ERP systems design process is different from the traditional systems development process. The ERP systems development process includes planning, requirements analysis, design, detailed design, implementation, and maintenance (see Table 3-2).

Planning starts with a needs assessment, which provides a business justification for the purchase of the software. This needs assessment phase is important because of the major investment in an ERP system and its business impact. The requirements analysis phase of an ERP project involves specifying the business processes to be supported by the ERP package. Most ERP vendors offer "best practices," which are models of functions supported by the ERP system.

TABLE 3-2	ERP Systems Design Process	
Step	*Activities*	*Tools and Techniques*
Planning	Conduct a needs assessment; provide a business justification, based upon the difference between the existing system and the proposed system	Interviewing; cost justification
Requirements analysis	Analyze current business processes and specify the processes to be supported; select the ERP system	Use best practices models to see what the company can gain by implementing the new system
Design	Re-engineer business processes around the best practices model of the ERP system or customize the software	Use the ERP methodology's best practices or customize
Detailed design	Choose standard models, processes, inputs, and outputs (e.g., customer lists, vendor lists)	Interactive prototyping
Implementation	Configure the system; migrate data from the old system to the new system; develop interfaces; implement reporting systems; conduct testing; implement controls, security; train end-users	Work with vendors to correct any "bugs" in the software; clean processes and data Use reporting tools
Maintenance and continuous improvement	Provide technical support; provide upgrades and enhancements	Add enhanced functionality to existing modules

In the design phase of the project, the project sponsors introduce the best practices, which the ERP system supports. This entails re-engineering business processes to fit the software. This is fundamentally different from the traditional systems development approach, in which the systems designer defines new business requirements and implements software to conform to these requirements. One of the fundamental design decisions in implementing an ERP package is whether to re-engineer the organization's business processes to fit the software or to customize the software to fit the organization's business practices.

PLANNING: MAKING THE BUSINESS CASE FOR ERP

The business justifications for ERP include tangible and intangible benefits, including inventory reduction, operating cost reductions, overdue accounts collection, process improvement, and reduction in cycle times (Ross, Vitale, and Willcocks, 2003). The technology and business rationales for ERP packages are illustrated in Table 3-3.

TABLE 3-3 Rationales for ERP	
Technology Rationales	**Business Rationales**
Ability to use timely operational data	Inventory cost reductions
Ability to integrate systems, instead of maintaining many separate systems	IT cost reductions
Ability to enhance systems without incurring the time and cost of custom development and modifications	Personnel cost reductions
Ability to implement new features, such as Customer Relationship Management (CRM)	Increased profitability
Access to on-line, real-time operational data	Productivity improvement
Reduction in the time and cost of systems development and maintenance	Better cash management

REQUIREMENTS ANALYSIS

Requirements analysis activities involve (1) analyzing business processes and (2) specifying the processes to be supported by the ERP package. Since the company is buying into the vendor's view of best practices, it is important to select a system which fits with the organization's goals and competitive strategy (Umble, Haft, and Umble, 2003). Most vendors offer best practices for specific industries, such as the chemical industry and oil industry.

The process of selecting the best ERP system entails working through a checklist of activities (see Table 3-4) (Umble et al., 2003).

Aside from the business issues, there are a number of technology factors to consider in selecting an ERP vendor and an ERP system (see Table 3-5).

DESIGN: RE-ENGINEERING VERSUS CUSTOMIZING

The fundamental decision in ERP systems design is re-engineering versus customizing. In the re-engineering approach, the team selects a commercial off-the-shelf ERP and re-engineers business processes to fit the package. In the customizing approach, the team selects a commercial ERP and customizes the ERP to meet unique requirements (see Table 3-6).

An in-depth analysis of the trade-offs between re-engineering and customizing an ERP system illustrates several important factors. Re-engineering the business to fit the software can disrupt the organization because this represents changes in procedures, work flows, and data. However, customizing an ERP can make upgrading to newer versions difficult since vendor-supplied versions will be based upon vanilla versions of the software (see Table 3-7).

ALTERNATIVE ERP DESIGN OPTIONS

ERP systems can be designed using various approaches. A complete vanilla ERP package is easiest to implement because the organization can follow the vendor-prescribed

TABLE 3-4	Selecting an ERP System	
Steps	***Activities***	***Complete Y/N***
Create the vision	Develop corporate objectives for ERP	
Create a feature/function list	Use a team who are familiar with company processes; map current processes to the new best practices	
Create a software candidate list	Narrow the field based on size of company, industry type; talk to existing buyers in the industry	
Narrow the field to four to six serious candidates	Conduct preliminary analysis of strengths and weaknesses; determine goodness of fit	
Create the Request For Proposal (RFP)	Develop a list of features and functions	
Review the proposals	Consider strengths and weaknesses of each proposal	
Select two or three finalists	Have the finalists demonstrate their packages	
Select the winner	Consider numerous factors (e.g., supplier support, closeness of fit, technological risk)	
Justify the investment	Conduct a cost-benefit analysis; tangible benefits include improved material control, reduced costs, increased productivity, increased on-time deliveries, improved customer service, inventory reduction, and elimination of redundant databases; intangible benefits include reduced cost, higher morale, and improved communications; make a GO, NO GO decision	
Negotiate the contract	Participate in contract review	
Run a pre-implementation pilot	Have the cross-functional team review the pilot	
Validate the justification	Involve the cross-functional team in a final GO, NO GO decision	

TABLE 3-5	Technology Factors to Consider in Selecting an ERP System
Technology Factors	***Questions***
Cost of technology	What are the start-up and recurring costs?
Installation	What consulting assistance is offered (time, cost)?
User interfaces	What interfaces are supported?
Upgradability	What is the frequency of upgrades?
Computing environment	What is the computing environment?
Personnel requirements	What expertise is needed for design and implementation (business analysts, consultants)?

TABLE 3-6   Re-engineering vs. Customizing

	Pros	*Cons*
Customizing approach	Supports unique business processes; strategic processes are maintained	An ERP may not support these unique business processes; re-inventing the wheel; customization is difficult, since modules are integrated; difficult to upgrade the software to newer versions, since upgrades are based on vanilla versions
Re-engineering approach	Is supported by an ERP solution; takes advantage of shared or generic processes within industries (e.g., industry templates); best practices may represent improved process changes; documents best practices; works well when there is minimal organizational change	Does not support strategic or unique business processes; resistance occurs when there is extensive organizational change

TABLE 3-7   Detailed Comparison: Re-engineering vs. Customizing Approach

	Re-engineering Approach	*Customizing Approach*
Re-engineering business processes	Supports re-engineering processes to fit the software system's best practices	Re-engineering is independent of the tool being implemented (e.g., its models, processes, outputs)
Organizational fit	Works well with minimal organizational change, but extensive re-engineering may disrupt the organization	May disrupt the organization less because software is designed to support current methods of work organization and structure
Evolution	Evolution depends upon vendor upgrades and enhancements to the system	Evolution can support unique user requirements
Timeliness	Software is available and ready to implement	May involve lengthy systems development activities
Cost	Implementation is cost-effective	May involve extensive cost of custom implementation
Requirements	Puts boundaries on the design; designs conform with business models and best practices	Provides greater flexibility for meeting unique requirements; not constrained by the tools' best practices; no boundaries for the design
Competitiveness	Other firms have access to the same design	Do not have to use software to which everyone in the industry has access
Fit	Requirements will be supported by an ERP system	Unique requirements may not be supported by an ERP system
External consulting	More of a turnkey approach, particularly using a vanilla implementation	May entail the expense of much external consulting

TABLE 3-8   ERP Modules and Level of Customization—Sweden

Module	Implementation Frequency	Customization Relative Implementation[*]
Purchasing	93%	60.5%
Order entry	92.4%	67.8%
Materials management	91.8%	60.7%
Production planning	90.5%	69.2%
Financial accounting	87.3%	50.7%
Distribution/logistics	84.8%	67.9%
Financial control	82.3%	53.1%
Asset management	63.3%	41%
Human resources	57.6%	33%
Quality management	47.5%	36%

[*]Percentage of firms which have customized the module.

methodology and use consultants with specialized vendor expertise. Firms are more successful in implementing ERP systems under budget or on-budget when the amount of customizing is kept to a minimum (Mabert, Soni, and Venkataramanan, 2000).

Nevertheless, many organizations customize ERP modules. A large percentage of firms surveyed in Sweden (Olhager and Selldin, 2003) decided to customize the ERP system they selected (see Table 3-8).

When an ERP system is customized, the time and cost of the project increases along with the risk associated with successful implementation. This is because the customized software cannot be as easily integrated with new versions of the ERP, which are introduced by the vendor over time. In their study of ERP implementation, Mabert, et al., found that firms which were able to implement ERP under budget or on-budget made fewer modifications than over-budget firms. Making modifications in the ERP software contributed to a 50% increase in project duration (Mabert, et al., 2000).

Some organizations decide to maintain their legacy systems and add ERP modules to support specific functions, such as Financial Accounting and Customer Relationship Management (CRM). Though this approach is cost-effective compared with a full-scale ERP implementation, it deprives the organization of the benefits of an integrated ERP that supports multiple business functions, and it leads to the maintenance of legacy and ERP systems. The one advantage of this approach is that it disrupts the organization less because users do not need to accept changes in business procedures.

Another approach to ERP implementation is to use outsourcing and to have an external vendor operate the system. One of the best ways of outsourcing ERP is to use an Application Service Provider (ASP), which provides the ERP software on a time-sharing basis to its customers (see Table 3-9). This enables the client to have access to technological expertise and is more cost-effective than a full-scale internal ERP implementation. However, any outsourcing decision is dependent upon the reliability and

TABLE 3-9	Menu of ERP Alternatives			
Option	**Time**	**Cost**	**Advantages**	**Disadvantages**
Vanilla implementation of a single vendor ERP	Moderate	Moderate	Easiest to implement	May forfeit internal systems which provide a strategic advantage
Single-vendor ERP with customization	High	High	Maintains strategic processes	Poses greater risk and higher cost because vendor modifications cannot be easily adopted
In-house with supplementary ERP modules	Moderate	High	Minimizes the extent of change that users have to accept	Higher cost because of maintaining legacy systems and new ERP modules; limited benefits because of lack of integration
ASP	Moderate	Moderate	Provides vendor support and expertise at lower cost	Creates dependence on the provider

stability of the vendor, and the organization is vulnerable (Ross, Vitale, and Willcocks, 2003). You will learn more about outsourcing ERP in Chapter 9.

The decision for which approach to use in implementing ERP should be based upon the extent to which the business benefits of ERP can be realized using each approach. If only partial business benefits can be achieved via an in-house system with supplementary ERP capabilities, then management should consider a full-scale implementation approach, using vendor-supported ERP implementation or an outsourcing approach to ERP services.

DETAILED DESIGN

In the project's detailed design phase, the team selects the models, processes, and information supported by the system. The best practices methodology provides models supporting the business processes for each functional area within the business (see Table 3-10). The process for using the best practices includes these steps:

1. Select applicable business processes.
2. Discard inapplicable business processes.
3. When business processes are not matched up with the system, they serve as a foundation for re-engineering (re-organizing processes, organization).
4. Identify any areas not covered by the best practices and which may require the development of customized models.

Detailed design involves interactive prototyping and extensive user involvement in determining systems design elements. In SAP's environment, the following elements can be implemented (see Table 3-11).

TABLE 3-10 Models Supporting the Best Practices

Model	Purpose	Characteristics	Example
Component model	What is done?	Shows the major functions supported by the system	Create material master
Organizational model	Who does what?	Shows the breakdown of organizational units	Sales
Data model	What information is needed?	Shows the information needed by the company	Material order
Interaction model	What information must be exchanged between different components?	Shows the major organizational units involved in information processing (e.g., sales, procurement, production)	Materials management

TABLE 3-11 SAP Design Elements

Entity	Definition	Example
Organizational element	Depicts the enterprise structure using an SAP application	Plant
Master data	Data that is created centrally and available to all applications	Customer master
Transactions	Application programs that conduct business processes	Create sales order
Output	Information that is released	Sending an order confirmation to a customer
Workflow	Optimizes activities	Processing a travel request form
Reporting	Generates reports	Financial analysis report

Figure 3-1 illustrates Customer master data, which provides relevant data to multiple modules, including financial accounting and sales.

Figure 3-2 illustrates sales transactions. When a sales order is created, the user must enter the customer number from the Customer master and the Material master numbers from the Material master for the items being ordered. This copies relevant customer data and material data to the sales order.

Figure 3-3 illustrates various reporting systems, including reports generated via information systems, such as financial, logistics, and human resources reports. In addition, tools for database query and ad hoc reporting are used to generate reports from separate databases. These advanced reporting systems are known as executive information systems and business warehouse applications. You will learn more about these reporting systems in Chapter 9.

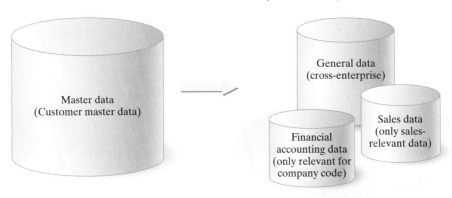

FIGURE 3-1   Master Data: Customer Master

Source: Copyright SAP AG.

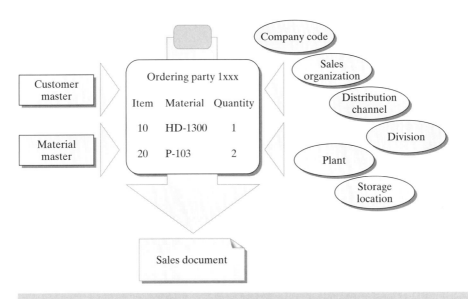

FIGURE 3-2   Sales Transactions

Source: Copyright SAP AG.

Implementation

ERP implementation includes addressing configuration issues, migrating data from the old system to the new system, building interfaces, implementing reports, and pilot testing. Many companies contract with a technical support specialist from the software supplier to assist in implementation.

Configuring the ERP system requires the project team to address a number of factors, including data ownership and data management, as shown in Table 3-12.

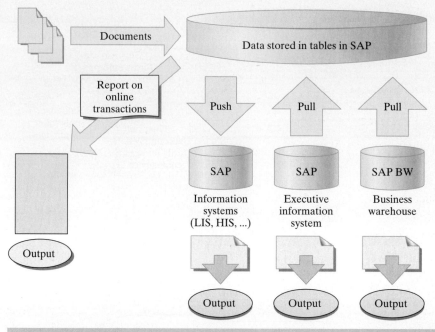

FIGURE 3-3 Reporting Systems

Source: Copyright SAP AG.

◆ ERP IMPLEMENTATION STEPS

ERP implementation includes establishing security and permissions, so users have the access they need. Migrating data from the old system to the new system means ensuring that data to be migrated are accurate and that data bridges work. Building interfaces to other systems, such as office systems (e.g., Lotus Notes), can be very important

TABLE 3-12 Factors to Consider in Configuring an ERP System

Factor	*Things to Consider*
Data ownership	Who is responsible for data integrity? (centralized responsibility versus local responsibility?)
Distribution of procedures	Which business processes should be centralized? Which processes should remain under local control?
Transactions	Does the ERP provide an audit trail of transactions at the traceable level? Does the ERP provide an audit trail of transactions at the aggregate level?
Data management	Will the ERP support centralized data management—a master repository? Will the ERP support local data management?

TABLE 3-13	Implementation Strategy (Swedish firms)	
Implementation Strategy		*Percent*
Big bang		42.1
Mini big bang		20.4
Phased by module		17.1
Phased by site		20.4

to successful operation. Documentation is provided by the vendor and should be reviewed. User training is also an important priority. Training end-users, which is critical to successful implementation, is often not extensive enough (Umble et al., 2003).

The issue of whether to cutover to the new system all at once, or to phase in modules sequentially, is an important one. The cutover approach, known as the big bang approach, is more rapid, but there might not be sufficient resources to accomplish it. Most large firms choose to phase in modules by module or by site. Smaller firms can implement the big bang approach with reasonable success. Based upon a survey of Swedish firms (see Table 3-13), a large percentage of firms use the big bang or the mini big bang approach, the latter being a partial vendor implementation (Olhager and Selldin, 2003).

Since ERP projects represent considerable time commitments and cost, many risks are involved in implementation, and these risks can trigger time and cost overruns. These risks can be reduced if the company decides to implement a complete vendor package because the vendor-tested implementation technique will be followed. However, if the organization does not choose a full vendor implementation, then risk assessment and analysis should become part of the implementation strategy. One risk assessment model proposes that at the beginning of each phase of the project, project managers should conduct a risk analysis to determine what might go wrong and what strategies will be used if problems occur. Having a plan of action and external resources available at the outset of the each project phase can minimize the implementation risk.

◆ SUMMARY

In ERP systems development, the project team specifies the functions to be supported by the ERP package and has the choice of re-designing the organization's business processes to fit the software or customizing the software. In addressing this question, the project team must determine the business benefits that can be achieved by implementing the vendor's best practices and the overall maintainability of the software. Critical success factors for ERP implementation include the commitment of top management and project management, organizational change management, an effective implementation team, data accuracy, and extensive education and training. You will find in-depth coverage of the management of ERP projects in Chapter 9.

Questions for Discussion •

1. How does the traditional systems development life cycle differ from the ERP information systems design and implementation process?
2. What are the advantages of the re-engineering method of implementing ERP? What are its disadvantages?
3. What are the advantages of the customizing method of implementing ERP? What are its disadvantages?
4. Dell wanted a more flexible architecture and the opportunity to select software from various vendors. What were the advantages and disadvantages to using this approach? (See: D. Slater, "An ERP package for you, and you, and even you," *CIO Magazine*, February 15, 1999.)
5. What are the advantages and disadvantages of using an ASP to implement ERP?

◆◆◆ Case

Response to Request for Proposal for an ERP System

The purpose of this project is to give students an opportunity to learn about various ERP systems and to present vendor characteristics and qualifications in response to a Request for Proposal (RFP). The RFP has been developed to meet the needs of a mid-sized manufacturing company, Wingate Electric.

In this project, the class will be organized into teams, and each team will represent one of four or more ERP vendors who are responding to an RFP for an ERP financial module, which can be integrated with a larger ERP system over time. The case provides selection criteria to evaluate the alternative ERP financial modules, and a brief description of the scoring method of evaluating the alternatives. Each team (representing one of the vendors) will have an opportunity to consult various resources, including the vendor web sites, on-line library resources, trade publications, and marketing publications.

The case includes directions for each team, which will give a presentation to a mock panel of user managers of the company considering the ERP options. The panel of user managers can be selected from local businesses or from the university community. The presentation will be reviewed by the panel of user managers using an

Evaluation Form, and the panel will make the selection decision based upon the "winning" team. The panel of user managers will provide feedback to each team with respect to the strengths and weaknesses of each of their presentations, and the rationale for their selection decision.

The materials for the Case Study include:

- Company Background
- The RFP
- The selection criteria to evaluate the alternative ERP modules supporting financial applications
- Scoring method, which describes the scoring method of evaluating the alternatives
- Team directions
- Team vendor assignments and resources for vendor research
- List of user managers (e.g., job titles, background)

A. COMPANY BACKGROUND

Wingate Electric is a mid-sized manufacturing company that makes small electric motors for appliances, lawn mowers, and small tractors. The company, founded by Bob Wingate, has been in business for 100 years. It is currently owned by his two sons, Dick and Steve Wingate, on a 50/50 basis. Dick, the CEO, handles the marketing and business development side of the business, and Steve, the Chief Operating Officer, is responsible for internal operations management.

The MIS systems at Wingate Electric are home-grown systems that have been patched together over the years. These systems support the major accounting and financial functions, including sales order processing, inventory control, accounts payable, accounts receivable, and general ledger. These applications use multiple legacy file systems, and much of the data are redundant. Since updates must be made to multiple files, some of the data are inconsistent. With little documentation, making queries to existing databases is difficult.

Competitors within the industry are adopting ERP systems to integrate financial and manufacturing data, and Wingate Electric is being left behind. Competitors are adopting web-based front ends for order processing, order tracking, and order follow-up, but Wingate cannot move in this direction because its back-office systems are in disarray.

The owners of Wingate Electric have decided to issue a RFP for an ERP system which supports their accounting and financial functions and which can be extended to support their production and manufacturing applications over time. The panel of user managers who will be reviewing the presentations in response to the RFP will be the following:

Dick Wingate, CEO

Steve Wingate, Chief Operating Officer

Robert Murdick, Chief Financial Officer

Richard Hayes, Marketing Manager

Kathryn Martell, Director of Accounting Operations

B. REQUEST FOR PROPOSAL

Date: February 1, 2005

Wingate Electric is a mid-sized manufacturing company that makes small electric motors for appliances, lawn mowers, and small tractors. The company, founded by Bob Wingate, has been in business for 100 years. The company is currently managed by its owners, Dick and Steve Wingate. Dick Wingate, the CEO, is responsible for overall business development and marketing. Steve Wingate, the COO, is responsible for operations management.

Wingate Electric currently does $400 million in sales. Its customers include major manufacturers of small appliances and vehicles, and they would like to have web-based order processing and order tracking capability, and this is one motivation for acquiring an ERP foundation for web-based applications.

The MIS systems at Wingate Electric are home-grown applications that have become fragmented over time. They are difficult to maintain, and they do not use an integrated relational database. Managers have trouble gaining access to data for query and reporting purposes.

Wingate Electric is interested in acquiring an ERP system, which supports its financial and accounting functions, including accounts receivable, accounts payable, and general ledger. The ERP financial system will be implemented first, and the company is interested in adding modules supporting production planning and manufacturing in the next phase. Ideally, the ERP system will also support Sales and Marketing, Human Resources, CRM, and eBusiness. These capabilities will be implemented in subsequent phases, depending upon the success of the ERP modules supporting financial and accounting functions.

The budget for ERP is estimated at $1,000,000, excluding the cost of acquiring the necessary upgrades in hardware, software, and networking facilities. In the current environment, the firm has 100 microcomputer workstations, a Windows NT network, and a Hewlett-Packard server supporting its legacy systems.

The timeline for selecting the ERP modules supporting finance and accounting is three months. The due date for the RFP response is March 1, 2005. Upon receipt of the proposals, four or more vendors will be asked to give presentations and to respond to questions. The selection committee will make a decision within 30 days after the presentations have been given. The selection criteria are listed below. Five of these criteria deal with supplier-related issues, and five of them deal with the evaluation of the

ERP modules supporting finance and accounting. Proposals and presentations should address each of these selection criteria.

C. SELECTION CRITERIA FOR ERP SUPPLIER

1. Corporate History, Experience, and Corporate Profile
   a. Overall History
   b. Number of Years of Experience
   c. Position in the Industry
2. Market Strategy and Strategic Direction
   a. Market Share
   b. Market Strategy
   c. Future Market Strategy
   d. Overall Strengths
3. Product Offerings, Integration, and Scalability
   a. Overall ERP Product Line
   b. Module Integration Strategy
   c. Web-based Application Strategy
   d. New Offerings (e.g., business intelligence, CRM)
4. Consulting Support
   a. Support for Configuration of Application Modules
   b. Technical Support for System Implementation
   c. Cost of Consulting Support
   d. Availability of Consulting Support
5. Availability of Training
   a. Training in Configuration
   b. Technical Training

Selection Criteria for ERP Modules Supporting Financial and Accounting Functions:

6. Fit with Current Business Processes
   a. Fit with Sales and Order Processing Processes
   b. Fit with Financial Accounting Processes (A/R, A/P, General Ledger)
   c. Fit with Managerial Accounting Processes
7. Reporting Applications
   a. Current Reporting Capabilities
   b. Availability of Tools for Database Query and Reporting
   c. Web-based Reporting Capability

8. User Friendliness
   a. Availability of Tutorials
   b. Availability of Application Module Documentation
   c. Technical Documentation
9. Cost
   a. Cost of ERP Modules
   b. Cost of Configuration and Implementation Support
   c. Cost of Training
   d. Cost of Maintenance Fees and Software Licenses
10. Ability to Integrate Finance and Accounting Module with other ERP Modules
    a. Integration with Production and Manufacturing Modules
    b. Integration with Sales and Marketing Modules
    c. Integration with Human Resources Modules
    d. Integration with web-based Applications

D. SCORING METHOD

The selection committee will use the score sheet (see below) to rate each vendor on each of the selection criteria. The selection committee will rate each presentation on the basis of the selection criteria, which include ten criteria in all. Five of these criteria pertain to ERP supplier characteristics, and five of these criteria pertain to the characteristics of the ERP modules under consideration. For each criteria, the selection committee will use a rating scale of 1 to 10, with 10 being the most possible points that can be scored in any one category.

In addition, the selection committee will rate each presentation on several bonus/penalty items, which can add or detract from the total scores. These bonus/penalty items will have a possible value of +5 or −5 points each, as illustrated on the score sheet below. These bonus/penalty items include the effectiveness of the overall presentation, and the special, value-added qualifications (noted below). The overall possible maximum score for each presentation is 110 points.

The selection committee will consist of individuals who will play the roles of user management. In addition, each of the teams will rate the other team presentations using the same score sheet.

E. DIRECTIONS TO TEAMS

Each team will assume the role of an ERP vendor responding to the RFP. Each team should have 3–6 students, with 5 students as ideal, and each team will have three weeks to prepare for the presentation to the selection committee. In preparation for the presentations, each team should do research on its ERP vendor's characteristics in order to address each of the selection criteria. For example, to respond to the corporate history, experience, and corporate profile criteria, the team will need to use external resources for research about the vendor.

The presentations should be accomplished in 25 minutes, with each team member having 5 minutes. There will be an additional 5 minutes for questions from the Selection Committee.

The teams can augment their oral presentations with audio-visual aids, including computer-based Powerpoint presentations. They can bring handouts, articles in trade publications about user experiences with the ERP modules under consideration, and information about external resources (e.g., web sites, trade reviews), which the Selection Committee might want to consult. The purpose of the exercise is to make the presentations as real as possible.

TABLE 1	Selection Committee Score Sheet

Team Members:

Score	Weight	Item	Criteria	Comments
	10	#1	Corporate history, experience, and profile	
	10	#2	Market strategy and strategic direction	
	10	#3	Product offerings, integration, scalability	
	10	#4	Consulting support (e.g., configuration, technical)	
	10	#5	Training availability (e.g., configuration, technical)	
	10	#6	Current business process fit	
	10	#7	Reporting applications (e.g., tools, web-based)	
	10	#8	User-friendliness (e.g., tutorials, documentation)	
	10	#9	Cost (e.g., modules, training, maintenance)	
	10	#10	Ability to integrate with other ERP modules	
	100 possible		Basic total score	
			Bonus/Penalty Items	
	+5/−5		Presentation effectiveness	
	+5/−5		Unique qualifications	
	110 possible max		Basic score +/− Bonus/penalty total	

At the end of the presentations, the selection committee will deliberate about each of the presentations, using the criteria that have been established on the score sheet. They will tabulate their scores and rank the presentations in sequence (e.g., first place, second place, third place). After reporting the results, the selection committee will give informal feedback to each of the teams.

F. TEAM VENDOR ASSIGNMENTS AND RESOURCES FOR VENDOR RESEARCH

Each team will represent a specific ERP vendor (see Table 2).

Each team will be responsible for developing their presentation in response to the RFP. In developing its proposal, each team should address each of the selection criteria as effectively as possible. To do so, it can use various resources, including vendor web sites, on-line library databases with articles in trade publications, vendor marketing materials, and trade reviews.

G. LIST OF USER MANAGERS (JOB TITLES, BACKGROUND)

The selection committee and will consist of five members: Dick Wingate, CEO; Steve Wingate, Chief Operating Officer; Robert Murdick, Chief Financial Officer; Richard Hayes, Marketing Manager; and Kathryn Martell, Director of Accounting Operations.

Dick Wingate, the CEO, handles marketing and business development. He is a natural salesperson and is extensively involved in community activities and charitable organizations, such as the Rotary Club, American Cancer Society, and Boy Scouts. He enjoys skiing and golf, and he owns a golf condo in Florida. Through his contacts, he has been instrumental in growing the sales of the business.

Steve Wingate, the Chief Operating Officer, is responsible for internal operations management. Steve is more internally focused than his brother, Dick. He earned a Bachelor's degree in engineering from Purdue University, and he has used his technical background to assume an important role in quality management. He is cautious about expenditures, and he scrutinizes the budget to avoid unnecessary expenditures and to control costs. He lives in the same middle-class neighborhood where he grew up, which speaks to his conservative lifestyle. Because of his cost-conscious mentality, Steve is hesitant to make a big investment in an ERP system.

Robert Murdick, Chief Financial Officer, came to Wingate Electric after spending ten years at Ernst and Young, a public accounting firm. He chose to join the management at Wingate Electric because the opportunity to work with a team to expand a mid-sized company offered considerable challenge. In his consulting career, Bob traveled extensively, and he finds that his career at Wingate Electric provides greater autonomy and flexibility. Bob's accounting background convinces him that an investment in an integrated financial and accounting system would be a good investment.

Richard Hayes, Marketing Manager, was one of the most productive members of Wingate's sales force before joining the management team. For seven years, Richard was the top sales performer in this industry niche in the country. Richard was able to earn this distinction through his dedicated commitment to serving the needs of his customers. Richard has a positive attitude toward automation. He encouraged his sales force to use laptops with computer-based sales prospecting software.

Kathryn Martell, Director of Accounting Operations, started at Wingate Electric as a clerk-typist 18 years ago. She is known for her strong work ethic and perfectionism. She is loyal to the company, and she works long hours. She organizes the company picnic and Christmas party each year. Kathryn is resistant to change, and she is skeptical about spending a lot of money on a computer-based information system. Her opinion is that most of the inefficiency can be remedied by adding staff members.

TABLE 2	Team Vendor Assignments	
Team	**Vendor Assignment**	**Financial Module**
A	Great Plains	Financial Management
B	Peoplesoft	Financial Management Solutions
C	Oracle ERP	Financials
D	SAP	Financial Accounting (FA)

References

Davenport, Thomas. 2000. *Mission Critical: Realizing the Promise of Enterprise Systems.* Cambridge, MA: Harvard Business School Press.

Gremillion, L.L., and P. Pyburn. 1983. "Breaking the systems development bottleneck." *Harvard Business Review* 130–137.

Langenwalter, G., 2000. *Enterprise Resources Planning and Beyond: Integrating Your Entire Organization.* Boca Raton, FL: St. Lucie Press.

Mabert, V.A., A. Soni, and V.A. Venkataramanan. 2000. "Enterprise resource planning survey of U.S. manufacturing firms." *Production and Inventory Management Journal* 41: 52–58.

Oden, H., G. Langenwalter, and R. Lucier. 1993. *Handbook of Material and Capacity Requirements Planning.* New York: McGraw-Hill.

Olhager, Jan, and Erik Selldin. 2003. "Enterprise resource planning survey of Swedish manufacturing firms." *European Journal of Operational Research* 146: 365–373.

Ross, Jeanne, Michael Vitale, and Leslie Willcocks. 2003. "The continuing ERP revolution: Sustainable lessons, new modes of delivery," in *Second-Wave Enterprise Resource Planning Systems.* Graeme Shanks, Peter Seddon, and Leslie Willcocks (Eds.), Cambridge: Cambridge University Press, 102–132.

Umble, Elisabeth, Ronald Haft, and M. Michael Umble. 2003. "Enterprise resource planning: Implementation procedures and critical success factors." *European Journal of Operational Research* 146: 241–257.

CHAPTER 4

ERP Systems: Sales and Marketing

Objectives

1. Understand the sales and marketing module.
2. Recognize the interrelationships among business processes supporting sales and marketing, production, accounting and finance, and human resources.

A s an introduction to this chapter on Sales and Marketing, sales and marketing functions can create problems, which lead to lack of responsiveness to customer needs, lack of productivity, and lack of profitability.

CASE: ATLANTIC MANUFACTURING

Atlantic Manufacturing is a manufacturer of custom configured small motors that go into jet skis, snowmobiles, and other recreational vehicles. Its customers represent major consumer manufacturing companies. In June 2004, it reported these problems in order acquisition, operations, distribution, and accounting.

SALES AND DISTRIBUTION

✓ Salespersons have to call the home office for quotations for many products because of many possible configurations.

✓ Salespeople are making quotas, but profitability is declining because the standard cost system is not providing accurate information with respect to costs.

✓ Customers are asking for reduced lead times, which could be achieved if Atlantic's engineers worked more closely with their suppliers.

CREDIT

✓ Recently, customers were put on "credit hold" when they were not able to pay on a timely basis. However, when the credit manager was out of town for several weeks, an order went through to this customer by mistake. Nothing could be collected on this account because the customer could not pay.

CUSTOMER SERVICE AND REPAIR

✓ Atlantic has a stand-alone system to take care of field service. When service technicians repair equipment in the field, they do not always bill the customer for the correct amount since the system does not have information indicating which replacement parts are covered by the warranty.

✓ Since the field service system is a stand-alone system and does not integrate with other systems within the company, quality control people mainly use anecdotal evidence to identify potential problems.

In contrast, Atlantic's competitors are offering their customers lower quotes and reduced lead times. Salespersons are creating quotes using laptops from their customers' offices. Credit checking is automatic on all new orders, and salespersons have immediate access to customer credit information. Field service technicians have access to data indicating which parts are covered by warranty to the customer and which parts are covered by supplier warranty.

In the Atlantic Manufacturing case, a number of problems are affecting order entry, credit management, and field service. The lack of an integrated system can cause incorrect credit, inadequate inventory, shipping delays, incomplete invoices, and accounts receivable delays (see Table 4-1). These problems can significantly affect profitability and customer service.

TABLE 4-1 Problems with Sales Order Processing

Subsystems	Problems
Sales order entry	Incorrect pricing; incorrect credit information; calls to customers to get the correct information
Inventory	Incorrect inventory; delays in inventory updates; inadequate inventory to fill orders; partial shipments
Shipping and delivery	Delays in shipping and delivery
Invoicing	Inaccurate or incomplete invoices
Payment processing	Customers may not include a copy of their invoice with their payment; incorrect posting of payments
Accounts receivable	Delays in accounts receivable posting; reminder letters are generated to customers who have paid

TABLE 4-2	Sales and Marketing Processes
Operational	Prospecting; contact management; telemarketing; direct mail
Management control	Sales management; product pricing; advertising and promotion; sales forecasting

◆ SALES AND MARKETING PROCESSES

Sales and marketing processes include operational-level and management control processes (see Table 4-2). Operational processes include daily activities, such as prospecting, contact management, telemarketing, and direct mail. Sales representatives need to create and maintain lists of prospects by location, by product category, and by sales potential and need to create and maintain a contact management system, which tracks customer preferences, sales history data, and the history of sales calls. When sales are done via telemarketing, telemarketing databases are used for contacts and follow-ups. Direct mail processes create and maintain mailing lists, some of which are designed for target markets.

Traditionally, sales and marketing operational functions are supported by sales order processing systems, which capture order data, and point-of-sale (POS) systems, which capture data at the point of sale. These systems are linked to inventory management systems, which update inventory levels for stock items based upon sales data.

◆ MANAGEMENT CONTROL PROCESSES IN SALES AND MARKETING

Management control activities in sales and marketing are designed to allocate sales and marketing resources in order to achieve maximum revenues. One of the most important areas is sales management.

SALES MANAGEMENT PROCESSES

Sales managers are responsible for creating territories and for allocating sales people's time to generate maximum revenue and service. The decisions which sales managers need to make include the following:

- How should territories be shaped?
- How can we allocate salesperson time to call on the highest potential accounts?
- Which customers are most profitable?
- Which products are most profitable?

The information that sales managers use to make decisions is largely based upon an analysis of past sales. Summary reports, comparative analysis reports, and exception reports are all useful tools in analyzing sales trends and determining how to best allocate resources. Examples include the following:

- Comparison of sales, product revenues, customer revenues, and territory revenues against benchmarks of success

- Comparison of the productivity of each salesperson to the average for the department
- Listing of the most profitable products in each territory
- Listing of the products that represent the highest percentage of sales for each salesperson
- Listing of the customers that represent the highest percentage of sales for each salesperson

See sales analysis reports examples in Figure 4-1 and 4-2.

Sales Management software is used by sales managers to assess the productivity of the sales force and the success of products, by salesperson, by territory, and by customer type. Specifically, sales management software achieves these and other objectives:

- To identify weak products in a territory
- To compare salesperson performance by product type and customer type

FIGURE 4-1 Sales Analysis Report

	A	B	C	D	E	F	G	H	I
1	Order Date 31-Oct-2099				Ord. No.2457				
2	No.	Product No.	Price	Quantity	Total	% of Total			
3	1	3108	72	36	2592	12.01%			
4	2	3123	79	14	1106	5.12%			
5	3	3127	488.4	17	8302.8	38.46%			
6	4	3150	17	27	459	2.13%			
7	5	3155	44	32	1408	6.52%			
8	6	3170	145.2	42	6098.4	28.25%			
9	7	3172	36	45	1620	7.50%			
10	Total				21586.2				
11	% of Total				0.59%				
12									
13	Order Date 31-Aug-2099				Ord. No.2439				
14	No.	Product No.	Price	Quantity	Total	% of Total			
15	1	1797	316.8	9	2851.2	12.87%			
16	2	1806	45	4	180	0.81%			
17	3	1820	54	9	486	2.19%			
18	4	1822	1433.3	13	18632.9	84.12%			
19	Total				22150.1				
20	% of Total				0.60%				
21									
22	Order Date 31-Aug-2099				Ord. No.2440				
23	No.	Product No.	Price	Quantity	Total	% of Total			
24	1	2289	48	19	912	1.29%			
25	2	2293	98	2	196	0.28%			
26	3	2302	150	2	300	0.43%			
27	4	2311	86.9	7	608.3	0.86%			
28	5	2322	23	10	230	0.33%			
29	6	2330	1.1	13	14.3	0.02%			
30	7	2334	3.3	15	49.5	0.07%			
31	8	2337	270.6	19	5141.4	7.28%			
32	9	2339	25	23	575	0.81%			
33	10	2350	2341.9	24	56205.6	79.64%			
34	11	2359	226.6	28	6344.8	8.99%			
35	Total				70576.9				
36	% of Total				1.92%				
37									
38	Order Date 29-Mar-2099				Ord. No.2414				
39	No.	Product No.	Price	Quantity	Total	% of Total			
40	1	3208	1.1	8	8.8	0.08%			
41	2	3216	30	7	210	1.95%			
42	3	3220	41	9	369	3.42%			
43	4	3234	39	11	429	3.97%			
44	5	3246	212.3	18	3821.4	35.40%			
45	6	3253	206.8	23	4756.4	44.06%			
46	7	3260	50	24	1200	11.12%			
47	Total				10794.6				
48	% of Total				0.29%				
49									

Sheet1 / Sheet2 / Sheet3 /

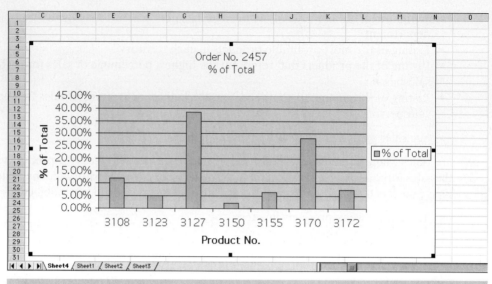

FIGURE 4-2   Sales Analysis Chart

- To compare salesperson performance against sales goals
- To analyze salesperson performance within territories
- To identify trends in customer purchases
- To identify potential shortages or excess stock in inventory

Sales analysis will drive decisions about how to allocate sales personnel, how to organize territories, how to serve customer needs, and how to train sales personnel to use their time more effectively to generate maximum revenues from the highest potential accounts.

SALES FORECASTING PROCESSES

Sales forecasting is important to determine the potential needs of customers in various market segments. Sales forecasting activities include segmenting the market into target groups of potential customers and planning products/services to meet the customers' needs. Sales forecasts can be developed for overall sales, for sales by territory, for sales by each product or service, for sales for new products/services, and for sales by sales representative. Sales forecasts use information on past sales history as well as information about competition, customer demand, and demographic trends.

ADVERTISING AND PROMOTION

Another important marketing process, which requires decisions about how to allocate resources, is advertising and promotion. The major questions are the following:

- Which advertising media and promotional channels should I use?
- Which advertising channels and media are most effective in addressing specific market targets?

The effectiveness of advertising campaigns needs to be constantly monitored.

PRODUCT PRICING SYSTEMS

What prices should I establish for products? This is a key question to be addressed as part of marketing management. To make pricing decisions, the marketing manager should know the expected product demand, the desired profit margin, the product production costs, and the competing products. Pricing depends upon pricing strategy. Pricing models are built from data from various forces that influence pricing, including consumer price indices, expected consumer disposable income, volume of products produced, labor costs, and raw materials costs.

◆ SALES AND MARKETING MODULES IN ERP SYSTEMS

Traditionally, sales and marketing software supports operational and management control processes, including contact management, sales management, and sales analysis/forecasting. The difference between Sales and Marketing modules within an Enterprise Resource Planning (ERP) system and traditional sales and marketing software is that ERP systems provide integrated marketing support systems, including contact files, order entry files, and sales history files. In addition, ERP systems provide Customer Relationship Management (CRM) software, which provides information to salespeople about the previous experiences of customers, including purchases, product preferences, and payment history.

With an ERP module, a customer places an order, and a sales order is recorded (see Figure 4-3). The system schedules shipping and works backward from the shipping date to reserve the materials, to order parts from suppliers, and to schedule manufacturing. The module checks the customer's credit limit, updates sales forecasts, and creates a bill of materials. The salesperson's commission is updated. Product costs and profitability are calculated. Finally, accounting data is updated, including balance sheets, accounts payable, ledgers, and other financial information.

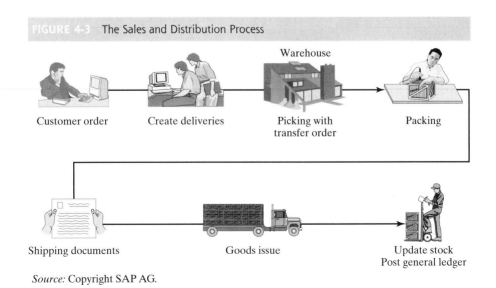

FIGURE 4-3   The Sales and Distribution Process

| Customer order | Create deliveries | Warehouse
Picking with
transfer order | Packing |

| Shipping documents | Goods issue | Update stock
Post general ledger |

Source: Copyright SAP AG.

TABLE 4-3   The Sales and Marketing Module and Related Modules

Subsystem	What It Does
Pre-sales	Tracks customer contacts; provides the customer with a price quote
Sales order processing	Uses the price quote to record items to be purchased; determines the sales price; records order quantities; configures quantity discounts; checks customer credit
Inventory sourcing	Checks the inventory database to see if items can be delivered on time; updates the production planning database to avoid any shortfalls
Delivery	Releases documents to the warehouse: items are picked; orders are packed and shipped
Billing*	Uses sales order data to create an invoice; updates accounting records; increases (debits) accounts receivable
Payment*	Accepts payment; decreases the customer's accounts receivable balance with the amount of payment

*Handled by the Accounting module.

The purpose of the Sales and Marketing module within ERP is to identify sales prospects, to process sales orders, to manage inventory, to handle deliveries, to provide billing, and to accept and process payments (see Table 4-3).

As with other ERP modules, the Sales and Marketing module provides the benefits of standard codes, a common database, standard documents, an audit trail, and data integration (see Figure 4-4 and Table 4-4). For example, a standard document number follows an order throughout its life cycle, including partial shipments, partial payments, and returns. This document flow prevents errors and inaccuracies and keeps accounting data relevant.

FIGURE 4-4   SAP Screen (Create Standard Order)

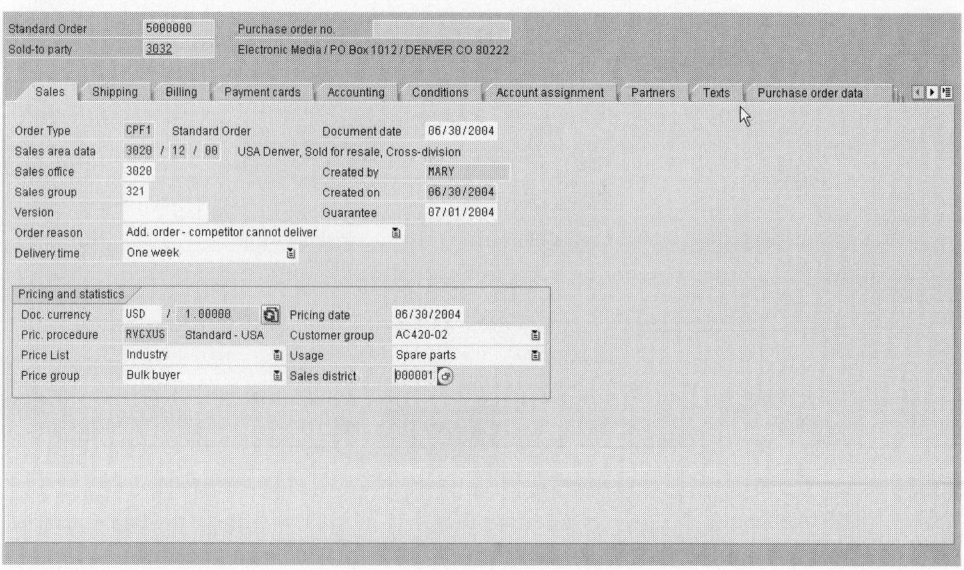

Source: Copyright SAP AG.

TABLE 4-4	Advantages of Sales and Marketing ERP Software

Feature	*Benefit*
Standard codes	Each customer has a standard code
Common database	Common database supports all modules
Standard documents	Standard document number (e.g., sales order number) sticks with the transaction throughout the process, including shipping and accounting
Audit trail	Standard document number helps track partial shipments, partial payments, returns
Data integration	Sales records are integrated with accounting records

◆ ERP AND CUSTOMER RELATIONSHIP MANAGEMENT

An ERP system supports back-office functions, such as sales, accounting, human resources, and manufacturing, and the ERP system provides a foundation for advanced applications, such as CRM, and Supply Chain Management (SCM). CRM represents the systems that interface with the customer, and SCM represents the systems which interface with the supplier. CRM, which provides an important front end to sales and marketing, is described in the next section.

CRM is a comprehensive sales and marketing approach to building long-term customer relationships. CRM relies upon the foundation of ERP. CRM provides a single interface to the customer, so a salesperson who has a customer will know about all the worldwide interactions for that customer. For example, if there is a problem with filling an order for a Wal-Mart store in Albany, New York, the salesperson calling on the Wal-Mart store in Carlsbad, California, will know about it.

Using the following scenario, you can see how a CRM can make the difference between losing and gaining business.

Scenario 1: You are on your way to see one of your company's best customers (they represent 5% of the company's total sales). When you get there, you learn the customer is angry. His entire firm has been at a standstill for 48 hours because he cannot get delivery on a part for a high-speed color laser printer; he has a critical deadline to meet on some marketing materials, and he's been on the phone for the past day to no avail. You have lost his business. Somehow, you had not heard about any of this.

Scenario 2: You are on your way to see one of your company's best customers (they represent 5% of the company's total sales). En route, you turn on your laptop, and you receive a customer alert that there has been an equipment failure on a high-speed color laser printer. When you arrive, your service tech is there installing the broken part. He was able to order the needed part via eBusiness and had it dispatched by courier. The customer admits that he probably needed a laser printer upgrade because he has been using excessive volumes. You have increased your revenue from this customer.

These two scenarios show how knowledge of customer needs can affect customer service and customer retention. CRM software had its roots in sales force automation software, which is designed to provide sales representatives with sales activity management, sales and territory management, contact management, lead management, configuration support, and knowledge management.

Sales Activity Management

Sales Activity Management guides sales representatives through each step of the sales process, including generating leads, contacting prospects, handling order placement, and assuring order follow-up.

Sales and Territory Management

Sales and Territory Management helps sales managers study the pipeline, monitor salespeople's activities, and optimize teams.

Contact Management

Contact Management helps sales representatives organize their contact data in databases, so they can query these databases and ask questions, such as "Who is the client's purchasing agent?" and "Which customers received a recent promotion for product XYZ?"

Lead Management

Lead Management enables sales representatives to monitor leads, to generate next steps, and to refine selling efforts by using on-line support. Managers can distribute leads to field sales representatives based upon the representative's product knowledge. Lead management enables sales people to track prospect attributes, such as product interests, budget amounts, and likely competitors. Query capability makes it possible to ask the following questions:

- At what step in the sales cycle do we lose our prospects?
- How many appointments did Mark have with XYZ company?
- What percentage of leads in the Eastern Michigan territory resulted in sales last month?
- How did order amounts for product ABC in San Francisco compare with order amounts in Seattle?

Configuration Management

Configuration Management provides product-specific configuration support to companies that must build products for their customers. Technology vendors, appliance vendors, and computer vendors are examples of companies which need to create product configurations, make price quotes, and communicate these electronically via a laptop, while sitting in the customer's office.

Knowledge Management

Knowledge Management offers access to information resources. Information resources in sales include the following: corporate policy handbooks, sales presentation slides, company phone lists, proposal templates, industry and competitor data, press releases, and transcripts of sales meetings. Some of this information can be made available via the corporate intranet. Before making a follow-up call to a customer who has

TABLE 4-5 Customer Relationship Management (CRM)	
Key Features	*Characteristics*
One-on-one marketing	Tailors products, pricing, and promotions to the customer
Telemarketing	Facilitates customer contact and call list management
Sales force automation	Maintains information on customer contacts in a database; forecasts customer's needs
Sales campaign management	Organizes marketing campaigns, including the creation of call lists
Call center automation	Enables queries to a product marketing database
e-Selling	Delivers on-line systems that enable customers to configure products on-line, including a shopping basket
Customer service	Handles customer service, from the customer request for service to the service technician reporting time and materials used

attended a sales presentation, it is useful to review the presentation along with any notes from prior meetings with the customer.

CRM systems build upon sales force automation capabilities and offer advanced functions that can be integrated with an ERP system. The major functions of a CRM system include one-on-one marketing, telemarketing, sales force automation, sales campaign management, call center automation, e-Selling, data warehousing, and customer service. Without an underlying Sales and Marketing ERP module, the CRM system could not acquire needed operational-level data on sales, orders, and sales order history to support CRM functions. CRM data are accessible via a data warehouse and are separate from the operational database supported by the ERP system. A data warehouse is a repository of integrated data, which enables sales representatives to make queries and to generate reports on customer-specific trends.

CUSTOMER SERVICE

The processes, which are part of customer service, are initiated when the customer calls with a service request. The service notification triggers a service order, which is dispatched to a service technician. Once the job is complete, the technician confirms the hours worked and the materials used. Based on the billing request from the service order, the Accounting Department generates a billing document.

INTEGRATION OF SALES AND DISTRIBUTION WITH OTHER MODULES

Sales and Distribution modules within SAP are integrated with other ERP modules (see Figure 4-5). First, the Sales and Distribution module is interfaced with the Financial Accounting module. In SAP, for example, you assign a billing transaction to a specific sales organization, a distribution channel, and a division. This information is transferred to Financial Accounting (see Table 4-6).

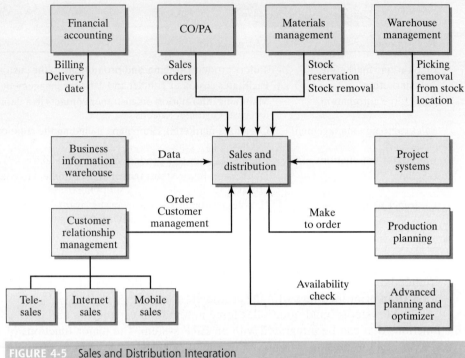

FIGURE 4-5   Sales and Distribution Integration

Source: Copyright SAP AG.

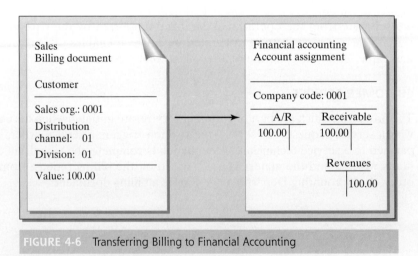

FIGURE 4-6   Transferring Billing to Financial Accounting

Source: Copyright SAP AG.

Data integration across functional modules saves time, facilitates customer service, and improves productivity and profitability. As an example of data integration, the Sales and Distribution modules interface with other SAP modules, including the Materials Management, Human Resources, Quality Management, Financial Accounting, and Controlling modules.

TABLE 4-6	Integration of Sales and Distribution with Other Modules	
Materials management	MM	Material master describes spare parts used in repairs and services sold to the customer
Human resources	HR	Matches technician's qualifications with requirements needed for specific service orders
Quality management	QM	Checks condition of materials being shipped back to a customer following repair
Financials	FI	Bills customers for service and receives payments
Controlling	CO	Service order can collect costs and become an input into profitability analysis

◆ SUMMARY

Sales and Marketing modules in an ERP system are designed to support sales order entry, inventory sourcing, delivery processing, billing, and payment processing. The core Sales and Marketing module is a foundation for CRM systems. CRM modules support sales management, contact management, lead management, and configuration management. In addition, interrelationships exist between sales and marketing modules and modules supporting materials management, human resources, financial accounting, management accounting, and quality management.

Questions for Discussion •

1. Gather information about the best practices which are associated with the Sales and Marketing modules within an ERP package. You can do this by (1) conducting research on the web; (2) interviewing a user of a Sales and Marketing package; (3) using an on-line database to find an article in a trade publication which describes the effective use of a Sales and Marketing module; or (4) using a Sales and Marketing module within an ERP system to identify new best practices.
   a. What are the best practices, which you have discovered?
   b. How do they contribute to overall productivity?
   c. What information for decision making do they provide?
2. The Sales and Marketing module within ERP is regarded as the module with the most interfaces to other modules, including Human Resources, Materials Management, Production Planning, and Financial Accounting. Describe the interfaces between the Sales and Marketing module and each of these other modules:

Module	*What Information Is Shared with Sales and Marketing*
Human resources	
Materials management	
Production planning	
Financial accounting	

Featured Article: Staples and Integrated ERP

Using the following excerpt, how is technology helping Staples achieve a competitive advantage?

STAPLES KIOSKS CONNECT CUSTOMERS AND MERCHANDISE

Customer service drives Paul Gaffney's commitment to integration. And profits show that commitment matters.

"Our most profitable customers are those who use the full range of the way we do business," says Gaffney, the CIO at Staples in Framingham, Mass. He adds that customers "want to get a very consistent and seamless experience. When you do the right thing for your best customers, good things happen."

The CIO of the office-supplies giant stresses that for those good things to happen, it's essential to have an overarching strategy that uses IT to advance the company's mission. Gaffney adds that "trying to be more holistic in our outlook is one of the things that separates great IT organizations from the rest of the pack."

One of the products of Gaffney's enterprisewide focus on the customer is the online kiosk, dubbed Access Point, that is installed in all of the company's 1,040 U.S. stores. Creating the kiosks required connecting the company's e-commerce website, Staples.com, with its point-of-sale (POS) system, order management system, distribution system and supply chain. On the people front, staffers from the retail, catalog, online, finance, distribution, merchandising and training areas, practically everyone but the cafeteria chefs, collaborated. For example, the kiosks offer customers the option of buying, say, an office chair at the kiosk using a credit card, then taking a bar-code printed receipt up front to the register to pay in real-time. Customers can also use the kiosks to access a library of information about products and services, view an inventory of 45,000 online products, and build PCs to order (eliminating the need for more than 35 percent of stores to carry computers). "We're letting customers do business the way they want to do business, not the way we want them to," says Gaffney.

But the benefits don't go solely to customers. For Staples, the multimillion-dollar Access Point project has introduced many customers to Staples.com. The company estimates that a customer who shops in both stores and one other channel (Staples.com or catalog) has a lifetime value of two and a half times that of a store-only shopper.

And the company's approach toward integration goes beyond customer-facing systems. Another major integration project involved consolidating the Staples and Quill fulfillment center facilities. Staples acquired Quill, a mail-order office products company, in 1998. To connect the two disparate order management systems, Staples could have gone the point-to-point route, which would have required building customized connections between the two sets of applications. But the Staples team chose instead to implement an integration layer built on IBM's MQ series. "That way, if we had a future acquisition, or needed more volume in the future, we won't have to do a new point-to-point integration project," says Gaffney.

Reducing the number of direct linkages between systems is one part of Gaffney's holistic strategy. Standardization is another. "Every IS organization is trying to deliver more business results for less money. One tool is reducing the number of different technologies that you need your staff to be proficient in. If you have four or five [technology] approaches, you've diluted your staff's proficiency. I think it's a productivity imperative," Gaffney says.

Staples is just starting to look hard at how it can standardize, but Gaffney pointedly says that Web services will play a key role. Because of that, Gaffney doesn't feel a need to standardize his platform on either Sun's Java 2 Platform Enterprise Edition (J2EE) or Microsoft's .Net, since Web services can work with both. "We believe it's more important to focus on good semantics, for example, getting the definition of the interface right on our next generation internal pricing service, than to get hung up on whether it's a J2EE or Microsoft deployment," he says.

To ensure that his IS organization continues to maintain a big- picture integration strategy, Gaffney has appointed a team, led by two vice presidents in IS but involving people from all business areas, to help Staples get a detailed look at its business processes. They also want to determine how people and technologies map against those processes (for example, to see if there are multiple groups of people using multiple technologies, all to produce a sales forecast). They can then use the information they uncover to move ahead on the integration projects that will have the most business impact.

SOURCE: Datz, Todd, "Strategic Alignment; Your business processes can't enable superior customer service or an efficient supply chain without integrated systems. The four companies profiled here demonstrate the benefits of a strategic perspective and long-term commitment to integration." *CIO,* Aug 15, 2002, p. 1–64.

References

Dyche, Jill. 2002. *The CRM Handbook. A Business Guide to Customer Relationship Management.* New York: Addison-Wesley.

Hasan, Matt. 2003. "Ensure success of CRM with a change in mindset." *Marketing News* 16.

Parke, Shep. 1998. "Avoiding the unseen perils of sales technology." *Sales and Field Force Automation.*

Rigby, D., F.R. Reichheld, and P. Schefter. 2002. "Avoiding the pitfalls of CRM." *Harvard Business Review,* 101–109.

Ruquet, Mark E. 2003. "Evaluating CRM: Many hurdles remain for carriers." *National Underwriters.* Cincinnati: National Underwriters Company.

Schultheis, Robert, and Mary Sumner. 1998. *Management Information Systems: The Manager's View.* 4th ed. Burr Ridge, IL: Irwin/McGraw-Hill.

ERP Systems: Accounting and Finance

5

Objectives

1. Understand the accounting and financial systems within ERP.
2. Recognize the interrelationships among business processes supporting sales and marketing, production, accounting and finance, and human resources.

Difficulties with accounting functions can create problems that lead to bottle-necks, mis-information, lack of responsiveness to suppliers, and poor control (see Table 5-1).

CASE: ATLANTIC MANUFACTURING

At the current time, Atlantic Manufacturing is experiencing similar issues with its paper-intensive accounting systems.

✓ Manufacturing sometimes ships products to customers with inaccurate paperwork, so Accounts Receivable has to track down the product specifications to ensure customers are making proper payment. In some cases, the original invoices are incorrect.

✓ Accounts payable to suppliers is bogged down, and Purchasing has to contact Accounting to get details about payment dates.

✓ Sales people report they could sell a large quantity of items at a reduced price. Should Atlantic submit a quotation? There is no management information to help sales managers determine if they can make a profit by selling items at a slightly reduced price.

In the Atlantic Manufacturing Case, problems occur when a lack of coordination exists between sales and accounting and between manufacturing and accounting. Many problems occur when accounting information is out of date or inaccurate. For example, when customer accounts receivable balances fall out of date, this results in mis-information to sales about customer credit limits.

TABLE 5-1	Problems without ERP

Subsystems	Problems
Credit management	Accounts receivable balances on customer accounts can fall out of date and result in mis-information in sales about customer credit limits
Product profitability	Inconsistent recordkeeping, keyed into multiple data-bases, may result in incorrect data on product profitability
Finished goods inventory	Delays in increasing finished goods inventory when finished goods are transferred from manufacturing into the warehouse
Inaccurate inventory costing	Difficulty providing information on cost variances (e.g., the difference between standard costs and actual costs)
Consolidating information from subsidiaries	Difficulty closing books at the end of accounting periods, which is complicated when multiple subsidiaries deal with multiple currencies; difficulty integrating financial information generated from incompatible systems, with different databases
Management reporting	Separate databases for marketing, production, and purchasing make it difficult to provide management with an integrated analysis of profitability and cash flow
Creating an audit trail	Difficulty creating an audit trail of transactions when multiple transactions use multiple databases

Business decision making about product profitability is difficult when financial information is maintained in separate databases for marketing, production, and purchasing. These multiple databases make determining product profitability difficult. Providing information on cost differences (e.g., standard costs versus actual costs) of inventory is difficult, and accurate inventory costing is the basis for determining product profitability.

◆ ACCOUNTING AND FINANCE PROCESSES

At the conceptual level, an accounting system supports operational and management control functions. At the operational level, an accounting system produces transactions, such as paychecks, checks to vendors, customer invoices, and purchase orders. You can see the workings of an accounting system by looking at the conceptual model provided (see Figure 5-1).

The accounting processes begin when a sales order is entered. This generates an inventory update to the inventory system, which maintains information about each item in stock and triggers the purchase of additional stock when stock levels reach certain points. The purchase order system creates purchase orders and tracks which purchase orders have been filled, which items are on back order, and when orders are expected to be received.

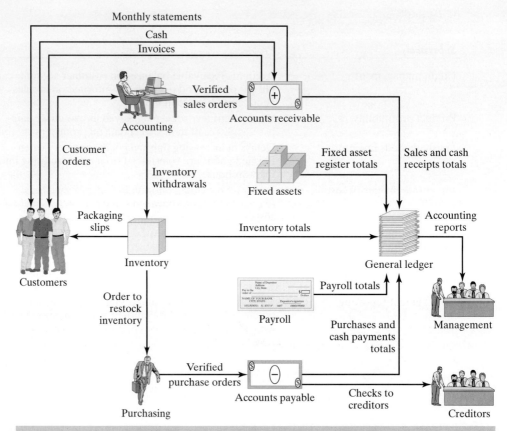

FIGURE 5-1   Conceptual Model of an Accounting System

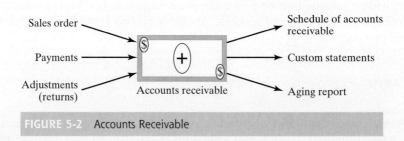

FIGURE 5-2   Accounts Receivable

The sales order generates an invoice to the customer from the Accounts Receivable System. When payments are made, the accounts receivable balance is updated. When payments are overdue, the Accounts Receivable System generates an Aging Report that shows account balances, which are 30, 60, and 90 days overdue. The inputs and outputs of the Accounts Receivable System include daily transactions (see Figure 5-2).

In the accounting system, payments to suppliers or vendors are made through the Accounts Payable System (see Figure 5-3).

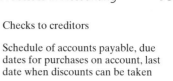

Purchase orders

Payments

Adjustments
(returns)

Accounts payable

Checks to creditors

Schedule of accounts payable, due
dates for purchases on account, last
date when discounts can be taken

List of bills due

FIGURE 5-3   Accounts Payable

◆ MANAGEMENT CONTROL PROCESSES IN ACCOUNTING

Control processes within accounting include budgeting, cash management, capital budgeting, and investment management. Budgeting processes entail tracking revenues and expenses and comparing these amounts to actual expenses and revenues. Budgetary analysis includes comparing current budget allocations to prior year's allocations and comparing current revenues and expenditures to prior years' revenues and expenditures. For example, a budget analyst can compare a department's travel expenses for the current year with the former year and find a 25% increase in travel expenditures. Another analysis may find that revenues generated from sales in one region are much greater this year than in prior years. In both of these cases, the budgetary analysis may raise further questions for investigation. For example, sales managers may want to take advantage of potential growth areas by assigning additional sales representatives or introducing new products into these regions.

CASH MANAGEMENT PROCESSES

Cash management ensures the organization has sufficient cash to meet its needs and to place excess funds into use through investments. A cash flow analysis shows the estimated amount of revenues and expenditures each month. Budget analysts can perform what-if cash flow analysis to determine the impact of different business conditions, such as decreased revenue, deferred expenditures, deferred hiring, and leasing fixed assets instead of purchasing them.

CAPITAL BUDGETING PROCESSES

Capital budgeting processes analyze the impact of possible acquisitions. Capital budgeting uses evaluation tools, such as net present value (NPV), internal rate of return (IRR), and payback period. In NPV analysis, the manager can determine the present value of future cash flows. For example, if the current discount or interest rate is 10%, then you would receive $1,000,000 on an investment of $909,090.90 a year from now. The present value of $1,000,000 to be spent one year from now is $909,090.90. In IRR, the organization can determine if it can make a better return by acquiring an asset now or by investing its money in another venture. A third form of analysis for capital budgeting is payback period. In this analysis, you determine the time at which the increase in revenues or savings in expenses will match the investment in the new asset.

TABLE 5-2	Summary of Accounting Processes
Operational	General ledger
	Fixed asset
	Sales order
	Accounts receivable
	Accounts payable
	Inventory control
	Purchase order
	Payroll
Management Control	Budgeting
	Cash management
	Capital budgeting

Table 5-2 summarizes the accounting processes at the operational and control level. In summary, operational processes produce daily transactions on a periodic basis. Management control processes, such as budgeting and cash management, support decisions on how to allocate resources to maximize profitability and to cut costs.

◆ ACCOUNTING AND FINANCE MODULES IN ERP SYSTEMS

Traditionally, computerized accounting systems provide operating-level software to produce invoices, checks, monthly statements, financial statements, and other financial outputs. Financial Accounting deals with financial statements required for external reporting purposes (e.g., balance sheets and P&L statements). External reporting requirements are established by general accounting standards, as well as legal requirements. Management accounting systems or management control systems provide information on product profitability and cost center profitability, which enables managers to make business decisions.

The difference between traditional computerized accounting systems and ERP modules supporting the Accounting and Finance departments is that financial information is shared in an integrated database (see Table 5-3). For example, when finished goods are transferred into the warehouse, financial statements are updated with up-to-date cost information. ERP modules provide up-to-date information on cost variances, so that product pricing and profitability decisions can be made with accurate information.

The Accounting module is an integral part of the entire ERP system, and most accounting entries are automated as different business transactions occur. One of the major benefits of using the Accounting module within an ERP system is that the system creates a document flow of all transactions. If the customer has a question about an invoice, an accounting representative can trace the data to the original order document (see Table 5-4).

FINANCIAL ACCOUNTING MODULES IN ERP

Financial Accounting deals with financial statements required for external reporting purposes (e.g., balance sheets and P&L statements). External reporting requirements

TABLE 5-3 How ERP Supports Accounting and Finance

Subsystem	*What It Does*
Credit management	Accounts receivable balances are automatically updated, so sales has up-to-date information on customer credit limits
Product profitability	Data is entered and stored in an integrated database, leading to uniform results
Finished goods inventory	ERP automatically updates the increase in the monetary value of finished goods when finished goods are transferred to the warehouse; financial statements are updated
Inaccurate inventory costing	Provides up-to-date information on cost variances, which enables the company to establish prices that will enable it to sell products profitably
Consolidating information from subsidiaries	Provides an integrated database with the capability of converting multiple currencies
Management reporting	ERP database is integrated, so all information is consistent, complete, and accurate; a data warehouse provides a comprehensive database for management reporting
Creating an audit trail	ERP provides interconnected document flow, which establishes an audit trail and makes it possible to research and link source documents

TABLE 5-4 Document Flow Creates an Audit Trail

Order placed	**Doc 789654**
Order requirements transferred to Materials Management	**Doc 667852**
Picking request tells warehouse what items are on order	**Doc 995380**
Goods removed from inventory	**Doc 345621**
Invoice generated	**Doc 786453**
Accounting entries posted	**Doc 094531**

are set by general accounting standards, as well as legal requirements. Financial Accounting modules post all accounting transactions, and these transactions are reflected in the general ledger (see Figure 5-4).

Within Financial Accounting is the Accounts Receivable subsystem. The Accounts Receivable module monitors customer accounts, accepts payments, updates accounts, generates due date lists, generates balance confirmations, and produces account statements. The accounts receivable module interfaces with Cash Management (see Figure 5-5).

Accounts Payable handles all payments to suppliers, including international payments, and takes advantage of available discounts (see Figure 5-6).

MANAGEMENT ACCOUNTING MODULES IN ERP SYSTEMS

Management accounting modules provide an internal accounting perspective for managers who are responsible for directing and controlling operations. Management accounting modules provide information about variances between planned versus

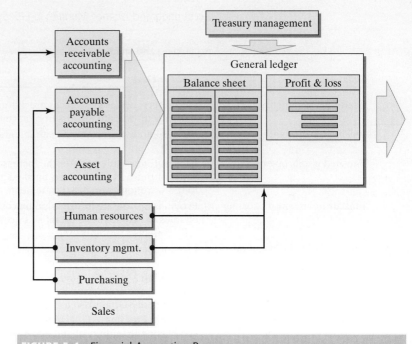

FIGURE 5-4 Financial Accounting Process

Source: Copyright SAP AG.

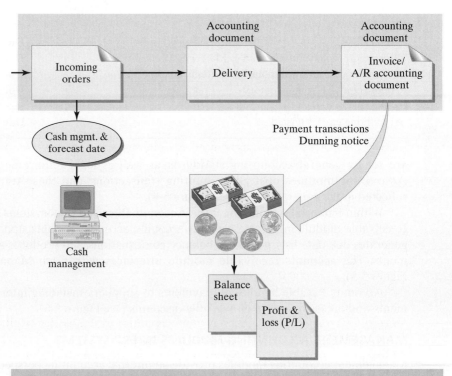

FIGURE 5-5 Accounts Receivable

Source: Copyright SAP AG.

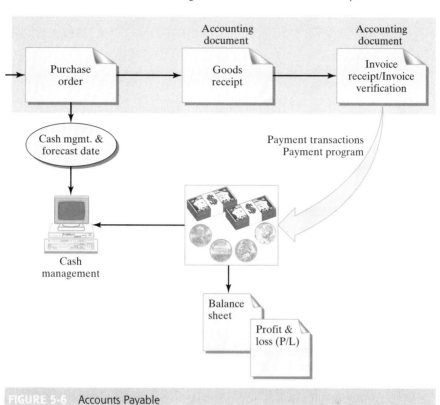

FIGURE 5-6   Accounts Payable

Source: Copyright SAP AG.

actual data, data are the basis for planning. Key management accounting activities include the following:

Cost Center Accounting: Cost centers are organization sub-areas treated as independent account assignment objects in cost accounting.

Internal Orders: Internal orders are used as a basis for collecting and controlling costs according to the job incurring the costs.

Activity-Based Costing (ABC): ABC monitors costs by business process rather than by cost center, so the cost of a business process can be determined.

Product Cost Controlling: Product cost controlling calculates the costs of manufacturing a product or providing a service. This provides information to Profitability Analysis to calculate contribution margins.

Profitability Analysis: Profitability analysis analyzes profit or loss by individual market segments, which include products, customers, and orders.

Profit Center Accounting: Profit center accounting evaluates the profit or loss of an organization's individual, independent areas.

Consolidation: Consolidation provides the ability to consolidate financial data for external and internal accounting perspectives.

- Profit center accounting, profitability analysis, and cost center analysis provide a company-wide view of costs and enable management to answer questions, such as

TABLE 5-5   Management Control Functions in ERP

Business Scenarios	Functions
Profit center accounting	Provides profitability reports with planned versus actual comparisons; provides profitability reports with a comparison of current period versus cumulative period
Profitability analysis	Identifies which products or markets have the highest contribution margins

the following:

- Which products are most profitable?
- Which divisions are most profitable?
- Which customers are most profitable?

These questions can be broken down further. For example, you could ask which customers in the New York territory are most profitable during the month of December. Which products in the Seattle territory are most profitable during the June through August timeframe? All of these questions enable management to allocate resources, including product development, sales force hours, and management time, so resources will be devoted to the highest-potential accounts and products. This maximizes overall profitability and business performance.

Increasingly, businesses are using profit centers, or responsibility centers, to manage operations. Each profit center manager is responsible for his/her own business, and for the profit and loss of the business. Profit center accounting creates reports on the performance of these profit centers (see Table 5-5).

FIGURE 5-7   Profitability Analysis

	A	B	C	D	E	F	G	H	I	J	K
1				MIDTOWN BRANCH			✛				
2				PROFITABILITY ANALYSIS							
3				26-Apr-04							
4											
5	SEVICE TYPE	NUMBER OF	TOTAL	UNIT	TOTAL		MARGIN				
6		TRANS	CHARGES	COST	COST	PROFIT	AS A % OF SALES				
7											
8	Money Order	12,000	2160	0.13	$1,560	$600	28%				
9	Wire Trans	120,000	40875	0.20	$24,000	$16,875	41%				
10	Trav Checks	87,000	7830	0.06	$5,220	$2,610	33%				
11											
12	TOTAL	219,000	50865		$30,780	$20,085					
13											
14											
15											
16											
17											
18											
19											
20											
21											

Sheet1 / Sheet2 / Sheet3 /

TABLE 5-6	Integration of Managerial Accounting and Control Systems with Other ERP Modules

Module	*Interface*
Financial Accounting	The source of data for Management Accounting (e.g., revenue postings to the general ledger)
Materials Management	Posts cost of goods to Management Accounting
Production Planning	Posts the cost of bills of materials, which are created in Production Planning
Personnel Administration	Posts expenses for payroll transactions
Sales and Distribution	Posts revenue from billing documents

The Managerial Accounting module within ERP is a central clearinghouse for accounting information that is created, updated, and used by many different functional areas of the business, including financial accounting, materials management, production planning, personnel administration, and sales and distribution (see Table 5-6).

THE NEW ROLE FOR MANAGEMENT ACCOUNTING

ERP systems provide on-line real-time data for decision making. With ERP, "Accountants are no longer at the back of the corporate ship issuing delayed reports about the history of the voyage . . . Instead, they will be on the bridge with the CEO, offering real-time cost information to help steer the ship into the future" (Kaplan and Cooper, 1998).

ERP systems offer two types of data. The first type of data is operational data, which provides feedback on the quality and efficiency of processes. Operational data, for example, includes information on cycle time and defects and the cost of people and machines used in operations.

With ERP, managers have access to activity-based cost (ABC) information. ABC information traces the costs from resources (e.g., people, machines) and applies these costs to specific products, services, and customers. Using ABC systems, managers can answer important questions, such as the following:

- How much does it cost to make a product?
- How profitable is a customer?
- How profitable is a product?

This information differs from operational information. A comparison of operational control systems and ABC systems is shown in Table 5-7.

ABC information, running as a part of an ERP system, provides managers with information on the profitability of customers and products with real-time data on sales and production. This information is strategic because it can guide decisions on marketing strategy and business strategy. For example, information indicating that a certain product line is profitable would lead sales managers to develop incentives for sales personnel to focus on marketing this product line.

To understand data within the proper context, managers need to link information coming from operational control systems with information coming from ABC systems.

TABLE 5-7 A Comparison of Operational Control and ABC Systems		
	Operational Control Systems	*ABC Systems*
Purpose	Provides information about process and business unit efficiencies	Provides strategic cost information about the underlying economies of the business
Data	Information must be timely, accurate, and specific to the work group	Estimates are sufficient; lower requirements for accuracy
How cost is defined	Relevant information on the cost of people, machines, energy, which are used in operating processes	Cost of resources across the value chain of providing a product or service (e.g., from suppliers to after-sale service)
Questions addressed	What scrap metal is left over from production?	How much does it cost to make a product and serve a customer? How profitable is a product? How profitable is a customer?
Scope	Specific to a responsibility center	Aggregates costs across multiple cost and responsibility centers
Example	Measure actual expenses of a specific process: a customer help desk	Measure what it costs to connect a customer to the Internet including customer help desk, credit check, dispatching, billing, and customer service

Adapted from: Kaplan, Robert and Robin Cooper. "The promise and peril of integrated systems," *Harvard Business Review,* July/August 1998, pp. 109–119.

The ABC system budgets the quantity and expense of committed resources and feeds this information into the operational control system, which monitors the actual expenses. As an example, an order entry department has eight clerks, and the ABC system uses the standard that each clerk can process 2,000 orders per month. Total departmental output is 16,000 orders per month. The operational control system tests the standard by examining the actual quantity of accomplished work. If the order entry department loses a person but can still process 16,000 orders without difficulty, then this information can be used to recalculate the capacity of order processing activity to 2,285 orders per month per person (Kaplan and Cooper, 1998).

Process standards must be updated based upon continuous improvements. When changes in efficiency are updated (e.g., the ability to process 2,285 orders per month), the system can update the activity cost driver rates. Increases in materials, energy, and wage rates can cause budgeted expenses to rise, and cost driver rates can be updated accordingly.

The implications of having real-time data for managerial accounting is of enormous importance. ERP systems provide a "coming of age" for managerial accounting because information on customer, product, and market profitability can be based on real-time information. However, these data must be used in context. Managers should not be using ABC systems for real-time operational control. Rather, they should link operational data and ABC data as a basis for guiding continuous improvement.

The partnership between ERP and ABC establishes a connection between the key enabler of management decision making (e.g., ABC) and the key enabler of information flow in the organization (e.g., ERP). Now that operational managers have access to on-line, real-time ABC data, they can focus on measuring product and customer profitability and reducing operating costs. The partnership between ABC and ERP allows management accountants to play the role of proactive business strategists rather than reactive, retrospective reporters (Shaw, 1998).

◆ SUMMARY

The purpose of the Accounting and Financial modules is to support financial accounting and management accounting functions. Financial information is created, maintained, and updated for external reporting purposes. Management accounting information is internal information designed to support management decision making. By analyzing profitability and business unit performance, managers can allocate resources to marketing the most profitable products and services, and this will increase revenues and reduce costs.

Questions for Discussion

1. Gather information about the best practices, which are associated with the Financial Accounting module within an ERP package. You can do this by (1) conducting research on the web; (2) interviewing a user of a Financial Accounting module; (3) using an on-line database to find an article in a trade publication that describes the effective use of an Financial Accounting module; or (4) using an Financial Accounting module within an ERP system to identify best practices.
   a. What are the best practices you have discovered?
   b. How do they contribute to overall productivity?
   c. What information for decision making do they provide?
2. The Financial Accounting module is often the first module to be implemented within an ERP system. Why do many companies start with the Financial Accounting module?
3. Many divisions of organizations seek decentralized financial control. How can an ERP system be implemented to ensure local financial decision making and control?
4. The Management Accounting module within ERP has interfaces to many other modules, including Human Resources, Sales and Distribution, Materials Management, Production Planning, and Financial Accounting. Describe the interfaces between the Management Accounting module and each of these other modules:

Module	*What Information Is Shared with Management Accounting*
Human Resources	
Sales and Distribution	
Materials Management	
Production Planning	
Financial Accounting	

5. The Mid-Level Market for ERP

The high-end accounting software vendors (e.g., SAP, PeopleSoft, BAAN, Oracle) see the potential of the mid-level market, and to edge into it, they have been scaling down their expensive and complex products. The mid-level market is variously described as organizations with annual revenue of between $20 million and $200 million or with more than 100 employees.

By removing some high-end functions and restricting users' ability to customize the remaining ones, the vendors can trim prices and, they claim, can accelerate implementation from an average of two years to between three to six months. For a mid-sized organization, this is a major plus because it usually lacks the information technology (IT) staff required to customize an ERP package.

Gather research on ERP packages that address the needs of the mid-level market. What challenges do mid-market companies face in implementing ERP software?

Source: Jones, Roberta Ann. "Spotlight on midlevel ERP software." *Journal of Accountancy.* v. 193, No. 5, May 2002, pp. 24–47.

Featured Article

Read these excerpts from the article, "The changing landscape of computerized accounting systems," and answer these questions: (1) Define each of the "in-technologies and systems." (2) What is their relationship to the success of ERP?

MORE POWER AND GREATER STANDARDIZATION

The world of accounting systems software used to be divided into two parts: the low end and the high end. This worked quite well before e-commerce, e-business, and enterprise resource planning came along. These, coupled with cheaper and more powerful computers, have given rise to a new breed of accounting systems beyond the high end. The good news, however, is that while the pricing of the new breed is not cheap, it is far less than the mainframe- and minicomputer-based systems that previously were needed to perform the same functions. Also, for the first time, database management within accounting systems is becoming standardized under the SQL-based client-server system. This means ease of movement for databases from one application to another.

The computer has revolutionized the way enterprises keep their accounting records. After transactions are recorded they can be manipulated sorted, analyzed, summarized, and turned into financial statements with ease. The

observer does not even know whether Luca Pacioli's double-entry concept is still being used. Accounting seems to be the perfect application for making the most of computing power.

As we face the 21st century and the third millennium, questioning what technology has in store for accounting systems is quite appropriate. With prices for consumer PC systems hovering around $600–1,000, and low-end accounting software priced at about $100, businesses can afford to have computerized accounting. But, are the old programs enough to run a business in the 21st century?

The New Marketplace. Today the computer accounting industry has three major levels, with the mid and lower levels each split into two groups.

ERP vendors dominate the highest tier of accounting systems, where software solutions can start at $150,000. The mid level (where previously high-end functions are found), with software costs at $8,000–$50,000, is divided into SQL-based systems and non-SQL-based systems. Lastly, the low-end systems, which still provide some bang for the buck, carry prices in the $100–5,000 range. This group is also broken down into two strata: the very low-end systems, and a class of "larger" systems that are more functional and robust but fall far short of the mid-level systems.

Another force at work is the introduction of e-commerce and e-business into the accounting systems mix. Most, if not all, mid- and high-end products provide some sort of communications interface with the Internet. Many of these interfaces are based on ODBC and the ability to have multiple software and hardware products communicate directly with the accounting system and its databases.

Even low-end vendors such as Peachtree offer an e-commerce module. Peachtree's PeachLink provides small businesses with the wherewithal to do business on the Internet. PeachLink allows the user to list products and services on the Web, take orders, and even receive payments.

THE 21ST CENTURY MARKETPLACE

Most of the major accounting systems manufacturers agree with the following view of the future accounting marketplace:

"In" technologies and systems

E-commerce and e-business

Best practices

SQL

GUI front ends

Web-enabled applications

Extended enterprise solutions

Value chain

Internet-based Commerce. Commerce conducted over, through, by, or with Internet-related technologies will be the single hottest technology in the next decade. Vendors that responded to an e-mail survey all stressed a vision of e-commerce or e-business solutions. Each and every non-respondent's website also stressed e-commerce or e-business.

A new feature in Quicken 99 exemplifies the attention that accounting vendors are paying the Internet. Quicken, the highly popular and simple to use home accounting system, now provides remote entry of transactions through the Web. This capability allows users of Quicken 99 to enter transactions through Intuit's (Quicken's publisher) site and store them for later retrieval.

E-business has been defined as the exchange of goods and services using electronic means. Electronic data interchange (EDI) and electronic funds transfer (EFT) are examples of

e-business primarily conducted at the commercial or wholesale level. E-commerce is the use of the Internet to conduct business. Amazon.com and online securities trading are examples of e-commerce at the retail level.

The use of SQL as the back-end database, and its ability to use ODBC as a methodology for transmitting information to and from other applications, makes using the Internet for business transactions easier than ever. Dell Computer Corporation currently handles $10 million in retail transactions per day over the Internet, according to Lettie Ledbetter of Dell Computer's public relations department.

Enterprise Resource Planning. Lynne Stockstad, director of global marketing at Great Plains software, sees the back office application of ERP as follows:

"This application category is the backbone of a strategic business management solution. . . . It typically includes fully integrated applications across financials, distribution, human resources/payroll, service management, and manufacturing. ERP solutions have predominantly been implemented by the Fortune 500 businesses. However, major midmarket vendors . . . are now offering this full scope of ERP solution[s]." ERP leaders SAP, PeopleSoft, and Baan have, as stated, moved into the middle tier of businesses, breaking into the Fortune 500 and beyond. They have done this by repositioning and restructuring their current selection of ERP products to run on the mid-tier platform of choice, Windows NT.

Nevertheless, the former high-end accounting products, which have been reclassified by these ERP vendors, should not be discounted. As Stockstad stated, ERP and the creation of programs that support this system of management are on the wish lists of the now mid-level accounting systems.

Solutions which in the past cost in the millions of dollars can now be achieved for less than $500,000. This new accessibility to ERP allows information power that was not previously available to be used by smaller corporations. Solutions geared toward specific industry sets or implementation of management theories (such as best practices) foster tighter integration of the accounting, managerial, and operational functions of the business.

The addition of the Internet to ERP and e-commerce has morphed even this newfound jargon with a new glossary of terms, most notably the extended enterprise solution (EES).

Best Practices. Arthur Andersen defines best practices as "simply the best way to perform a process." The boom in ERP and e-commerce gives rise to the need to institute best practices, to both improve the bottom line and create an air of control over what is to be a new explosion in information. From accounting to marketing data, inventory control to depreciation schedules, it is the art of data warehousing that is enabling the small and large business to manage growth in changing economic times. By implementing best practices, from planning to implementation, companies are able to reengineer their business and maximize productivity. A best practice forces a reexamination of the business from all points of view, essentially requiring the corporate entity to redefine itself.

The largest mistake made during the implementation of a new accounting system, especially a manufacturing requirement processing (MRP) or ERP system, is to redesign the new system to work in the old environment. This is often done without a thorough examination of the effectiveness of existing procedures and an

evaluation of where best practices can optimally be employed.

Structured Query Language. As mentioned previously, SQL is quickly becoming the database of choice. Vendors from Peachtree to Accountmate are rolling out SQL-based accounting systems, offering improved management of increasing amounts of data. The use of SQL standardizes the database aspect of these upper-end accounting systems. Before the acceptance of SQL, every vendor either used disparate database systems or created or modified their own database system. This made it difficult to share information with other systems located on shared resources.

THE RULER OF THE ROOST

Today, and most certainly tomorrow, ERP rules the roost, requiring CPAs' and businesses' accounting staffs to retool and reeducate themselves in this new management philosophy. ERP, best practices, and ad hoc SQL queries will exist not only in large enterprises but also in mid-sized companies.

SOURCE: Honig, Susan, "The changing landscape of computerized accounting systems," *CPA Journal*, v. 69, n. 5, May, 1999, pp. 14–20. Copyright: Copyright New York State Society of Certified Public Accountants 1999.

References

Baxendale, Sidney, and Farah Jama. 2003. "What ERP can offer ABC." *Strategic Finance* 85: 54–57.

Connolly, James. 1999. "ERP: Corporate cleanup." *Computerworld* 33: 74–78.

Kaplan, Robert, and Robin Cooper. 1998. "The promise and peril of integrated systems." *Harvard Business Review* 109–119.

Schultheis, Robert, and Mary Sumner. 1998. *Management Information Systems: The*

Manager's View. 4th ed. Burr Ridge, IL: Irwin/McGraw-Hill.

Shaw, Russell. 1998. "ABC and ERP: Partners at last?" *Management Accounting* 80: 56–58.

Smith, Mark. 1999. "Realizing the benefits from investment in ERP." *Management Accounting* 34: 34.

Stein, Tom. 1999. "Making ERP add up." *Information Week.* 59.

•CHAPTER•

ERP Systems: Production and Materials Management

6

Objectives

1. Understand the production and materials management systems within ERP.
2. Recognize the interrelationships among business processes supporting sales and marketing, production and materials management, accounting and finance, and human resources.

As an introduction to this chapter on Production and Materials Management, we will go back to the Atlantic Manufacturing case and see how difficulties with production and materials management functions create capacity problems, supplier problems, and order filling delays.

CASE: ATLANTIC MANUFACTURING

Issues occur in the Materials and Manufacturing processes, as well as in the Purchasing processes.

MATERIALS AND MANUFACTURING

✓ Materials and manufacturing people at Atlantic are constantly dealing with shortages, capacity problems, and supplier problems. A capacity problem forced them to air express a shipment to a customer to meet the promised delivery date, incurring much greater costs.

✓ A last-minute change in specifications failed to make it to the shop floor before the order was assembled and shipped. This caused a time delay in delivering the correct merchandise.

✓ The product design process is basically sequential, so it takes between 9 and 12 months from concept to production. Competitors can design and manufacture products with shorter lead times.

✓ When engineering starts to design a product, it often does not have detailed information from Marketing about the details of what customers want.

✓ Excess inventory is a problem.

PURCHASING

✓ Purchase requisitions get lost in the approval process, because paperwork is all manual. It is difficult to track some of the paperwork down, so buyers sometimes create multiple purchase requisitions.

In this chapter, you will learn about how Production and Materials Management can help companies control costs and provide efficient order fulfillment, from customer orders to purchase requisitions.

◆ BACKGROUND

The history of manufacturing systems shows the evolution of systems that were designed to re-order inventory using a re-order point to systems, which adapt production schedules to meet customer needs. Increased flexibility, increased responsiveness to customer demand, and increased integration are themes associated with manufacturing system evolution.

The manufacturing systems of the 1960s, 1970s, and 1980s were designed to manage high-volume production of a few products. These systems used large mainframe-based databases and were designed to implement large-scale production plans to address constant demand. If too much was manufactured, however, then excess inventory could become a significant problem. These systems were not flexible enough to provide customized products in limited quantities quickly.

By the late 1980s, the rules of thumb governing manufacturing changed. Customers expected their suppliers to create new products and services to meet their needs. This meant that production schedules needed to be more changeable and flexible to accommodate changing customer demands. Manufacturing Execution Systems (MES) provided continuous feedback and control of manufacturing processes, so changing market needs could be addressed. MES provided components to manage machine resources, to prioritize production schedules, to control workflow, to manage labor, and to automate document flow.

In the 1990s, ERP systems were instrumental in integrating manufacturing processes with other business processes. ERP systems manage processes across the supply chain so that customers' needs for information about products and services are met. ERP systems achieve operational efficiency through integration of data.

Prior to ERP, customers primarily dealt with distributors and retailers; the manufacturer was far removed from the customer. With ERP, the supply chain becomes more integrated, and many manufacturers sell directly to customers. This enables manufacturers to develop a better sense of customers' needs and to adapt to their needs more efficiently.

TABLE 6-1	Problems in Production Planning and Materials Management
Subsystems	***Problems***
Production Planning	Production planning may not be linked to expected sales levels; difficulty in adjusting production to reflect actual sales; difficulty in meeting anticipated sales demand
Production	Materials costs and labor costs can deviate from standard costs, and this will change manufacturing costs
Purchasing/Materials Management	Production manager may not be able to give the Purchasing/ Materials Management manager a good production forecast
Accounting	Differences occur between standard costs and actual costs

Many of the problems with traditional systems occur because of lack of integration between production planning, sales, purchasing, and accounting. If production plans are not linked to expected sales levels, then there may not be sufficient inventory to meet demand. There may be too many slow-moving items because customers no longer demand these items. This is particularly true in industries where buyer preferences change, such as clothing, consumer electronics, and computers.

Inaccurate production forecasts trigger incorrect purchasing decisions by Materials Management, leaving excess raw materials and finished goods inventory. Excess inventories impact the cash flow and profitability of the business because they represent significant costs (see Table 6-1). To minimize excess inventory, production must be based upon an accurate sales forecast.

◆ PRODUCTION PLANNING AND MANUFACTURING PROCESSES

Production Planning and Manufacturing Processes include all the activities necessary to ensure production. Production systems achieve these objectives:

1. Producing the production plan
2. Acquiring raw materials
3. Scheduling equipment, facilities, and workforce to process these materials
4. Designing products and services
5. Producing the right quantity and the required level of quality at the time required by production goals

The production planning and manufacturing processes, which achieve these goals, include operational-level and managerial-control processes (see Table 6-2).

Operational-level processes handle daily activities, such as purchasing, receiving, Quality Control (QC), and inventory management. The function of purchasing is to obtain the right quantity of raw materials and production supplies. In receiving, items are inspected and received, and information about their status is passed along to accounts payable, inventory, and production. QC identifies vendors who ship badly made or unreliable materials. QC continues to monitor the quality of production goods as they move from raw materials, to goods-in-process, to finished goods inventory. In

TABLE 6-2	Production Planning and Manufacturing Processes
Operational	Purchasing
	Receiving
	Quality Control (QC)
	Cost accounting
	Materials management
	Inventory management/control
Management control	MRP
	Just-in-time (JIT) manufacturing
	Capacity planning
	Production scheduling
	Product design

Total Quality Management (TQM) environment, emphasis is placed on anticipating and preventing defects. Continuous feedback about quality is critical.

In modern production planning and manufacturing, information systems support these processes. Shop floor data collection systems are used to enter data about the status of goods-in-process, including the amount of worker time devoted to each phase of the production process. In factory floor automation, microcomputers with keyboards enable factory floor personnel to enter data about the time spent on a job order, piece counts, and the amount of scrap materials.

Materials Management systems provide information on inventory levels of production materials, usage of these materials in production, and location of materials. Bill of Materials (BOM) systems provide a list of ingredients for the final product, including raw materials, subassemblies, and component parts.

Inventory management systems maintain inventories at their proper levels. Traditionally, a re-order point system makes certain that sufficient production materials are ordered with sufficient lead time to arrive at the plant when they are needed in the production process. Another inventory management tool is economic order quantity, which identifies the economic order quantity for each item.

Finally, cost accounting systems collect and report information about the resources used in production processes to determine accurate production costs, including the cost of personnel, materials, equipment, and facilities (Schultheis and Sumner, 1998).

◆ MANAGEMENT CONTROL PROCESSES IN PRODUCTION AND MANUFACTURING

MATERIAL REQUIREMENTS PLANNING (MRP)

Material Requirements Planning (MRP) supports these processes:

- Identifying stock that planned production calls for
- Determining the lead time to get the stock from suppliers

TABLE 6-3	MRP Vocabulary
MRP	The amount and timing of raw materials orders to support the Master Production Schedule (MPS)
BOM	The recipe of materials needed to make a product
Lead times	The time for the supplier to receive and process the order, and ship it to the manufacturer
Lot sizing	Production quantities
MPS	Master Production Schedule
Gross requirements	Raw materials needed for production
Planned orders	Sufficient raw materials for production

- Calculating safety stock levels
- Calculating the most cost-effective order quantities
- Producing purchase orders for needed stock items in the right amounts

MRP uses inputs from the Master Production Schedule (MPS). The MPS uses the sales forecast to identify the products needed and when they are needed.

It is useful to have some basic vocabulary for production and manufacturing processes (see Table 6-3).

The ideal production and manufacturing environment is a just-in-time (JIT) system, in which enough inventory is on hand to serve needs. To make a just-in-time system work, suppliers need to deliver enough material to meet the production schedule. The company needs to develop close working relationships with suppliers to make this work. Suppliers can use Electronic Data Interchange (EDI) or the Internet to monitor the manufacturer's inventory levels by linking into their inventory systems. In this way, they can replenish the manufacturer's inventory on a JIT basis.

CAPACITY PLANNING PROCESSES

The purpose of capacity planning is to determine if there is enough production capacity, in terms of personnel, space, machines, and other production facilities, to meet production goals. Capacity planning requires detailed information about human resources, BOM, goods-in-process inventories, finished goods inventories, lot sizes, status of raw materials, orders in the plant, and lead time for orders. The result is time-phased plans for each product and for each production work area. Additionally, personnel capacity planning estimates the number and type of workers, supervisors, and managers needed to meet the master production plan.

Production Scheduling information systems allocate specific production facilities for the production of finished goods to meet the master production schedule. This allows managers to control projects and project completion times/dates and to determine the impact of problems on projected completion dates.

Product Design and Development information systems integrate information about component costs into product design/engineering in order to reduce costs. For example, a product designer can compare component costs from two or three alternative sources and build the most cost-effective component into the product design before the product goes into manufacturing (Schultheis and Sumner, 1998).

The introduction of ERP extends the production information system to finance, marketing, human resource management, and other functions. ERP modules for production planning and manufacturing support materials requirements planning, shop floor control, inventory management, and capacity planning. The ERP system accesses cost accounting data through integration with the financial accounting system.

The ideal computer-integrated manufacturing system is designed to integrate all software and hardware used in manufacturing by merging manufacturing databases. This concept eliminates paperwork and bottlenecks associated with non-integrated data. The objective is to decrease design costs, to decrease lead time, to increase productivity of engineering and design processes, to decrease work-in-process inventory, and to decrease personnel costs.

With an ERP system, sales forecasts are used to determine production levels and to develop a production plan. Sales forecasts are an input into the sales and operations plan, which determines resource requirements for production. Demand Management creates an MPS, which determines the quantities and dates for finished products that are needed. The MRP component develops a detailed material plan, which is a set of planned orders for materials to be purchased or for materials to be transferred from a plant (see Table 6-4).

The MRP module determines what needs to be ordered at what time in order to fulfill the requirements of the MPS, and this triggers the purchasing of needed raw materials and/or subassemblies. The MRP function develops the planned orders, and these orders are sent to Production as work orders. Each work order includes a list of required materials from the BOM, and the manufacturing operations, which need to be performed. Materials are issued to these work orders in the manufacturing process.

TABLE 6-4   How ERP Supports Production Planning

Subsystems	*How an ERP Works*
Sales Forecasting	Production has access to sales forecasts, so it can adjust production levels to actual sales if sales differ from expectations
Sales and Operations Planning	Determines if production facilities can produce enough to meet consumer demand
Demand Management	Breaks down the production plan into weekly production; produces the MPS, which is the production plan for finished goods
MRP	Determines the amount and timing of raw materials orders or subassemblies to support the MPS
Purchasing	Generates Purchase Orders for raw materials
Detailed Scheduling	Schedules production based on demand
Production	Uses the detailed schedule to manage operations
Accounting	ERP captures data on the shop floor for accounting purposes

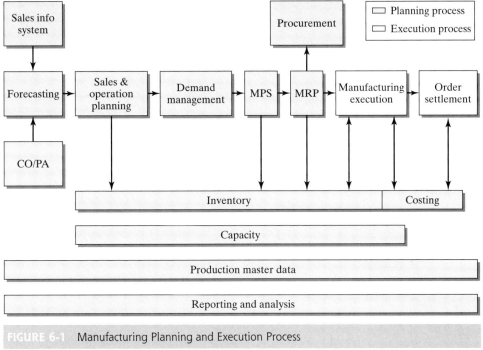

FIGURE 6-1   Manufacturing Planning and Execution Process

Source: Figure 108, SAP01, SAP Overview, p. 331.

SAP's modules in Production Planning support Sales and Operations Planning, Demand Management, the MPS, MRP, Manufacturing Execution, and Order Settlement (see Figure 6-1). Each of the modules provides important inputs into the next module (see Table 6-5).

TABLE 6-5   SAP Modules in Production Planning

Module	Function
Sales and Operation Planning	Determines the rate at which the company provides manufacturing, engineering, and financial resources to support the sales plan
Demand Management	Links forecasting functions to the MPS and the MRP
MPS	Creates planned orders for top-level items to satisfy requirements from Demand Management
MRP	Determines which material you need, in what quantity, and at what time; generates replenishment schedules for all manufactured components, purchased parts, and raw materials
Manufacturing Execution	Creates production orders from planned orders; production orders contain data on production objectives, material components, required resources, and costs
Order Settlement	Confirms production order operations; collects data on quantities produced, completion dates

	A	B	C	D	E	F	G	H	I	J	K
1											
2											
3		Lewis Manufacturing									
4		Sales for first quarter 2004									
5											
6	Stock no.	Current Sales	Projected	Percent							
7			Sales	on target							
8											
9	TR223	$643,861.00	$665,000.00	96.82%							
10	TR224	$628,693.00	$629,000.00	99.95%							
11	TR226	$80,311.00	$84,500.00	95.04%							
12	TR230	$95,556.00	$45,000.00	212.35%							
13	TR322	$788,966.00	$877,600.00	89.90%							
14	TR323	$88,156.00	$93,400.00	94.39%							
15											
16	Totals	$2,325,543.00	$2,394,500.00	97.12%							
17											
18											
19											
20											

Sheet1 / Sheet2 / Sheet3

FIGURE 6-2 Sales Forecast

The Sales and Operations Plan, which determines what manufacturing resources are needed to support the sales forecast, is an input into Demand Management (see Figure 6-2). Demand Management links the forecast to the MPS and MRP. MRP determines which materials are required, in what quantity, and at what time, and then creates the necessary orders through the procurement process. Procurements converts the planned order into a purchase requisition, or production planning converts the planned order into a production order.

The MPS and MRP are inputs into Manufacturing Execution, which creates the production orders. The production orders have data on production goals, materials, resources, and costs. Manufacturing Execution is an input to Order Settlement, which collects data on production amounts, times, and completion dates.

◆ MATERIALS MANAGEMENT MODULES IN ERP SYSTEMS

The Procurement Process determines needs, identifies potential sources of supply, compares alternative quotations, creates a purchase order, tracks the status of a purchase order, receives goods, and verifies invoices upon receipt of goods (see Table 6-6).

An ERP system provides needed integration between the Materials Management subsystem and other subsystems (see Table 6-7). For example, all purchase orders are assigned to a cost center in the Management Accounting module. In Production Planning, the inventory function posts components needed to fill Production Orders. Purchasing and Financial Accounting share common vendor data.

TABLE 6-6	The Procurement Process
Activity	***Description***
Determine requirements	Determines needs, based upon re-order point, regular checking of stock, and forecasting based upon usage
Source determination	Identifies potential sources of supply
Vendor selection	Compares alternative quotations
Purchase order processing	Uses information from a purchase requisition to create a purchase order
Purchase order follow-up	Provides status of purchase orders
Goods receiving and inventory management	Confirms the receipt of goods
Invoice verification	Matches invoices with information on goods which have been received

TABLE 6-7	Integration of Materials Management with Other Subsystems
Interface With	***Interface Type***
Management Accounting	Purchase orders are assigned to a Cost Center
Financial Accounting	Purchasing maintains vendor data which are defined jointly with Financial Accounting
Sales and Distribution	When a Purchase Requisition is created, it is assigned to a sales order
Production Planning	Inventory Management posts components needed for production orders

THE FUTURE OF ERP IN MANUFACTURING AND THE SUPPLY CHAIN

Manufacturers are moving toward JIT manufacturing environments since companies want to carry less inventory and want to produce more customized products. Emerging developments in manufacturing are the convergence of manufacturing execution systems and ERP, the use of advanced planning and scheduling systems, advanced data collection strategies, and eBusiness.

MANUFACTURING EXECUTION SYSTEMS (MES) AND ERP

The convergence of MES and ERP systems is a recent development. MES are factory floor information and communication systems which provide feedback from the factory floor on a real-time basis. MES support data collection, detailed scheduling, labor management, quality management, maintenance management, product tracking, and performance analysis. These systems provide feedback from the factory floor on a real-time basis (Manetti, 2001).

ERP vendors are expanding their modules to extend closer to the plant floor, and MES vendors are expanding their shop floor solutions to include front-end and back-end applications such as order fulfillment and warehouse management systems. A partnership between MES and ERP systems yields outstanding results: better shop floor to front office communication, better customer service, and improved information for decision making.

ADVANCED PLANNING AND SCHEDULING (APS) SYSTEMS

APS Systems work with ERP systems by providing business analysis and decision support capabilities. The majority of ERP systems are still transactions-oriented and have limited decision support features. An APS system leverages the data residing in a company's ERP system to provide decision support for production planning, demand planning, and transportation planning (Kilpatrick, 1999).

DATA COLLECTION

In the past, data collection focused on using a network of bar code readers to gather inventory movement and shop activity on the plant floor. To reduce on-hand inventories and transaction costs, today's data collection goes far beyond bar codes and the network of collection stations. Real-time data are gathered directly from the shop floor using mobile and Internet-enabled devices, bar-coding capabilities, and easy interfaces (Turbide, 2000). Automating routine data collection with mobile user interfaces optimizes the flow of information 300% or more (Turbide, 2000). Choosing a data collection system that integrates tightly with a powerful ERP package gives companies a competitive edge.

eBUSINESS STRATEGIES IN MANUFACTURING ERP

The business world is looking for less inventory and more customized products. Manufacturing is moving toward JIT manufacturing, whereby the exact supplies needed for manufacturing are acquired on a timely basis. eBusiness offers the potential to improve materials management by facilitating communications between all links in the supply chain.

Business-to-business (B2B) electronic commerce increased in transaction value from $43 billion in 1998 to $1.3 trillion by 2003. This is ten times the value of business to consumer electronic commerce (Manetti, 2001). B2B applications enable procurement organizations to interact with a multitude of suppliers, creating more competitive bidding. Technology allows buyers to provide suppliers with their material resource planning forecasts and, using this information, suppliers can make bids to meet a company's specific needs.

eBusiness buyers benefit from the rise of eMarketplaces or exchanges. eMarketplaces aggregate buyers, sellers, content, and business services, making traditionally fragmented markets more efficient. eMarketplaces lower the cost of doing business by eliminating inefficient processes which are part of traditional paper-based supply chains. By reducing search costs, eMarketplaces enable buyers to evaluate alternative supply sources. eMarketplaces offer a number of advantages, including lower prices, lower transaction costs, improved electronic communications, and community features, such as discussion forums. eMarketplaces maintain neutrality, rather than favoring sellers over buyers or pushing one seller over another.

Web technology enables suppliers to see Requests for Proposals (RFPs), technical specifications, and purchasing requirements so they can respond more quickly to meet these requirements. Some companies reduce supply chain lag times by giving suppliers a chance to obtain real-time demand forecasts, so these suppliers can ship raw materials and parts without waiting for a purchase order.

Finally, eMarketplaces have transformed the role of purchasing agents. Prior to the emergence of eMarketplaces, purchasing agents spent a good deal of their time processing purchase orders and expediting shipments. With eBusiness, purchasing agents can devote their efforts to more strategic activities, such as organizing e-partnerships and analyzing alternative sourcing possibilities.

♦ SUMMARY

The discussion of Production and Materials Management illustrates how the production plan is based on the sales forecast. Once the sales plan is developed, then the Demand Management function determines the quantities and dates required for finished products. The MPS satisfies the requirements of Demand Management, and the MRP system determines what is needed, in what quantity, and at what time to fulfill the requirements of the MPS. In the next step, Purchasing or Procurement generates purchase orders for materials or subassemblies, which are needed for the production process. All of these Production and Materials Management processes are essential to ERP.

Questions for Discussion ●

1. Many people argue that MRP is a precursor to ERP, and that ERP systems were designed to integrate MRP systems with financial and accounting systems.
   a. Given the interrelationship between MRP and ERP, does it make sense for a non-manufacturing company to adopt an ERP system?
   b. Have manufacturing systems been the basis for all ERP systems?
2. Gather information about the best practices, which are associated with the Production Planning and Materials Management modules within an ERP package. You can do this in one of four ways: (1) Conduct research on the web; (2) Interview a user of a Production Planning/Materials Management module within an ERP package; (3) Use an on-line database to find an article in a trade publication which describes the effective use of a Production Planning/Materials Management module; or (4) Use a Production and Materials Management module within an ERP system.
   a. What are the best practices you have discovered?
   b. How is the ERP system with Production and Materials Management modules superior to a non-integrated Manufacturing system (i.e., where the Financial Systems and MRP systems are separate).
   c. What information for decision making does the integrated system provide?

3. The Production Planning and Materials Management modules within ERP have interfaces to other modules, including Human Resources, Sales and Distribution, and Financial Accounting. Describe these interfaces:

Module	What information is shared with Production Planning and Materials Management
Human Resources	
Sales and Distribution	
Financial Accounting	

Featured Article

The article "What ERP can offer ABC" describes the integration of manufacturing and accounting data, which is made possible through the use of ERP. Based upon this article, answer these questions:

1. What manufacturing data is used by the managerial accounting module within ERP?
2. How is this information used to control costs, to maximize productivity, and to streamline operations?
3. How does this data integration support managerial decision making?

"WHAT ERP CAN OFFER ABC"

One of the greatest stumbling blocks in implementing an activity-based costing (ABC) system is finding the right activity cost driver to use in attributing the cost of an activity to products or other cost objects. The nonfinancial measures that are typically used as activity cost drivers are rarely found in the accounting system. Measures such as number of sales orders, number of material moves, and number of engineering change notices per type of product are more likely found elsewhere.

Because the activity cost drivers aren't under the control of the accounting system, the activity cost-driver information isn't subject to the same process controls used to add reliability to the accounting numbers. In the early days of ABC-based costing, activity cost-driver information was often derived from a "back-of-an-envelope" information system.

Enterprise Resource Planning Systems

Enterprise resource planning (ERP) systems can significantly increase the availability and reliability of activity cost-driver information. ERP systems have become popular in recent years because they typically integrate financial accounting, managerial accounting, cost accounting, production planning, materials management, sales and distribution, human-resource management, quality management, and customer service using a relational database. The use of a relational database permits functional areas to share information without reentering the data or duplicating the data in databases throughout the organization.

One of the more dramatic ways that ERP systems provide reliable activity cost-driver information is by integrating production planning, materials management, and cost and management accounting. In cost and management accounting, activity-based costing is used to increase the accuracy of the product-cost information and to develop activity-based budgets. Before ABC, the materials handling costs and other materials management costs were often allocated to products based on a percentage of the direct material costs associated with each product. The percentage amount used in the allocation was based on the relationship between budgeted materials management costs and the expected total cost of direct materials.

Turning Overhead Costs into Direct Costs

To simplify this presentation, we will focus on ABC support in the widely used R/3 System from SAP. It's important to note that ERP systems from other vendors typically include an ABC feature with degrees of integration that vary from company to company. Check your vendor's support team for specifics.

SAP's R/3 system links production planning's bill of materials with material movement information that is available in the materials management portion of the system. It permits the establishment of standards for material handling. In fact, in many respects, the use of the R/3 system results in material handling cost as a direct cost rather than as the traditional indirect (overhead) cost.

The R/3 system is capable of regarding materials handling as a process whose activity cost driver is the "number of pallet moves." The cost of the materials handling process is then attributed to a product based on the various direct materials that are moved in the manufacture of the product specified in a production order. The bill of materials (BOM) for the production order will reveal direct material part numbers that will be needed. Materials management personnel will have already entered into the R/3 system information about the number of units of each direct material part number that will fit on a pallet. One unit of direct material part number B123 might require 1/20th of a pallet (20 units per pallet), and one unit of direct material part number A456 might require 1/50th of a pallet (50 units per pallet).

If we assume that a unit of product PDQ requires one unit of direct material B123 and one unit of direct material A456, then the R/3 system can calculate a standard direct cost that includes material handling costs. Those material handling costs formerly would have been regarded as indirect (overhead) costs. Table 1 shows the direct costs associated with a production order for 1,000 units of product PDQ. Those direct costs were calculated using an activity-based costing approach to product costing.

In costing the bill of materials for the production of 1,000 units of product PDQ, the R/3 system would link production planning's BOM for PDQ with material management's "bill of services," which specifies the portion of a pallet required by each unit of the various raw materials. That BOM would be related to the standard direct material costs maintained by the financial accounting portion of the R/3 system for inventory costing purposes. The associated bill of services would be related to the activity cost-driver charging rate for the materials handling process as determined by the ABC system. These relationships are possible because the data resides in the R/3 system's relational database. Using this relational database, each direct material part number on the BOM is converted to its related cost based on the standard direct material costs maintained by the financial accounting portion of R/3 for inventory valuation purposes. Further, the quantity of required direct materials is converted into required pallet moves, and the required pallet moves are costed using the activity cost-driver charging rate calculated by the ABC system.

R/3 Support for Activity-Based Budgeting

These same relationships between production planning, materials handling, and accounting,

TABLE 1 Calculation of Standard Cost for a Production Order	
Direct material B123	1,000 products × 1 unit × $10.00 per unit = $10,000
Direct material A456	1,000 products × 1 unit × $25.00 per unit = 25,000
Materials handling:***	
1,000 products × 1 unit of B123 × 1/20 × $50*	= 2,500
1,000 products × 1 unit of A456 × 1/50 × $50*	= 1,000
Total Direct Product Cost**	$38,500
Direct Cost per Unit of Product	$38.50

* This $50 represents the activity cost-driver rate for the material handling process. This amount is calculated by dividing the annual budgeted costs of the materials handling process by the annual capacity of the process in terms of the number of pallet moves.

** This example has omitted other direct costs for simplicity purposes.

*** If a direct material required only a portion of a pallet, the number of pallets would be increased to the next whole number of pallets.

TABLE 2	Budgeted Pallet Moves for Product PDQ
Direct Material B123	$1,000 \times 1/20 = 50$ pallet moves per production order
Direct Material A456	$1,000 \times 1/50 = 20$ pallet moves per production order
Total for Product PDQ	70 pallet moves per production order of 1000

If 100,000 units of product PDQ require 100 production orders, then the budgeted annual production of product PDQ will require 7,000 pallet moves.

as represented in the R/3 system, are a tremendous benefit when the ABC system is used for budgeting purposes. Activity-based budgeting (ABB) attempts to anticipate the demands on a process, such as materials handling, given the estimated production of various products in standard batch sizes. Table 2 shows the required number of pallet moves by the materials handling process given a budgeted annual production of 100,000 units of product PDQ in lot sizes of 1,000 units.

When the budgeted production of all products (product PDQ and others) is considered, the R/3 system will have estimated the quantity of the various direct materials and the number of pallet moves required to support the total budgeted production. The activity-based budget will already have an estimated budgeted cost and an estimated practical capacity in terms of pallet moves for the materials handling process. Let's assume that the budgeted annual cost for materials handling was $5 million and the budgeted annual capacity at that budgeted level was 100,000 pallet moves (resulting in the $50 activity cost-driver charging rate mentioned earlier). If the production budget estimated that 120,000 pallet moves would be required for the year, the activity-based budgeting system would reveal that the demands on material handling would be 20,000 pallet moves in excess of the budgeted capacity. This should certainly result in a reevaluation of the materials handling process and its budget.

This reevaluation could result in process improvements, including placing more units of raw material on each pallet or reducing the average length of each move. If no process improvements are possible, the manufacturer may have to increase the capacity of pallet moves by increasing the resources budgeted for the materials handling process. The final budget for materials handling cost and materials handling capacity will determine the activity cost-driver charging rate for each pallet move. Thus, the $50 activity cost-driver charging rate used in determining the direct cost for product PDQ could change as a result of a shift in the budgeted practical capacity and/or the budgeted cost.

Other Processes

SAP's R/3 system collects a multitude of nonfinancial measures that are potential activity cost drivers for use in ABC systems. It can count and record the number of line items on a sales order, the number of sales orders for each type of product, the weight of each item on a shipping document, the number of shipping containers per sales order, and more.

This information is collected as part of a formal process that has built-in controls designed to ensure reliability. These controls include automatic counting of line items on a sales order. As the sales-order information is entered into the R/3 system, the system counts and records the number of different products that are included on the sales order. As the orders are processed, the system counts the number of sales orders for each product type. Another control includes the mandatory inclusion of information in the master record. For example, the master record for direct material B123 must include the maximum number of units of the direct material that will fit on a pallet (20 units for B123) before the master record will be incorporated into the ERP system.

Bar coding of product information is another control that adds integrity to the system. SAP's R/3 can record information directly into the system by reading bar-code information concerning direct materials input and product output. A feature of R/3 is the use of sensing devices on machines that will record data in the system without human intervention. With this feature, every time a punch press makes a "punch," the system automatically records the number of pieces created by the "punch."

SAP's R/3 system has an abundance of non-financial measures that may be used by activities as activity cost drivers. These measures have a high degree of integrity because of the way they are collected and recorded. Now, activity-based costing can move beyond the back-of-an-envelope information for determining the activity charging rates used to assign activity costs to products or other cost objects. Integrating the ERP information with the ABC process saves time and resources.

SOURCE: Baxendale, Sidney J; Jama, Farah, "What ERP can offer ABC," *Strategic Finance*, v. 85, no. 2, August, 2003, p. 54–57. Copyright: Copyright Institute of Management Accountants, Aug. 2003.

References ●

Fitzgerald, K. 1999. "Buyer's interest keeps growing." *Purchasing: The Magazine of Total Supply Chain Management* S8–S12.

Kilpatrick, J. 1999. "Advanced planning systems spark the supply chain." *APICS: The Performance Advantage* 25–28.

Liker, Jeffrey, Ed. 1997. *Becoming Lean: Inside Stories of U.S. Manufacturers.* Portland, OR: Productivity Press.

Manetti, J. 2001. "How technology is transforming manufacturing." *Production and Inventory Management Journal* 42: 54–64.

Pine, B. Joseph, and Stan Davis. 1999. *Mass Customization: The New Frontier in Business Competition.* Cambridge, MA: Harvard Business School Press.

Rondeau, P.J., and L.A. Litteral. 2001. "Evolution of manufacturing planning and control systems: From reorder point to enterprise resource planning." *Production and Inventory Management Journal* 42: 1–7.

Schultheis, Robert, and Mary Sumner. 1998. *Management Information Systems: The Manager's View.* 4th ed. Burr Ridge, IL: Irwin/McGraw-Hill.

Turbide, D. 2000. "Welcome to the new millennium." *Midrange ERP: The Management Magazine for Midsized Manufacturers* 10–16.

ERP Systems: Human Resources

Objectives

1. Understand the Human Resources (HR) processes supported by an ERP system.
2. Recognize the interrelationships among business processes supporting human resources, financial accounting, and other modules.

CASE: ATLANTIC MANUFACTURING

Atlantic Manufacturing is facing a number of issues relevant to Human Resources (HR), in terms of recruiting, retention, and cost control of benefits.

RECRUITING

✓ In recent years, recruiting talented sales representatives has become increasingly difficult. In addition, turnover among sales representatives is very high. Often, Atlantic makes an investment in training a new sales representative, and that investment is lost when the sales rep leaves the firm.

✓ It is difficult to make queries to the HR files to identify good candidates for job openings within the firm. For example, the firm had an opening for a web designer several months ago, and it was impossible to go through the various personnel files to identify possible internal candidates.

HUMAN RESOURCES DATA ADMINISTRATION

✓ Paperwork supporting the HR function seems to grow and grow. This has meant adding administrative staff to maintain and to update employee and job salary history data and to provide numerous governmental reports associated with affirmative action, the Family Medical Leave Act, and OSHA.

COMPENSATION AND BENEFITS ADMINISTRATION

✓ The firm needs better data on the most relevant compensation packages for certain hard-to-find job descriptions, such as sales managers. They want to be able to offer competitive compensation packages that will enable them to retain qualified personnel, but they do not want to offer unnecessary programs that will increase their costs.

✓ The cost of employee benefits has increased dramatically over the past several years. Atlantic is interested in developing strategies, which will control the costs of these health benefits. A better information system would enable them to assess the costs and benefits of alternative health insurance programs, early retirement plans, and educational program reimbursements.

A number of problems are affecting the quality and responsiveness of the HR function (see Table 7-1). Most of these problems deal with the lack of access to information about employees, skill sets, job descriptions, turnover data, retention data, and benefits plans that will enable managers to make queries and to generate reports for external agencies, including government agencies.

◆ HUMAN RESOURCE MANAGEMENT PROCESSES

The business processes supporting HR can be categorized into operational and decision-making processes (see Table 7-2). Operational-level processes include creating and maintaining employee information, position information, and handling the

TABLE 7-1 Problems with Human Resources

Subsystems	*Problems*
Employee information	Need to query employee information to identify candidates with required skill sets
Applicant selection and placement	Need to develop selection criteria to provide a more stable workforce
Government reporting	Need to maintain and update data for government reporting requirements
Job analysis and design	Need to design positions, which will minimize turnover by providing breadth and depth of responsibilities
Compensation	Need to develop competitive salary and benefits packages for key positions
Benefits administration	Need to analyze alternative benefits scenarios to minimize costs and maximize employee loyalty and satisfaction

TABLE 7-2	Business Processes Supporting Human Resources

HR Processes	
Operational	Employee information; position control; application selection/placement; performance management info; government reporting; payroll information
Management control	Job analysis and design; recruiting information; compensation; employee training/development

job application screening and placement process. Other important operational-level activities include government reporting, payroll administration, and performance management (Schultheis and Sumner, 1998).

Managers need information to make decisions in order to allocate human resources effectively to achieve organizational goals. This means designing job specifications that enable the organization to recruit and retain highly qualified individuals. Designing compensation packages to attract and retain employees is important to achieving organizational goals. Employee training and professional development are critical to maintain appropriate skill sets, to improve productivity, and to maintain loyalty and morale.

Future workforce planning entails determining future workforce requirements and emerging skill sets. The gap between current workforce profiles and future skill sets needs to be analyzed so these skill sets can be developed. This may mean retraining internal candidates, acquiring external expertise, and outsourcing certain functions.

◆ HUMAN RESOURCES INFORMATION SYSTEMS

HR information systems have evolved in much the same way as information systems supporting finance, sales and marketing, and production and manufacturing. Historically, there has been a reliance on stand-alone, specialized applications supporting applicant tracking, compensation and benefits planning, skills training, and time and attendance reporting. This proliferation of applications leads to redundant data, which are difficult to maintain. Another shortcoming of legacy human resource management systems is their failure to link HR data with financial data. HR software that maintains and updates information on benefits, payroll, and labor without a tie-in to financial systems has limited value. By blending HR and financial data, the value of the HR function has increased for the organization as a whole.

An HR module within an ERP system offers the linkage between HR applications and financial systems and a standard set of processes based on best practices. However, as with any other ERP solution, it is not advisable to customize the system.

◆ HUMAN RESOURCE MODULES IN ERP SYSTEMS

The components of HR modules within an ERP system include HR Management, Benefits Administration, Payroll, Time and Labor Management, and Employee/Manager Self Service (Ashbaugh and Rowen, 2002).

- HR Management records personnel activity from the job application to retirement. Advanced systems can read résumés and enter pertinent data into the database.
- Benefits Administration links employee data to benefits data, including employee benefit election data. Advanced systems enable employees to elect and update benefits' preferences via the web.
- Payroll produces paychecks, tax reports, and sends accounting data to the general ledger.
- Time and Labor Management collects data for time/work reporting.
- Employee Self Service provides web-based self-service reporting for travel reimbursement, personnel data changes, benefits enrollment, and training classes enrollment.

An ERP system can support these HR processes (see Table 7-3).

TABLE 7-3   Human Resource Processes Supported by ERP

Subsystem	How ERP Works
Employee information	Maintains personnel information, including job history, salary, and retirement and benefit choices
Skills inventory	Maintains information on special skills, work experience
Position control	Defines each position within the organization; provides common job categories, descriptions, and specifications which can be used across the organization
Application selection/placement	Maintains information for recruiting, screening, evaluating, and selecting candidates for employment
Compensation	Maintains compensation data; maintains employee compensation changes (e.g., salary increases, salary history, job evaluation results, appraisal results)
Performance management	Maintains performance appraisal data and productivity data
Training and development systems	Tracks information about courses, instructors, students, and registrations; identifies training deficits and enables employees to book appropriate training
Government reporting	Provides reports in response to government statutes, including the Age Discrimination Act, the Equal Pay Act, the Occupational Safety and Health Act, the Family Leave and Medical Act
Payroll	Generates payroll and various statements

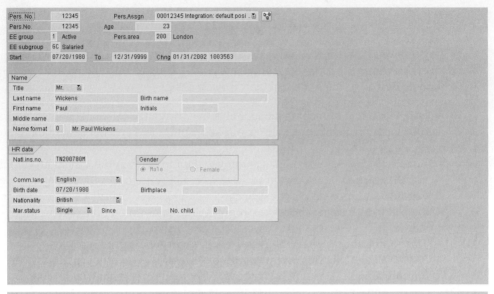

FIGURE 7-1 SAP Screen (Display Personal Data)

Source: Copyright SAP AG.

One of these operational-level processes, Display Personal Data, is shown in Figure 7-1.

In addition to supporting these capabilities, ERP modules support attendance reporting, determination of overtime and bonus wages, and tracking of absences, which are due to vacation, illness, or leave. HR systems handle booking of travel services and associated expense reimbursement. You can see an SAP screen for creating Display Travel in Figure 7-2.

ATTRIBUTES OF HUMAN RESOURCE MODULES IN ERP SYSTEMS

The attributes of a HR module within an ERP system include integration, a common database underlying all individual modules, and a common relational database, which promotes ad hoc query and reporting capabilities. ERP modules provide flexible and scalable technology, an audit trail, which provides the ability to review the history of changes to the database, and drill-down capability, which is the ability to reach the source document of the prior step in the process. Workflow management depicts the electronic routing of documents within the HR module. As with other ERP modules, the HR module provides process standardization.

Additional ERP attributes include security, user friendliness, web features, and document management and imaging capability. Security, including login security and record security, limits access to certain screens. User friendliness is supported by standard menus and flexible reporting tools. ERP modules provide web capabilities, enabling job seekers to download employment applications and to submit résumés online. Document management and imaging, which provides access to repositories of electronically stored documents, is an increasingly important feature of ERP (Ashbaugh and Rowen, 2002).

Pers.No.	12345	Pers.Assgn	00012345 Integration: default posi A..
Name	Mr. Paul Wickens		
EE group	1 Active	Pers.area	200 London
EE subgroup	6C Salaried		
Start	01/01/2001	to	12/31/9999 Chng 12/03/2001 1003563

Personnel action

Action Type	Trvl.exp (mini master)
Reason for Action	Initial hiring

Status

Customer-specific	
Employment	Active
Special payment	Standard wage type

Organizational assignment

Position	99999999	Integration: default posi
Personnel area	200	Corporate - United Kingdom
Employee group	1	Active
Employee subgroup	6C	Salaried

Additional actions

Start Date	Act.	Action Type	ActR	Reason f.Action
01/01/2001	56	Trvl.exp (mini master)		Initial hiring

FIGURE 7-2 SAP Screen (Display Travel)

Source: Copyright SAP AG.

MANAGEMENT CONTROL MODULES IN ERP SYSTEMS

Beyond maintaining databases on employees, positions, skills, applicants, and perfor-mance, a HR information system provides information that enables the organization to manage workforce characteristics. The objective of a good HR strategy is to acquire, place, train, and develop employees to meet organizational needs. HR information sys-tems support managerial decision-making needs by offering query and reporting tools for what-if analysis, (see the questions in Table 7-4).

An SAP screen which enables management to make a Compensation Change based upon a compensation review is illustrated in Figure 7-3.

A comprehensive HR module within an ERP package maintains and updates employee files, skills inventory files, job analysis files, design files, affirmative action files, and occupational health and safety files. These operational data provide a founda-tion for HR applications that support organizational effectiveness. Strategic HR appli-cations are Human Capital Inventory, Position Control, Labor/Management Relations, and Business Intelligence (Ashbaugh and Rowen, 2002).

Human Capital Inventory. A human capital inventory enables the organization to track employees from application to retirement, including information on skills track-ing, career planning, and linkage between performance evaluations and organizational goals. For example, tracking skills needed by IT personnel who develop mission-critical applications may provide a rationale for a strategic decision to invest in training designed to maintain these skills.

Position Control. When position control is linked to budgeting, managers can plan and budget for personnel costs. For example, if a strategic decision is made to limit the

TABLE 7-4	Human Resource Decisions Supported by an ERP System
Subsystem	**Questions and Decisions**
Recruiting	Do we have any internal candidates with a B.S. in Marketing and with Spanish-speaking ability?
	What are our most effective recruiting sources (e.g., universities, web sites, referrals, search firms)?
Job Analysis	What are the characteristics of our most effective managers (e.g., educational background, experience)?
	What are the characteristics of information technology (IT) professionals whom we retain?
	What jobs experience the highest turnover?
	What skill sets are missing among our HR professionals?
Compensation	What salaries and compensation packages do we need to offer our sales representatives to be competitive in our industry?
	What is the impact of various pay plans on retention and promotion of personnel?
	What do external market surveys say about job pricing?
Benefits	How can we control the cost of employee health benefits?
	Can we reduce employee benefit costs by providing self-selection of benefits?
Workforce development	What replacement personnel need to be planned for because of retirements?
	What should the future workforce look like? What new skill sets will we need?
	What additional human resources will we need in the short-term and long-term?
	What are the implications of workforce needs for training and development?
	What is the impact of a proposed merger on workforce development and retention?
	What is the availability of a skilled workforce in various locations under consideration for the placement of a new factory?

cost of contract plant maintenance personnel, then a link to budgets is essential to measure if this strategy is being followed.

Labor/Management Relations. HR modules provide accurate information such as tracking of seniority lists and disciplinary actions and tracking and analysis of grievances and worker's compensation. Data depicting trends in employee absences, costs for overtime work, and trends in employee benefits' costs, are particularly valuable in labor negotiations.

Business Intelligence is the use of advanced analytical tools to provide insight into organizational trends. Many interesting organizational trends are occurring in HR, including turnover analysis, recruitment and training analysis, and salary/workforce planning. Business intelligence is important to understanding these trends and developing human resources policy.

Pers.No.	12345	Pers.Assgn	00012345 Integration: default posi A..	
Name	Mr. Paul Wickens			
EE group	1 Active	Pers.area	200 London	
EE subgroup	6C Salaried			
Start	06/01/2004 to	12/31/9999		

Personnel action

Action Type	Change of Pay	
Reason for Action		

Status

Customer-specific		
Employment	Active	
Special payment	Standard wage type	

Organizational assignment

Position	99999999	Integration: default posi
Personnel area	200	Corporate - United Kingdom
Employee group	1	Active
Employee subgroup	6C	Salaried

Additional actions

Start Date	Act.	Action Type	ActR	Reason f.Action	

FIGURE 7-3 SAP Screen (Compensation Change)

Source: Copyright SAP AG.

◆ INTEGRATION OF HR MODULES WITH OTHER MODULES

One of the major benefits of an ERP system is the integration of modules. In the case of HR, the payroll, compensation, and expense reimbursement subsystems are integrated with the Financial Accounting Subsystem. This saves needless duplication of effort and provides a cost basis for making HR decisions.

◆ SUMMARY

HR management, decision making, and workforce development are among the most strategic areas of focus today. In the past, many human resource management systems have focused upon creating, maintaining, and updating personnel records. This process was so time-consuming that it was difficult to use these data for decision making. With the introduction of comprehensive, integrated ERP systems with HR modules, it is now possible to participate in short-term and long-term workforce development so personnel can be recruited, developed, compensated, and retained to meet overall organizational objectives.

Questions for Discussion •

1. Compensation for sales representatives is an important issue in many industries. If compensation packages are inadequate, salespeople will move to other firms with more attractive compensation packages. What information can a HR module provide to enable managers to develop compensation strategies to attract and retain successful sales representatives?

2. How can an HR system enable an organization to meet reporting requirements that are consistent with the following government statutes?
   a. Age Discrimination in Employment Act
   b. Equal Pay Act
   c. Family Leave and Medical Act
   d. Occupational Safety and Health Act (OSHA)
   e. Title VII of the Civil Rights Act of 1978
   f. Vocational Rehabilitation Act of 1973
3. Collect information about the best practices, which are associated with the HR module within an ERP package. You can do this by (1) conducting research on the web; (2) interviewing a user of an HR package; (3) using an on-line database to find an article in a trade publication that describes the effective use of an HR module; or (4) using an HR module within an ERP.
   a. What are the best practices which you have discovered?
   b. How do they contribute to overall productivity?
   c. What information for decision making do they provide?
4. Many organizations purchase the HR module from one ERP vendor (e.g., Peoplesoft) and the Financial Accounting modules from another ERP vendor (e.g., SAP).
   a. What do you see as the advantages of this approach?
   b. What do you see as the disadvantages of this approach?
5. Turnover among IT professionals has been a big issue for many years. There is a tremendous investment made in training IT professionals, and this is why turnover represents a considerable cost. What information will enable the manager to understand turnover and to develop human resources strategies to minimize turnover among IT professionals?

Featured Article

Please read the following article, "Keep Track of Your Employees," and answer these questions:

1. What are the benefits of automated time and attendance records?
2. What advantages might accrue to employees using these systems?

Though companies have been squeezing labor costs the past couple of years, many large businesses still do so without a clear picture of their employees' time, attendance, and skills. Tracking those factors is often done through a hodgepodge of manual processes or legacy applications.

"The time-keeping task has been neglected at many companies," says Paul Hamerman, an analyst at Forrester Research. "Most have a piecemeal approach of manual or disconnected dumb time-card systems or some automation in some places, but most companies haven't invested in end-to-end solutions." Hamerman estimates that only about a third of midsize to large companies have standardized and automated time and attendance systems. The market for software that provides company-wide automation of time and attendance hit about $275 million in 2002, with almost 8% growth predicted for this year, Hamerman says. "Any company with a large contingency of hourly employees needs to do this," he says. Industries such as health care, retail, financial services, manufacturing, and hospitality are among prime targets for such systems.

The most obvious benefit from automating time and attendance is the elimination of the time-consuming and error-prone manual process of figuring out time sheets and time cards and relaying that information to a payroll unit. "Another advantage is better analysis and control over labor allotment, costs, and scheduling," Hamerman says.

Banner Health realized those benefits when it recently rolled out Kronos Inc.'s time- and labor-management software. The operator of 19 hospitals, six long-term care centers, and other services, including family clinics and home-care services in seven states, has deployed the Kronos Workforce Central application suite to 15,000 employees. It will soon be rolled out to nearly all 26,000 workers, says Kathy Schultz, Banner's director of application development.

Using Kronos, Banner employees log on for work at badge terminals, the Web, or an interactive voice-response phone application. This information goes into Banner's payroll systems and is available to managers in real time. For example, nursing supervisors can adjust staffing plans based on factors such as which employees have worked overtime or the skills needed for a shift.

It was a culture change that also provided employees with a financial benefit: Those with direct deposit can access their pay a day earlier, Schultz says. Under the old process, Banner's bank sometimes didn't get payroll data in time to credit employees' accounts so that funds were available on payday.

Smurfit-Stone Container Corp.'s standardization of workforce management on Workbrain Inc.'s Web-based ERM3, an employee-relationship management software system, is part of a larger effort to consolidate systems and processes. The $7.5 billion-a-year container maker also is implementing SAP financial apps and has installed PeopleSoft Inc. as the standard package for payroll processing.

Smurfit-Stone wants to optimize scheduling and tracking of more than 30,000 employees in the 275 North American facilities of its packaging-products manufacturing business. ERM3 interfaces with the PeopleSoft apps, so time and attendance information is sent from ERM3 to PeopleSoft payroll.

While Kronos and Workbrain are leading providers of time and attendance solutions, other vendors include CyberShift Inc. and Stromberg LLC, Forrester's Hamerman says. Large ERP packages also include time-tracking modules.

SOURCE: Marianne Kolbasuk McGee, "Keep Track of Your Employees," *Information Week,* June 30, 2003, p. 59.

References

Ashbaugh, Sam, and Miranda Rowen. 2002. "Technology for human resources management: Seven questions and answers." *Public Personnel Management* 31: 7–20.

Schultheis, R., and M. Sumner. 1998. *Management Information Systems: The Manager's View.* Burr Ridge, IL: McGraw-Hill/Irwin Publishing.

Managing an ERP Project

Objectives

1. Recognize the importance of project management and control in minimizing the risk factors associated with implementing ERP systems.

2. Understand the process of organizational change and its application to enterprise system development, implementation, and operations.

ERP projects often represent the single largest investment in an information systems project for many companies and, in many cases, the largest single investment in any corporate-wide project. The magnitude and complexity of these projects poses considerable risk, which explains the "war stories" connected with implementing ERP systems (see Table 8-1).

◆ WHAT RESEARCH SHOWS ABOUT ERP PROJECT IMPLEMENTATION SUCCESS

In their study of firms that have implemented ERP systems, Mabert, Soni, and Venkataramanan, 2001, described the firms' implementation experiences, determined the business returns from ERP, and determined what factors influenced these experiences and returns (Mabert et al., 2001). Their sample included firms ranging from large firms with annual revenues of more than $5 billion with more than 20,000 employees to smaller firms with revenues of less than $500 million per year and fewer than 20,000 employees. SAP/R3 was the most frequently reported ERP, representing 65.3% of the sample. J.D. Edwards followed at 12.9%, and Oracle with 8.9%.

The overall data suggest that the firms felt they achieved more than 65% of the expected business case targets. The firms which were able to implement ERP either under-budget or on-budget attained a greater proportion (i.e., by 11%) of the planned business case than the overbudget firms (Mabert et al., 2001).

Although the response data indicated that 70% of the firms felt their ERP system was a successful project, the majority of firms (55.5%) indicated the actual ERP system implementation cost exceeded the original estimated budget by an average of 60.6%. The range of experiences included a low of 10% to a high of 200% (Mabert et al., 2001).

TABLE 8-1 War Stories	
Project	**What Happened**
FoxMeyer Corporation SAP ERP System	Drug distributor FoxMeyer claimed that the bungled ERP installation in 1996 helped drive it into bankruptcy
W.W. Grainger, Inc. SAP ERP System	Grainger spent $9 million on SAP software and services in 1998 and 1999; during the worst six months, Grainger lost $19 million in sales and $23 million in profits
Hershey Foods Corp. IBM-led installation and integration of SAP, Manugistics Group Inc., and Siebel Systems, Inc. software	To meet 1999's Halloween and Christmas candy rush, Hershey compressed the rollout of a new $112 million ERP system by several months; sales fell 12% in the quarter after the system went live
Tri Valley Growers Oracle ERP and application integration	An agricultural cooperative, Tri Valley bought at least $6 million worth of ERP software and services from Oracle in 1996; Tri Valley stopped using the Oracle software and stopped paying the vendor; Oracle denied all claims; the case was settled in January 2002
Universal Oil Products LLC ERP with Andersen Consulting	After a 1991 ERP deal with Andersen resulted in unusable systems for Universal Oil, the industrial engineering firm cried fraud, negligence, and neglect in a $100 million lawsuit in 1995

Certain factors influence whether firms are under/on budget or overbudget for implementation. First, under-budget or on-budget firms make fewer modifications than the overbudget firms. According to their survey data, these modifications contribute to a 50% increase in project duration. In addition, under-budget or on-budget firms establish greater authority for project implementation and implement more effective communications. Finally, the under-budget and on-budget firms manage their ERP implementations better, and they manage their businesses better. This enables them to generate additional revenues to cover the cost of ERP implementation (Mabert et al., 2001).

In general, ERP systems projects bring about a host of new questions. Some of these questions and issues are the following:

- What technology challenges (e.g., hardware, software, and networking) are encountered in implementing an enterprise-wide information management system?
- What organizational challenges (impact on business processes) are addressed?
- What people challenges (e.g., recruitment, training, retraining, and retaining) are encountered?
- What challenges are associated with project size and scope?
- What are the strategies for minimizing the risks associated with the technology, organization, people, and size/scope?

◆ CAUSES OF INFORMATION SYSTEMS PROJECT FAILURES

Much has been written about the causes of information systems project failures. Poor technical methods is only one of the causes, and this cause is relatively minor in comparison to larger issues, such as communications failures and ineffective

TABLE 8-2 Causes of Project Failures		
Failure	**Cause**	**Result**
Resource failures	Conflicts of people, time and project scope due to insufficient personnel	Incorrect systems with poor reliability, difficulty with maintenance, and dissatisfied users
Requirement failures	Poor specification of requirements	Leads to developing the wrong system with many changes in requirements downstream
Goal failures	Inadequate statement of system goals by management	Leads to developing the wrong system by leading to requirement failures
Technique failures	Failure to use effective software development approaches, such as structured analysis/design	Causes inadequate requirements specification, poor reliability, high maintenance costs, scheduling and budget problems
User contact failures	Inability to communicate with the system user	Causes inadequate requirements specification, and poor preparation for accepting and using the information system
Organizational failures	Poor organizational structure, lack of leadership, or excessive span of control	Leads to poor coordination of tasks, schedule delays, and inconsistent quality
Technology failures	Failure of hardware/software to meet specifications and failure of the vendor to deliver on time, or unreliable products	Cause schedule delays, poor reliability, maintenance problems, and dissatisfied system users
Size failures	When projects are too large, their complexity pushes the organization's systems development capabilities beyond reasonable limits	Caused by insufficient resources, inadequate requirements specifications, simplistic project control, poor use of methodology
People management failures	Lack of effort, stifled creativity, and antagonistic attitudes cause failures	Time delays and budget overruns occur, poor project specifications, and system is difficult to maintain
Methodology failures	Failure to perform the activities needed while unnecessary activities are performed	This type of failure can lead to any of the consequences of system failure
Planning and control failures	Caused by vague assignments, inadequate project management and tracking tools	Work assignments may overlap, deliverables may be poorly defined, and poor communication may result
Personality failures	People clashes	Passive cooperation and covert resistance, with possible acts of vengeance

leadership. In Robert Block's analysis, twelve categories classify most system failures (see Table 8-2).

In summary, Block points out that successful projects are on time, within budget, reliable, maintainable, and meet the goals and requirements of users. Block also points out that managers who succeed do an initial evaluation of a project. They evaluate the rules, players, goals, constraints, and project manager's responsibility and authority, and the feasibility of success (Block, 1983).

Studies dealing with risk factors in information systems projects describe issues of organizational factors, skill set, management support, software design, user involvement, technology planning, project management, and project escalation.

Some risk factors are associated with organizational factors, including the extent of changes being proposed, sufficiency of resources, and magnitude of potential loss (Barki, Rivard, and Talbot, 1993). Project managers may have to address issues over which they have no control, such as changing scope/objectives and conflicts between user departments (Keil, Cule, Lyytinen, and Schmidt, 1998). Lack of development expertise, lack of application-specific knowledge, and lack of user experience contribute to project risk (Barki et al., 1993; Ewusi-Mensah, 1997).

Lack of senior management commitment (Keil et al., 1998) and lack of agreement on a set of project goals/objectives (Ewusi-Mensah, 1997) lead to time/cost overruns. Misunderstanding requirements and continuously changing requirements contribute to project risk. Lack of an effective methodology and poor estimation can lead to cost and time overruns (Keil et al., 1998). Software risk factors include developing the wrong functions, developing the wrong user interface, shortfalls in externally furnished components, and shortfalls in externally performed tasks (Boehm, 1991).

Lack of user commitment, ineffective user communications, and conflicts among user departments are sources of risk (Keil et al., 1998). Lack of adequate technical expertise and lack of an adequate technology infrastructure to support project requirements contribute to escalating time and cost overruns and are associated with project abandonment (Ewusi-Mensah, 1997). Technological newness (e.g., need for new hardware, software), application size (e.g., project scope, number of users, team diversity), application complexity (e.g., technical complexity, links to existing legacy systems) and failure of technology to meet specifications are project hazards (Barki et al., 1993).

Project risk assessment is based upon project size, technological experience, and project structure (McFarlan, 1981), and managers need to control these risks. Project management and control failures, caused by inadequate planning and tracking, can contribute to unrealistic schedules and budgets and to project failure (Boehm, 1991). In information technology (IT) projects, there is a tendency to discount problems and their severity may remain unknown for a long period of time. When projects run into difficulty, there is a tendency to escalate projects because of societal norms (e.g., needing to save face) and to keep pouring resources into a failing project. This creates a greater risk of failure. (Keil and Montealegre, 2000).

Managers should recognize and implement strategies to minimize the risk of project failure, as outlined in the above description. If they recognize the nature and magnitude of the risks they face in implementing ERP systems, they can minimize these risks by employing project management and control strategies to address the challenges they face.

◆ RISKS IN IMPLEMENTING AN ERP SYSTEM

TECHNOLOGY RISKS

Implementing an ERP system poses unique challenges and risks. These risks involve technology, organization, people, and project size. The technology risks depend upon how consistent the new technology is with the current corporate infrastructure and operating system environment (see Table 8-3). When an organization introduces technology that is inconsistent with current database, operating system, and network management environments, the risk is greater.

ORGANIZATIONAL RISKS

The second area of risk deals with organizational factors. When business processes are re-designed to fit the package, the risk of excessive time and cost investments decreases (see Table 8-4). Customization poses the risk of extra, if not excessive project costs.

PEOPLE FACTORS

The third area of risk deals with people resources (see Table 8-5). If the IT professional staff is familiar with the application-specific modules, then the likelihood of implementing the system effectively will be enhanced. However, if the current skill mix of the IT staff does not include knowledge of application-specific ERP modules, the organization will incur significant costs in re-skilling the workforce or in acquiring external consultants.

TABLE 8-3 Fit with Organizational Technological Expertise

	Lower Risk	*Higher Risk*
Technology fit	System consistent with current technology infrastructure	System implementation will require major changes in technology infrastructure
Fit with technological expertise	Technical requirements (e.g., database, operating system, network) for the system are consistent with technology expertise	Technical requirements (e.g., database, O/S, network) for the system are not consistent with technology know-how

TABLE 8-4 Organizational Factors in ERP Projects

	Lower Risk	*Higher Risk*
Business process re-design	Extensive re-design of business processes to fit the package	Extensive customization to align package with existing business processes
Scope of business processes	Scope of project affects 0–25% of business processes	Scope of project affects 50–100% of business processes

TABLE 8-5	People Factors in ERP Projects	
	Lower Risk	*Higher Risk*
Knowledge of IT staff	IT staff knowledgeable in application-specific modules	IT staff has limited knowledge of application-specific modules
Knowledge of user staff	User representatives fully involved in the project	User representatives have limited involvement in the project

PROJECT SIZE

The fourth source of risk deals with project size. As already mentioned, an ERP project can be the largest single investment in a corporate technology project that an organization undertakes. The sheer size of these projects, as measured in time, staff commitment, budget, and scope, poses considerable risk and causes increased concern for accountability on the part of users and senior management.

◆ MANAGING LARGE-SCALE ERP PROJECTS

We can learn from experience in managing commercial off-the-shelf software projects. Large-scale projects involving software packages are MRP projects and ERP projects. Package implementation is different from custom implementation because users are likely to want to customize programs in the package to fit their unique needs, and users are dependent upon the vendor for assistance and updates (Lucas, Walton, and Ginzberg, 1988). Some of the variables associated with the successful implementation of packages are greater vendor participation in implementation and support, a higher rating of user/customer capabilities by the vendor, and a higher rating of user skills by MIS management.

The experience implementing large-scale MRP and ERP packages provides a better understanding of lessons learned. Commitment from top management and adequate training are critical success factors for implementation (Duchessi, Schaninger, and Hobbs, 1989). Lack of training leads to difficulties in MRP system implementation (Ang, Yang, and Sum, 1994).

ERP projects, which are commercial off-the-shelf packages, pose unique challenges. As in all large-scale projects, top management support, presence of a champion, good communication with stakeholders, and effective project management are critical success factors in ERP projects (Bancroft, Seip, and Sprengel, 1998). Unique ERP implementation factors include re-engineering business processes, understanding corporate cultural change, and using business analysts on the project team.

Based upon interviews with senior members of ERP implementation teams, Parr, Shanks, and Darke identified factors necessary for successful implementation of ERP systems, where success is understood to be adherence to time and budgetary constraints (Parr et al., 1999). Management support of the project team, a project team with the appropriate balance of technical/business skills, and commitment to change by all the stakeholders were important.

TABLE 8-6 Summary of Risk Factors in ERP Projects	
Risk Category	**Risk Factor**
Organizational fit	➤ Failure to re-design business processes ➤ Failure to follow an enterprise-wide design which supports data integration
Skill set	➤ Insufficient training and re-skilling ➤ Insufficient internal expertise ➤ Lack of business analysts with business and technology knowledge ➤ Failure to effectively mix internal and external expertise ➤ Lack of ability to recruit and retain qualified ERP systems developers
Management strategy	➤ Lack of senior management support ➤ Lack of proper management control structure ➤ Lack of a champion ➤ Ineffective communications
Software design	➤ Failure to adhere to standardized specifications which the software supports ➤ Lack of integration
User involvement and training	➤ Insufficient training of end-users ➤ Ineffective communications ➤ Lack of full-time commitment of customers to project management and project activities ➤ Lack of sensitivity to user resistance ➤ Failure to emphasize reporting
Technology planning/integration	➤ Inability to avoid technological bottlenecks ➤ Attempting to build bridges to legacy applications

Source: Sumner, M. 2002. "Risk factors in managing enterprise-wide/ERP projects." *Journal of Information Technology* 15: 317–327.

A summary of the risk factors affecting the management of ERP projects described in case studies of major corporate ERP implementations (Sumner, 2002) is in Table 8-6.

MANAGING THE RISK FACTORS IN ERP PROJECTS

Strategies for controlling the risk factors in ERP projects include management commitment to re-designing business processes, obtaining business analysts with knowledge of application-specific modules, obtaining top management support, and making a commitment to using the vendor-sponsored project management methodology (see Table 8-7). In addition, technical expertise is needed to plan and monitor client-server implementation and upgrades (Sumner, 2002).

COMPARISON OF SUCCESSFUL VERSUS UNSUCCESSFUL ERP PROJECTS

A number of research projects address the question of what factors distinguish successful ERP projects vs. unsuccessful ERP projects. These factors include customization,

TABLE 8-7	Strategies for Controlling Risk Factors in ERP Projects
Type of Risk	**Strategies for Minimizing Risk**
Organizational fit	➤ Commitment to re-designing business processes ➤ Top management commitment to restructuring and following an enterprise-wide design which supports data integration
Skill mix	➤ Effective recruiting and retaining of specialized technical personnel ➤ Effective re-skilling of the existing IT workforce ➤ Obtaining business analysts with knowledge of application-specific modules ➤ Effective use of external consultants on project teams
Management structure and strategy	➤ Obtaining top management support ➤ Establishing a centralized project management structure ➤ Assigning a champion
Software systems design	➤ Commitment to using project management methodology and best practices specified by vendor ➤ Adherence with software specifications
User involvement and training	➤ Effective user training ➤ Full-time commitment of users to project management roles ➤ Effective communications
Technology planning/integration	➤ Acquiring technical expertise ➤ Acquiring vendor support for capacity planning and upgrading ➤ Planning for client-server implementation, including client workstations

Source: Sumner, M. 2002. "Risk factors in managing enterprise-wide/ERP projects." *Journal of Information Technology* 15: 317–327.

the use of consultants, supplier relationship management, change management, and use of business impact measures. Project-related factors associated with success versus failure include the way projects are divided, project leadership, project focus, the project champion role, and the flexibility of the project schedule. Additional factors are management reporting needs, user training, and technological challenges.

Customization

It costs more and takes much longer to implement ERP when the modules are modified (Mabert et al., 2003). Customization increases project time and cost dramatically, Brown and Vessey note, and implementing the best practices embedded in the vendor package greatly increases the chance of project success (Brown and Vessey, 2003). One of the primary benefits of ERP is business process re-engineering that can be gained by adopting best practices, but many organizations do not achieve this benefit because they modify the ERP system to avoid having to change.

Use of External Consultants

Effective management of external consultants is important for ERP project success because the consultants can offer valuable expertise in cross-functional business processes, in system configuration, and in application specific modules, such as financial modules (Brown and Vessey, 2003). However, problems can occur when management outsources the entire ERP project to a contractor, without involving internal IT people. Organizations should use consultants but take advantage of opportunities to develop internal knowledge (Willcocks and Sykes, 2000).

Supplier Relationship Management

Because of the dependence on external vendors and consultants in the ERP implementation process, it is important to build effective relationships, facilitate contracts, and monitor contracts (Willcocks and Sykes, 2000). Successful ERP projects use a vendor-accelerated implementation strategy to help implement the system on time (Mabert et al., 2003).

Change Management

In implementing ERP, companies often fail to address resistance to change, especially resistance to changes in job design. Individuals need to understand the interrelationships the ERP system creates. For example, if you enter bad data in one place, the data will affect others (Ross, Vitale, and Willcocks, 2003). Since ERP implementation entails changes in business processes, change management is essential (Brown and Vessey, 2003). An organizational culture that fosters open communications is important to avoid resistance to change (Scott and Vessey, 2002).

Business Measures

Since many firms fail to establish specific benefits in measurable terms at the outset of an ERP project, it is difficult to determine the benefits (Ross et al., 2003). This can make it difficult to acquire ongoing resources. Success strategies are continuously monitoring project outcomes, and capitalizing on small successes (Scott and Vessey, 2002).

PROJECT-RELATED FACTORS

Project Division

Comparisons of successful versus unsuccessful ERP projects indicate that a good idea would be to subdivide the project into smaller projects and to achieve tangible business benefits for each project (Motwani, Mirchandanai, Madan, and Gunasekaran, 2002; Willcocks and Sykes, 2000).

Project Leadership

Project leadership is an important issue, and project leaders need to have a proven track record (Brown and Vessey, 2003). One of the lessons learned in case studies of ERP projects is that a strong project leader needs to keep the project on track, even when changes require following contingency plans (Scott and Vessey, 2002).

Project Focus

There is often too much focus on technology rather than on the business benefits of ERP. Focusing on user needs over technology is a success strategy for ERP implementation (Willcocks and Sykes, 2000).

Role of the Project Champion

A project champion is essential (Willcocks and Sykes, 2000). Beyond this, project team members need to have the authority to make decisions on behalf of their functional area (Brown and Vessey, 2003).

Project Schedule

Some slack needs to be built into the project schedule because unforeseen issues will arise in an ERP project. In more successful projects, managers create contingency plans and measure achievements (Scott and Vessey, 2002).

ADDITIONAL FACTORS

User Training

User training is critical to ERP success. Organizations must be willing to invest in user training because people's jobs will change. User training should focus on business processes, not just technical training in how to use the software (Willcocks and Sykes, 2000).

Management Reporting Needs

Many organizations ignore management reporting requirements. This is because ERP systems do not always have effective query and reporting tools (Ross et al., 2003). However, excellent query and reporting tools for ERP systems can be acquired from third-party vendors.

Technological Challenges

Technological challenges can be complex. To be successful in implementing ERP, firms need to recognize the complexity of data conversion and interface development (Scott and Vessey, 2002).

A summary of factors contributing to successful versus unsuccessful ERP projects is illustrated in Table 8-8.

TWO PROJECTS: FOXMEYER VERSUS DOW CHEMICAL

In 1993 and 1995, FoxMeyer Drug and Dow Chemical initiated ERP projects. The FoxMeyer Drug project was a failure and has been blamed for the company's bankruptcy in 1996. There were some similarities between the two projects. Both companies implemented a vanilla version of SAP R/3 software. Both companies experienced similar challenges, such as insufficient ERP skills and conversion from a mainframe to a client-server infrastructure. Neither company invested in change management, and neither seemed to have a good project planning strategy. Even though the Dow Chemical project experienced difficulties, it was ultimately successful. The two case studies demonstrate that overcoming the risks inherent in implementing ERP is important (Scott and Vessey, 2002).

The comparison between the FoxMeyer Drug project and the Dow Chemical project reveals some interesting differences. FoxMeyer lost a major customer, Phar-Mor, in 1993, and signed a new customer, University HealthSystem Consortium (UHC),

TABLE 8-8	Factors Contributing to Successful versus Unsuccessful Projects	
	Successful Projects	*Unsuccessful Projects*
Customization	Did not modify the ERP modules (Mabert et al., 2003) Compromise on a vanilla implementation, by implementing best practices embedded in the vendor package (Brown and Vessey, 2003)	
Use of consultants	Effectively manage external consultants to fill in gaps in expertise (Motwani et al., 2002, Brown and Vessey, 2003)	Outsource the entire ERP project without involving the internal IT group (Willcocks and Sykes, 2000)
Supplier relationship management	Effectively manage supplier relationships, including contract monitoring and contract facilitation (Willcocks and Sykes, 2000) Follow the vendor accelerated implementation strategy (Mabert et al., 2003)	
Change management approach	Effectively manage change (Brown and Vessey, 2003) Foster a culture with open communications (Scott and Vessey, 2002)	Fail to address resistance to change, including changes in job design (Ross, Vitale, and Willcocks, 2003)
Business measures		Fail to establish specific benefits in measurable terms (Ross et al., 2003)
Project division	Subdivide the project into smaller projects, with tangible business benefits (Willcocks and Sykes, 2000; Motwani et al., 2002)	
Project leadership	Obtain project leaders with a proven track record (Brown and Vessey, 2003), who can keep the project on track (Scott and Vessey, 2002)	
Project focus	Focus on business benefits of ERP (Willcocks and Sykes, 2000)	Focus on technology (Willcocks and Sykes, 2000)
Project champion	Obtain a project champion from the business side (Willcocks and Sykes, 2000)	
Project schedule	Create slack in the schedule (Scott and Vessey, 2002)	
Management reporting		Ignore management reporting needs (e.g., query and reporting tools) (Ross et al., 2003)
User training	Focus on business processes, not just technical training (Willcocks, 2002)	Focus on teaching technical skills (Willcocks and Sykes, 2000)
Technological challenges	Recognize the complexity of converting data and creating interfaces (Scott and Vessey, 2002)	

but the contract with UHC required changes to the software, causing the overall SAP project cost to go over $100 million. At the same time, FoxMeyer embarked on implementing new warehouse automation software. Technical issues clouded the SAP implementation. For example, project managers did not run tests to discover that SAP could not process the 420,000 transactions per day that had been processed on the mainframe (Scott and Vessey, 2002).

Dow Chemical experienced project implementation difficulties, but was able to overcome the risks. Dow Chemical's project had a strong project leader and a project champion (see Table 8-9). Even though they did not have a good project plan in place at the outset, Dow Chemical was able to adjust the project scope when difficulties occurred and to maintain control over the project (Scott and Vessey, 2002). Dow Chemical fostered open communications, and this contributed to project success, whereas employees at FoxMeyer did not express their concerns openly even though

TABLE 8-9   Differences between FoxMeyer Drug versus Dow Chemical's ERP Implementation

	FoxMeyer	*Dow Chemical*
Corporate characteristics	Wholesale drug distribution business	$2.5 billion producer of silicone products
Business environment	Lost a major customer (Phar-Mor) in 1993 and signed up a new customer (UHC)	Faced lawsuits from silicone breast implants
Project characteristics	Initiated SAP R/3 project in 1993	Initiated SAP/R3 implementation in 1995
Project portfolio	Installed a warehouse automation system at the same time	
Organizational culture	Less open culture; employees did not express concerns to management	Culture more accepting of change
Viewpoint regarding business benefits of ERP	Unrealistic expectations about the return on investment in ERP	Focused on small wins
Business factors	UHC contract required major changes in the software	
Project planning/management	Inadequate project planning	Adjusted scope when project difficulties occurred; maintained control over the project
Relationship with external consultants	Used external consultant (Andersen Consulting)	Relied on internal people to design processes and configure the system
Project champion	Project did not have a champion	Strong leadership from a project champion

Adapted from: Scott, Judy and Vessey, Iris, "Managing risks in enterprise systems implementations," *Communications of the ACM,* Vol. 45, No. 4, April 2002, pp. 74–81.

they had concerns about the project. Finally, FoxMeyer had unrealistic expectations about the return on investment in ERP and even underbid contracts based upon its perception that costs would decrease. In contrast, Dow achieved small wins.

If there is a lesson to be learned from the comparison of the FoxMeyer versus the Dow Chemical projects, it is that sound management is a critical success factor. Risks will be encountered in any ERP project, and these risks must be addressed through sound leadership and effective project management.

◆ SUMMARY

ERP projects tend to be large and complex, and require expertise that is not typically found internally within the organization implementing the ERP system. As such, these high-risk projects require multiple strategies to minimize risks (Applegate, McFarlan, and McKenney, 1999). A steering committee, responsible for system selection, monitoring, and managing external consultants, must be involved throughout the project (Bingi, Sharma, and Godla, 1999). External consultants with knowledge about specific modules (Piturro, 1999) are critical, but their knowledge should be transferred to internal employees.

Selecting a vendor may be a lifelong commitment (Davenport, 2000). ERP implementations require companies to adapt the organization to the package through business process re-engineering. A close fit between the software vendor and the user organization is positively associated with successful package implementation (Janson and Subramanian, 1996). User training is important, so frontline workers will be able to handle the demands of the new ERP system (Sweat, 1999).

Most important, ERP systems integrate information and standardize processes. If organizations find this consistent with their overall business strategies, then they will perceive greater value from ERP.

Questions for Discussion

1. Use articles in trade publications which are available in the library or through on-line data-bases to explore factors contributing to the problems encountered in these ERP projects. The timeframes are given so you can find articles during the appropriate timeframes:
   a. FoxMeyer Drug (project cancelled in 1996)
   b. Dow Chemical (project cancelled in 1998)
   c. Dell Computer (project cancelled in 1998)
   d. Hershey's (project in 1999–2000 timeframe)
2. Use articles in trade publications which are available in the library or through on-line data-bases to explore factors contributing to the successful implementation of ERP projects. In your analysis, include the following:
   a. Technology factors
   b. Project management factors
   c. User-related factors
3. Using Microsoft Project, do the following:
   a. You will see a project management schedule for an ERP project below. This project management plan has been created using Microsoft Project.

FIGURE 8-1 Project Management Plan

ID		Task Name	Duration	Start	January / Jan.	February / Feb.	March / Mar.	April / Apr.	May / May	June / June	July / July	August / Aug.
1		Finalize vendor decision	4 days	Mon 1/19/04								
2		Hire SD (sales/distrib.) consultant	7 days	Wed 1/28/04								
3		Develop internal project team	7 days	Wed 1/28/04								
4		Select client-server system	14 days	Thu 1/29/04								
5		Implement client-server system	4 wks	Thu 2/19/04								
6		Develop SD interfaces	8 wks	Thu 2/19/04								
7		Hire MM (materials mgmt.) consultant	1 wk	Thu 2/19/04								
8		Install SD module	3 wks	Mon 3/29/04								
9		Test SD module	2 wks	Mon 4/26/04								
10		Bring SD module into production	1 wk	Mon 5/3/04								
11		Develop MM interfaces	8 wks	Thu 4/1/04								
12		Install MM module	3 wks	Wed 6/2/04								
13		Test MM module	2 wks	Mon 6/28/04								
14		Bring MM module into production	1 wk	Mon 7/5/04								
15		Develop SD training	6 wks	Mon 5/3/04								
16		Develop MM training	6 wks	Mon 7/5/04								

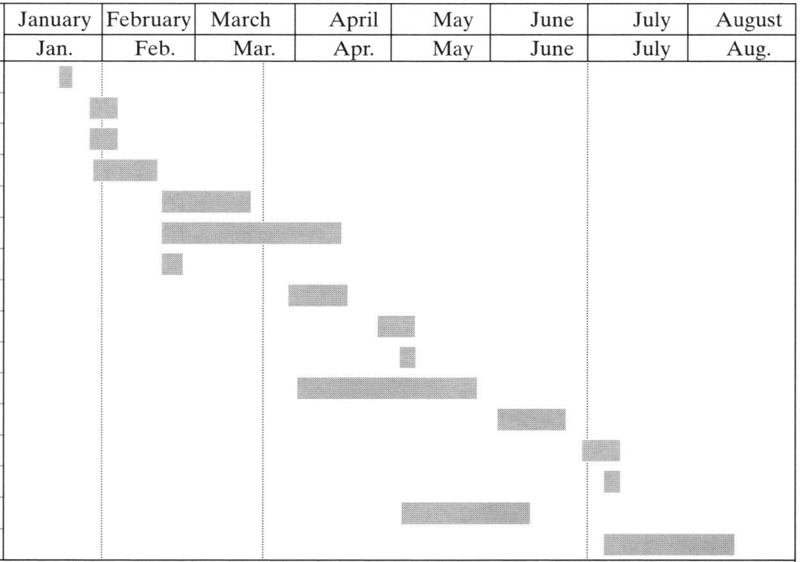

Task		Milestone	External tasks
Split		Summary	External milestone
Progress		Project summary	Deadline

Project: ERPprojectmanagementplan
Date: Mon 3/22/04

Page 1

b. Create a project management schedule for an ERP selection decision using Microsoft Project. Use these parameters:

ID	Activity	Duration
A	Create a list of software features which are needed	3 months
B	Create a list of ERP software candidates	3 months
C	Narrow choices down to 3 or 4 candidates	3 months
D	Develop a Request for Proposal	1 month
E	Participate in Vendor Presentations	3 months
F	Review Vendor Proposals	1 month
G	Evaluate and Select the Best Alternative	1 month
H	Negotiate for Pricing and Licensing Agreements	2 months
I	Develop implementation schedule	2 months

Featured Article

"FOXMEYER'S PROJECT WAS A DISASTER. WAS THE COMPANY TOO AGGRESSIVE OR WAS IT MISLED?"

CASE

Divide the class into two teams, one arguing on behalf of FoxMeyer that SAP was to blame, and one arguing on behalf of SAP that FoxMeyer's management was to blame. Each team should address these questions:

1. Was FoxMeyer misled?
2. What strategies could have been put into place to avoid the project disaster?
3. What business misjudgments occurred?
4. Was FoxMeyer's failure due to technology failure or business failure?

"Don't know whether the deficiencies resulted from the fact that the systems just didn't work or from the fact that there was poor implementation," says Bart A. Brown Jr., a Wilmington, Del.-based bankruptcy trustee appointed to oversee the case of FoxMeyer Drug Co., Carrollton, Tex. But if even 20% of what he has read of the situation in previous media accounts is true, Brown says, "then it sounds like there is a claim there."

Then the nation's fourth largest distributor of pharmaceuticals to both druggists and hospitals, FoxMeyer in the early '90s bet its future on a massive enterprisewide software and warehouse-automation project and lost. In August 1996 the company filed for protection under Chapter 11 of the federal bankruptcy code.

The bankruptcy court must decide whether FoxMeyer—which expected to save $40 million annually from a massive overhaul of its computer systems that were designed to serve a rapidly expanding customer base—was misled by any of the software companies and systems integrators it dealt with. They are: SAP AG, Walldorf, Germany, which supplied enterprisewide financial and logistics software; Andersen Consulting, which provided implementation expertise through an on-site team that at one point numbered about 50 people; and Pinnacle Automation Inc., St. Louis, which through its operating subsidiaries supplied conveyors, carousels, and a warehouse-management system for FoxMeyer's distribution center in Washington Court House, Ohio.

FoxMeyer executives complained to the bankruptcy trustee earlier this year that the technology vendors had oversold their capabilities during the sales process. Bankruptcy trustee Brown expects to decide by year-end whether his office will pursue legal action against the vendors on behalf of FoxMeyer or to allow the right to make a legal claim to revert to Avatex Group of Dallas, the new name of FoxMeyer Health Corp., the parent firm of FoxMeyer Drug.

One thing no one disagrees on is that FoxMeyer Drug crashed and burned. Once a $5 billion company, FoxMeyer filed under Chapter 11 shortly after taking a $34 million charge to cover uncollectible costs related to shipping and inventory troubles.

The reason for FoxMeyer's collapse, though, remains a subject of debate. A FoxMeyer spokesperson told the *Wall Street Journal* in late 1996 that computer-integration problems related to the company's IT effort-whose total price tag ultimately topped $100 million were "a significant factor leading to the bankruptcy filing."

While executives at Avatex declined comment, some technology experts who were on the scene agreed to be interviewed for this article. Christopher Cole, chief operating officer at warehouse-automation vendor Pinnacle, says the FoxMeyer mess was "not a failure of automation. It was not a failure of commercial software per se. It was a management failure."

To understand what happened at FoxMeyer, it's best to start with the company's business strategy and plans for technology to support it. FoxMeyer was afraid its customer orders—involving some 300,000 items daily, according to one person who worked on the technology overhaul—would soon outgrow the capacity of its aging Unisys mainframe. To gear up to handle continued growth in the business, the company embarked upon a search for a client/server based system that would enable it to relieve the stress on this system while keeping up with anticipated growth in business volume.

A key concern that the FoxMeyer project team had to address early on was the system's ability to handle the sheer magnitude of FoxMeyer's business. FoxMeyer was taking and filling orders from thousands of pharmacies and hospitals each day. Because each pharmacy could order hundreds of items at once, it was common for the company to process hundreds of thousands of transactions daily.

To make sure the new systems were up to handling that volume, SAP's software was tested on client/server hardware supplied by both Digital Equipment Corp., Maynard, Mass., and Hewlett-Packard Co. (HP), San Jose, the latter of which ultimately was selected. "But there are a lot of variables in doing benchmarking and volume testing," says Kenneth Woltz, president of Woltz & Associates Ltd., Chicago-based consul-

tants, "and I believe that just increased the risk. I would hate to guess how many HP systems they had coupled together and what changes had to be made to the Oracle database to process their huge volume."

Woltz, who advised FoxMeyer during the early stages of the project, contends that the implementation appeared troubled almost from the start. "Andersen had been selected as the SAP partner," he recalls. "And I remember a meeting where a presentation was being made that laid out a schedule for the entire implementation to be completed in 18 months."

Woltz says he challenged that goal as totally unrealistic. "Many IT personnel put forth these master schedules where each of the modules is to be implemented in two to three months," he explains, "but I've never seen that happen in reality in a large, complex organization."

A successful implementation of a new general-ledger accounting system sometimes takes up to a year by itself, Woltz argued. He believed FoxMeyer lacked available users on staff with the sophistication to handle a fast-track installation. "My position was, 'Go slower.' Competition was tough in this industry, but many companies underestimate how long it takes to implement changes in core business processes," he says.

Andersen's role, Woltz says, was to install SAP. "They put together the master schedule for implementing SAP financials and logistics modules," he adds.

Comments an Andersen spokesperson, "We delivered, the work we performed was successfully completed, and we were paid in full."

SAP officials agree that volume was an issue at FoxMeyer and continues to be a source of some concern at McKesson Corp., San Francisco, which bought FoxMeyer Drug's assets in October 1996. (The value of potential claims against SAP, Andersen, and Pinnacle were excluded from this transaction.)

However, Robert Pawlick, who served as project manager for SAP America Inc. at the FoxMeyer site, says that thanks to the test runs conducted at FoxMeyer, "there was some measurement evidence that these systems could perform at that level."

SAP's functionality came under close scrutiny as well. At that time, SAP was regarded are as a supplier of accounting and

Chronology of a Crash	
Date	*Event*
March 1993	FoxMeyer seeks solutions to system capacity issues. SAP introduced to FoxMeyer account by Digital
May 1993	SAP R/3 package selected; Phar-Mor, a major customer, seeks bankruptcy protection
July 1993	Questions regarding SAP's capacity to handle FoxMeyer's order volumes are raised; benchmark testing process begins
Jan.–Mar. 1994	FoxMeyer picks Hewlett-Packard hardware platform; signs Andersen Consulting as its SAP implementation partner
Feb. 1995	SAP financial, sales, and distribution modules begin coming on-line to serve University HealthSystem contract
May 1995	Washington Court House distribution center scheduled to open
Feb. 1996	Thomas Anderson, FoxMeyer's Health's president and CEO (and champion of the company's integration/warehouse automation projects), is asked to resign due to delays in new warehouse and realizing the SAP system projected savings
Aug. 1996	FoxMeyer Drug files for Chapter 11 protection from its creditors
Oct. 1996	McKesson buys FoxMeyer Drug business
March 1997	Status of FoxMeyer Drug bankruptcy shifts to Chapter 7 liquidation
Dec. 1997	Projected date for bankruptcy trustee Bart A. Brown Jr. to decide if his office will pursue claims on behalf of FoxMeyer Drug against SAP, Andersen, and Pinnacle

manufacturing software than a developer of systems with extensive functionality for warehouse management. So FoxMeyer elected to go with a warehouse system from McHugh Software International (formerly McHugh-Freeman), which it purchased through Pinnacle.

SAP, though, thinks it could have provided both systems. "Part of our claim to fame is that we have an excellent sales-and-distribution set of functionality," says Peter Dunning, SAP America's executive vice president for global accounts. "I think the slight wrinkle [at FoxMeyer] was that they were in more of a high-volume, complex-pricing environment." As a result, "There were certainly some differences that they wanted in the software." SAP solved them without holding up any software-implementation deadlines, he says.

Regardless, the decision to go with two different vendors for two of the company's most important business systems added still greater complexity to an already challenging situation. "Now you had two major packages that needed to be integrated," Woltz asserts, "and that is a

tough [job], in part because it is difficult to get two diverse vendors' knowledge of the nitty-gritty of their products in order to design a real-time integration. Despite the difficulty in assessing the internals of application packages, we did get into enough depth to know that there were many functional holes."

A significant change in FoxMeyer's business added to the problems. In July 1994 the company won a contract to supply University Health-System Consortium (UHC), a nationwide network of major teaching hospitals, in a deal that was expected to yield up to $1 billion in revenues annually for five years.

Once this pact was signed, recalls Pawlick, who now is SAP America's global support manager, "the focus of the project dramatically changed from giving them headroom on their current mainframe system, which had been one of FoxMeyer's driving factors, to satisfying the needs of the University HealthSystem Consortium."

Prior to this contract, explains SAP's Dunning, FoxMeyer had planned to have a small amount of capacity left on the Unisys platform once the SAP implementation was complete. "But with this new contract," he says, "their volumes would severely increase, and they ran out of capacity on their mainframe." The throughput capacity of the SAP project had to be increased, Dunning says.

SAP claims to have met such technical challenges in a manner that FoxMeyer found satisfactory. "In fact, FoxMeyer was a selective, but very good reference for SAP," Pawlick maintains.

Adds Dunning, "McKesson reinforced the work we had done at FoxMeyer." Shortly after purchasing FoxMeyer's assets, he explains, McKesson, planning an SAP implementation of its own, examined the FoxMeyer installation and was so impressed that it decided not only to keep the equipment, but also to speed up its own project. "They had SAP fully installed," says Buzz Adams, senior vice president for process improvement at McKesson. "McKesson has learned some useful lessons from FoxMeyer."

McKesson was fortunate to avoid the corporate migraines that accompanied the troubled start-up of FoxMeyer's Washington Court House distribution facility. "I don't think some of the things were thought through well enough," says Pinnacle's Cole, regarding this portion of the installation. (His company supplied hardware that FoxMeyer and Andersen integrated into a 340,000-sq-ft warehouse designed to service hospitals and pharmacies unrelated to the UHC contract.) "As an example, we were told to design a system that could ship in X number of hours, and we designed a system that could do that. Then later, it became a requirement that they be able to ship in one-third to one-half that time."

By the same token, he says, "I remember there being an enormous issue on balancing system traffic." While FoxMeyer initially counted on a typical shipment or package to make three or four stops along its automated route within the warehouse, in reality, this figure could wind up at eight or nine, a condition that sometimes caused conveyors to gridlock. But Cole contends that "the problem wasn't that the conveyor shut down; it was that the way they were running orders through there was such that they were gridlocking the system."

Pinnacle does accept responsibility for problems such as the occasional motherboard failure, although Cole states that such glitches

were "never the pacing issue." Rather, he says that the inhouse Unisys-based management-information system under which FoxMeyer was trying to run the new equipment "choked and died." For example, he reports that between the existing system and the new SAP implementation, "they had an enormous amount of trouble feeding us the information we needed on a timely basis." Nor did the facility debut on time. Slated to open in May 1995, the warehouse began shipping goods that August, and even that date was one FoxMeyer had difficulty meeting as a result of labor problems. Workers from other Ohio warehouses that the Washington Court House center was supposed to replace already had begun leaving their jobs en masse.

"The transition from closing old warehouses did not go smoothly," Cole recalls. Equipment outages resulted in the shipping of numerous half-finished orders. Then, when customers would complain about missing items, FoxMeyer representatives, unaware of what was happening on the warehouse floor, would authorize makeup shipments that turned out to be duplicates but were never reported as such by recipients.

FoxMeyer also suffered losses in transferring inventory to the new center. Because of a debilitating morale problem among departing workers, Cole explains, a lot of merchandise was dumped into trucks and arrived at Washington Court House with packages damaged or broken open or otherwise unsalable as new product. "That led to a huge shrinkage in inventory," Cole states. "As an outsider looking at it, I would imagine that they lost a lot there, as well as with the problems of their own internal computer system."

Meanwhile, FoxMeyer was faring poorly elsewhere in its business. The UHC contract, which initially had helped boost the distributor's stock value, ultimately delivered neither the volumes nor the profit margins expected.

"FoxMeyer was the price cutter in the industry," says Adam Feinstein, a research associate who follows the drug and medical-supply wholesale industry for Salomon Brothers in New York. That factor, combined with the information-system and warehouse-management initiative, pushed the company over the edge, he says. "They spent a lot of money and tried to put together a progressive management-information system," he says, "but they overspent and bit off more than they could chew."

Woltz offers a somewhat similar assessment. "Most companies would be wise to sell what they can currently deliver, perhaps with modest enhancements required to close the deal, but certainly not commit to a fast-track schedule on a technology implementation that has not been proven," he asserts.

As for the system's anticipated savings, Dunning says the $40 million figure FoxMeyer executives liked to use didn't come from SAP. "We generally don't do calculated savings to that extent, especially when it involves a lot of software that's not ours."

Dunning sums up SAP's involvement in the FoxMeyer fiasco this way: "It's one of those stories where the operation was a success, and the patient died."

Trying to win market share by price-cutting based on anticipated savings from new computer systems proved not to be a smart strategy. "If you put in new systems hoping [that] will give you efficiencies, without improving your overall processes, it rarely works," says McKesson's Adams.

SOURCE: Jesitus, John, "Broken promises?" *Industry Week,* v. 246, n. 20, Nov 3, 1997, p. 31–36. Copyright: Penton Publishing, 1997.

References ●

Ang, J.S.K, K.K. Yang, and C.C. Sum. 1994. "MRP II company profile and implementation problems: A Singapore experience." *International Journal of Production Economics.*

Applegate, L.M., W.F. McFarlan, and J.L. McKenney. 1999. *Corporate Information Systems Management. Text and Cases.* 5th ed. Burr Ridge, IL: Irwin/McGraw-Hill.

Bancroft, N., H. Seip, and A. Sprengel. 1998. *Implementing SAP R/3.* 2nd ed. Greenwich,CT: Manning Publications.

Barki, H., S. Rivard, and J. Talbot. 1993. "Toward an assessment of software development risk." *Journal of Management Information Systems* 10: 203–225.

Bingi, P., M.K. Sharma, and J.K. Godla. 1999. "Critical issues affecting an ERP implementation." *Information Systems Management* 16: 7–14.

Block, Robert. 1983. *The Politics of Projects.* Englewood Cliffs, NJ: Yourdon Press, Prentice-Hall.

Boehm, B.W. 1991. "Software risk management: Principles and practices." *IEEE Software* 8: 3241.

Brown, Carol, and Iris Vessey. 2003. "Managing the next wave of enterprise systems: Leveraging lessons from ERP." *MIS Quarterly Executive* 2: 65–77.

Computerworld. 2002. "35 years of IT leadership: The best and the worst." *Computerworld* 36: 74.

Davenport, T. 2000. *Mission critical: Recognizing the promise of enterprise systems.* Cambridge: Harvard University Press.

Duchessi, Peter, Charles Schaninger, and Don Hobbs. 1989. "Implementing a manufacturing planning and control information system." *California Management Review* 75–90.

Ewusi-Mensah, Kweku. 1997. "Critical issues in abandoned information systems development projects." *Communications of the ACM* 40: 74–80.

Janson, M.A., and A. Subramanian. 1996. "Packaged software: Selection and implementation policies." *INFOR* 334: 133–151.

Keil, Mark, Paul E. Cule, Kalle Lyytinen, and Roy C. Schmidt. 1998. "A framework for identifying software project risks." *Communications of the ACM* 41: 76–83.

Keil, Mark, and Ramiro Montealegre. 2000. "Cutting your losses: Extricating your organization when a big project goes awry." *Sloan Management Review* 41: 55–68.

Lucas, H., E. Walton, and M. Ginzberg. 1988. "Implementing packaged software." *MIS Quarterly* 537–549.

Mabert, V. A., A. Soni, and M. A. Venkataramanan. 2001. "Enterprise resource planning: Measuring value." *Production and Inventory Management Journal* 42: 46–51.

Mabert, V.A., A. Soni, and M. A. Venkataramanan. 2003. "Enterprise resource planning: Managing the implementation process." *European Journal of Operations Research* 146: 302–314.

McFarlan, F.W. 1981. "Portfolio approach to information systems." *Harvard Business Review* 59: 142–150.

Motwani, J., D. Mirchandanai, M. Madan, and A. Gunasekaran. 2002. "Successful implementation of ERP projects: Evidence from two case studies." *International Journal of Production Economics* 75: 83–94.

Parr, A.N., G. Shanks, and P. Darke. 8/21-22/1999. "Identification of necessary factors for successful implementation of ERP systems," in Ngwerryama, Ojelanki; Introna, Lucas; Myers, Michael; DeGross, Janice, "New Information Technologies in organizational processes: Field studies and theoretical reflections on the future of work." IFIP TC8 WGB8.2 International Working Conference on New Information Technology in Organizational Processes: Field Studies and Theoretical Reflections on the Future of Work. St. Louis, MO.

Piturro, M. 1999. "How midsize companies are buying ERP." *Journal of Accountancy* 188: 41–48.

Ross, Jeanne, Michael Vitale, and Leslie Willcocks. 2003. "The continuing ERP Revolution: Sustainable lessons, new models of delivery," in *Second-Wave Enterprise Resource Planning Systems*. Graeme Shanks, Peter Seddon, and Leslie Willcocks (Eds.), Cambridge: Cambridge University Press, 2003. pp. 102–132.

Scott, Judy, and Iris Vessey. 2002. "Managing risks in enterprise systems implementations." *Communications of the ACM* 45: 74–81.

Somers, T., and K. Nelson. 2003. "The impact of strategy and integration mechanisms on enterprise system value: Empirical evidence from manufacturing firms." *European Journal of Operational Research* 146: 315–338.

Sumner, Mary. 2002. "Risk factors in managing enterprise-wide/ERP projects." *Journal of Information Technology* 317–327.

Sweat, J. 1999. "Learning curve." *Information Week* 746: 209–231.

Willcocks, Leslie, and Helen Margetts. "Risk assessment and information systems." *European Journal of Information Systems* 3: 127–138.

Willcocks, L.P., and R. Sykes. 2000. "The role of the CIO and the IT function in ERP." *Communications of the ACM* 43: 22–28.

CHAPTER 9

Supply Chain Management and the eMarketplace

Objectives

1. Understand the links in the supply chain from raw materials to the retail customer.
2. Recognize the interrelationships among business processes supporting sales and marketing, production and materials management, and accounting and finance that exist in order to support the supply chain.
3. Recognize the role of ERP in supporting eBusiness applications.
4. Understand how business intelligence tools are used for decision analysis and management reporting.

◆ SUPPLY CHAIN MANAGEMENT (SCM)

Market competition, changing markets, changing customer demands, short product life cycles, and global competition characterize the current business environment. The purpose of Supply Chain Management (SCM) is to achieve integrated planning through the activities of the supply chain (see Figure 9-1). SCM is defined as *the planning and control of the flow of goods and services, information, and money through the supply chain from the acquisition of raw materials to the final product in the hands of the customer.*

Through SCM, customers and suppliers can partner with each other to achieve the objective of maximizing responsiveness and flexibility, while eliminating paperwork and cost. The objective is to gain a sustainable competitive advantage by eliminating duplication and facilitating the sharing of information across the supply chain (see Figure 9-2).

SCM entails managing the flow of information between partners in the supply chain. Coordination among partners in the supply chain requires exchange of information via networks. For example, when products leave the retailers' shelf, notice is sent to the manufacturer, who replenishes the products. When the manufacturer provides inventory, this enables the retailer to reduce inventory.

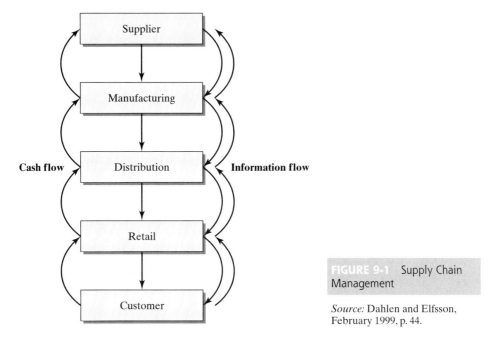

FIGURE 9-1 Supply Chain Management

Source: Dahlen and Elfsson, February 1999, p. 44.

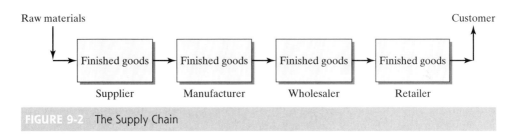

FIGURE 9-2 The Supply Chain

A "moment of information," according to Lummus and Vokurka, occurs when the company gets information from the customer about demand. Information on consumer purchases updates sales forecasts, triggers requests for on-hand inventory, and generates production schedules needed to fulfill future customer requirements (Lummus and Vokurka, 1999).

In the old supply chain, companies supplied customers with stock from on-hand inventory. In the new demand chain, companies use information about customer needs to manufacture products for which demand is known (see Figure 9-3).

In the new supply chain relationship, the retailer's inventory can be maintained by the manufacturer. Sales at the retailers' sites are deducted from on-hand balances through point-of-sale (POS) transactions transmitted every day. Then, the manufacturer replenishes the product. Hallmark uses a continuous replenishment model that

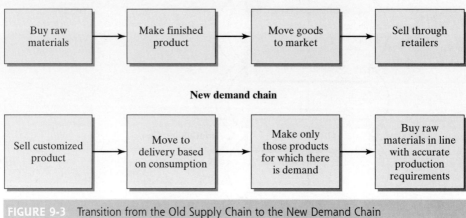

FIGURE 9-3 Transition from the Old Supply Chain to the New Demand Chain

includes forecasts of demand to ensure that retailers have the right products in stores, especially for the holidays.

In Wal-Mart's case, its supplier links into its POS system and decides when to resupply Wal-Mart's inventory. An innovative strategy called cross-docking eliminates the shipment of stock from the supplier to a retailer's distribution center. In cross-docking, merchandise moves directly from inbound trucks to outbound trucks, without being stored at the distribution center. This maximizes cash flow from the retailer's standpoint and reduces handling costs.

SCM creates linkages between suppliers and retailers that translate into lower costs, better customer service, and profitability for both partners. For companies to respond to changes in customer demand, managers must have information on POS activity, demand forecasts, growth projections, manufacturing plans, inventory balances, and product movement through the supply chain. The purpose of using this information is to meet customer demand by adapting production schedules.

For the supply chain to work, the information must be timely and must be shared by demand chain partners. Table 9-2 depicts information which needs to be shared among supply chain partners, including consumers, retailers, distributors, carriers, manufacturers, and suppliers (Lummus and Vokurka, 1999).

TABLE 9-1 Case Studies in SCM

Case Study	Links Along the Value Chain
Wal-Mart	Supplier, Procter & Gamble (P&G), links into Wal-Mart's POS system and decides when to resupply Wal-Mart's inventory
Ford and General Motors	Auto manufacturers have on-line links to suppliers' order-entry systems
Hallmark	Uses a continuous replenishment system to ensure that retailers have the right products in stores

TABLE 9-2	Shared Information				
Consumers	*Retailers*	*Distributors*	*Carriers*	*Manufacturers*	*Suppliers*
Demand (forecast)	On-hand inventory	On-hand inventory	In-transit inventory	On-hand inventory	On-hand inventory
	Consumer sales data (POS)	Retailers' orders	Planned shipments	Material production schedule	Material production schedule
		Shipping notices	Delivery schedules	Actual production completed	Actual production completed
				Distributors' orders	Manufacturers' orders
				Shipping notices	Shipping notices

TABLE 9-3	Key Performance Indicators: Best in Class versus Median Performers			
Metric		*Median*	*Best in Class*	*Difference*
Total SCM cost (% of revenue)		11.6	6.3	46%
Inventory (days of supply)		66	34	48%
Cash-to-cash cycle time		87	31	64%
On-time delivery to customer request date (%)		81	94	16%
Upside production flexibility (days to implement an unplanned 20% increase in end-product supply)		26	4	85%

Source: Mistry, Prafal. Benchmarking Study Shows Dramatic Reduction in Costs Using Best Practices for Supply Chain Management, *Insight,* PRTM, Weston, MA: Winter 1997.

SCM's purpose is to respond to customer demand. When all partners along the supply chain have access to customer information, each entity will benefit. SCM software provides information to translate sales transactions into production processes and material requirements.

IMPACT OF SCM ON PRODUCTIVITY

What has happened in industries that have moved toward a SCM approach? Moving toward a SCM approach seems to bring about remarkable results in terms of cost reduction, inventory reduction, cycle time improvement, and customer service.

In comparing the "Best in Class" companies with the "Median Performers," Pittiglio, Rabin, Todd, and McGrath found that for a company with annual sales of $500 million and a 60% cost of sales, the difference between being at the median in terms of performance and being in the top 20% is $44 million in available working capital (see Table 9-3). This occurs because of reduction in SCM costs by 46%, reduction in inventory holding costs by 48%, reduction in cycle time by 64%, and faster on-time

TABLE 9-4	Issues to Be Addressed in Integrating the Supply Chain	
Factor	**Objective**	**Issues to Be Addressed**
Strategy	Align supply chain management with the overall business direction	What level of customer service is needed?
Process	Integrate business processes	How can linkages be established with suppliers and customers throughout the supply chain?
Organization	Integrate organizational units	What level of cross-functional integration is necessary?
Technology	Use technology to achieve goals	How can advanced communications provide data integration across the supply chain?

delivery to customers by 16%. Production flexibility, or days needed to implement an increase in supply, is increased by 85%. These benchmarks illustrate significant productivity improvements associated with supply chain integration (Mistry, 1997).

Integrating the supply chain requires a commitment to strategy, process, organization, and technology. The major issue to be addressed in integrating the supply chain is what linkages can be established with suppliers and customers. Advanced communications and data integration are technology factors, which enable supply chain integration (see Table 9-4).

THE EVOLUTION OF PARTNERSHIPS

Suppliers and manufacturers did not always work together closely. In the past, manufacturers would negotiate with many different suppliers in order to get the best price. The same was true with manufacturers and customers. Customers would negotiate with different manufacturers to get the best price.

Over the past ten years, partnerships between suppliers and manufacturers and between manufacturers and their customers, have begun to emerge. Vendor-managed inventory (VMI) transfers the daily responsibility of inventory management from the customer to the supplier. In VMI, the supplier monitors inventory levels of their items and replenishes inventory to maintain adequate supply levels.

Vendor-managed inventory has great advantages over traditional inventory management, in which the retailer waits to re-order stock until their inventory is low, thereby risking stockouts. When the manufacturer can monitor inventories, response time drops. The retailer and the manufacturer realize advantages. The retailer can cut inventory costs and administrative costs, while assuring that adequate stock in on hand. The manufacturer benefits because VMI increases the volume of business coming from the retailer. In addition, the manufacturer does not have to expedite orders to retailers because of rush orders. The incidence of returned goods to the manufacturer from the customer decreases because customers are only receiving stock that they need.

Different strategies exist for coordination between suppliers, manufacturers, and customers across the supply chain (see Table 9-5).

SCM can evolve to multi-level or full collaboration. In these models, electronic linkages between the manufacturers' scheduling system and the suppliers' order system facilitate the transfer of parts, subassemblies, and components that are needed on a just-in-time (JIT) basis. These forms of collaboration reduce costs, improve response times, and increase responsiveness to customer needs.

◆ eBUSINESS AND ERP

INTRODUCTION TO eBUSINESS

The emergence of eBusiness has established interactive relationships between customers and suppliers and between suppliers and distributors. The eBusiness value chain, known as the virtual value chain, provides information-based channels for selling and buying products and services. The eBusiness value chain uses an information technology infrastructure (e.g., the Internet and communications networks) to support the primary value activities (see Table 9-6).

TABLE 9-5   Evolution of Coordination Across the Supply Chain

Phase	Characteristics
Open Market	Manufacturer negotiates with many vendors for required items; adversarial relationship between customer and manufacturer, and manufacturer and vendor
Cooperation	Beginning of a partnership between customer and manufacturer, and manufacturer and supplier
Single-Level Coordination	Single-source, long-term commitments (e.g., VMI)
Multi-Level Coordination	On the supply side, the manufacturers' scheduling system is linked electronically with the suppliers' system; on the demand side, the same capabilities exist
Full Collaboration	Full partnership across all functions of the business, including joint development of new products; multi-company design teams are electronically linked across the supply chain

TABLE 9-6   The eBusiness Value Chain

Inbound Logistics	Production	Management	Marketing and Sales	Customer Support
Extranets	ERP software	Intranets	eBusiness	Internet
Lower costs; increased speed	Lower costs; customized production	Lower costs; faster communications	Lower costs; enables newcomers to enter the marketplace	Lower costs; faster service

TABLE 9-7	The eBusiness Value Chain at Coca-Cola

Inbound Logistics	Production	Management	Marketing and Sales	Customer Support
Extranets	ERP Software	Intranets	eBusiness	Internet
Links between Coke and its suppliers	Links Coke with its bottling partners	Improves worldwide communications	Use cellular-linked vending machines	Provide more timely delivery to trade customers

TABLE 9-8	Evolution of eMarket Relationships

	Transaction	Contract	Partnership
Basis of interaction	Buyer/seller exchange	Prior contract governs exchange	Collaborative goals and processes (e.g., collaborate product development)
Level of integration	Low	Medium	High
Coordination	Based on supply and demand	Contract determines level of coordination	Inter-organizational processes
Information exchange	One-way exchange	Information exchange defined in contract	Two-way, interactive exchange of information

If we apply the eBusiness value chain to a company: Coca-Cola, you will see how eBusiness can create stronger relationships with suppliers and customers and provide a competitive advantage (see Table 9-7). As you can see with the example of Coca-Cola, eBusiness facilitates linkages between Coke, its suppliers, and bottling partners, which results in lower costs and increased responsiveness to the needs of bottling partners and customers.

eBusiness has changed market relationships dramatically. The basis for market relationships has evolved from transaction-based relationships, to contract-based relationships, to partnerships (see Table 9-8). New models of business are emerging on the Internet. eBusiness has facilitated the evolution of business from vertically integrated firms, in which all value chain activities are performed within the firm, to selective sourcing, in which some value activities are outsourced to eBusiness partners. The ultimate evolution occurs in the virtual corporation, in which the core firm outsources every line of business, including inbound logistics, manufacturing, logistics, marketing, and after-sale services to its eBusiness partners.

BUSINESS-TO-BUSINESS (B2B) MARKETPLACES IN THE SUPPLY CHAIN

eProcurement is one of the major breakthroughs of eBusiness. To understand the extent of the breakthrough, we can compare how an auto manufacturer acquired parts, before and after eProcurement.

Before eProcurement, the procurement of car parts could take months, and the cost of the process could exceed the purchase cost. In the traditional paper process, the automaker would need to decide how much inventory was needed and analyze which suppliers carried the parts needed. The purchasing agent would make 20 or 30 calls, issue a request for bids, and wait for bid responses from dozens of vendors. All of this would take time and involve cost.

With eProcurement, the automaker can rely upon JIT inventory, which means building products by demand. Using an Extranet, the company can communicate with its suppliers and submit purchase orders directly to the suppliers' inventory system over the web. This dramatically reduces costs and improves negotiations with the supplier.

Companies are doing away with approved supplier lists and posting requests directly on the web, inviting potential suppliers to bid. This makes the bidding process more competitive so prices are lower. Free-market bidding levels the playing field and lets smaller suppliers participate in the bidding process in a fast and economical way.

B2B marketplaces expand the choices available to buyers and reduce the transactions costs for all players (Kaplan and Sawhney, 2000). In Kaplan and Sawhney's classification of B2B marketplaces, businesses buy manufacturing inputs (e.g., raw materials and product or process components) and operating inputs, which are not part of finished products (e.g., office supplies, spare parts, airline tickets, services, cleaning, copier paper, etc.). Products are bought via systematic sourcing, which involves negotiated contracts with qualified suppliers, and spot sourcing, which involves buyers fulfilling an immediate need at the lowest possible cost.

The B2B hubs (e.g., exchanges) have a two-way classification scheme (see Table 9-9). A B2B hub that facilitates systematic sourcing of operating inputs, such as office printing supplies, is www.suppliesusa.com. A B2B hub that enables spot sourcing of operating inputs, such as freelance temporary help, including creative, information technology, business/consulting, and office/administration, is www.guru.com.

B2B hubs for manufacturing inputs exist as well. B2B hubs, like www.PlasticNet. com bring many suppliers together at one web site to offer manufacturing inputs, in this case plastics. Other B2B exchanges provide spot sourcing of manufacturing inputs, such as paper products (www.Trade-india.worldbid.com).

In these cases, the B2B hubs bring together buyers and sellers via a web site and reduce transactions costs by using one-stop shopping. This works well when the supplier universe is fragmented, and the cost of shopping around and processing a purchase order is high relative to the cost of the items being purchased.

In general, B2B hubs automate transactions and reduce transactions costs between buyers and sellers. Autodaq.com is an example of a B2B used-car auction market,

TABLE 9-9	The B2B Matrix		
	Operating Inputs	*Manufacturing Inputs*	
Systematic sourcing	www.Suppliesusa.com	www.PlasticsNet.com	
Spot sourcing	www.guru.com	www.Trade-india.worldbid.com	

which has advantages to buyers and sellers. Autodaq.com is meant for large-volume sellers, such as rental car companies and manufacturers. The buyers are auto dealers, not individuals. In the physical world, large volume sellers physically auction cars to dealers. In the eBusiness world, Autodaq inspects and describes the cars on-line, accepts bids from dealers, and transports the cars to the winning dealer. Buyers and sellers reap the benefits of Autodaq.com, including reduced transactions time, reduced cost, and a broader arena (Kaplan and Sawhney, 2000).

The eMarketplace improves SCM by facilitating alliances between partners, and this cuts the cost of exchanging goods. For example, an airline needing pretzels can release an order to an eMarketplace exchange, giving its order to the supplier most capable of filling it. Collaborative trading exchanges result in reduced costs and faster time to market and enable the company to tailor products to specific niches of customers.

◆ eSUPPLY CHAIN AND ERP

The ERP system is the foundation for the eMarketplace. A case in point is an on-line clothing retailer. In this scenario, customers input retail purchases into the system which is integrated with the ERP system. Summary data on customer orders are transferred via an extranet to the headquarters' ERP system. Since headquarters fills orders by electronic interfaces with clothing suppliers, the order information is transferred from the headquarters' ERP system to another extranet, linking headquarters with 50 suppliers. The suppliers receive information on forecasted demand. The suppliers replenish headquarters' inventory and adjust their ERP requirements to meet anticipated demand (see Figure 9-4).

The whole eSupply chain, ranging from customer to retailer through to the suppliers, facilitates real-time updates from the consumer through to the suppliers. The result is the ability to fill orders that might not have been filled, leading to greater customer satisfaction and a better understanding of customer needs.

FIGURE 9-4 The eSupply Chain

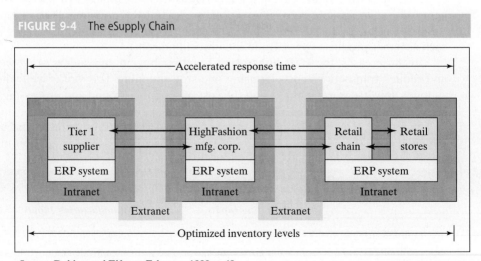

Source: Dahlen and Elfsson, February 1999, p. 49.

The advantages of the eSupply chain are the following: reduced cycle time, closer linkage with supply chain partners, increased revenue, increased speed, reduced costs, reduced production times, optimized inventory management, more efficient distribution, and collaborative business processes.

SAP'S mySAP.com

In the SAP System, mySAP.com was introduced as an eBusiness platform in 1999. The mySAP.com platform supports these objectives:

- ✓ Links manufacturers, suppliers, distributors, customers, partners, and employees
- ✓ Establishes collaborative business networks
- ✓ Provides integration of users, processes, and data within the enterprise as well as across the electronic marketplace
- ✓ Enables employees, customers, suppliers, and business partners to work together

The mySAP.com platform is implemented via each of the components of the SAP ERP system, beginning with mySAP Workplace, which is the enterprise portal, which provides users with access to all SAP applications, including mySAP Customer Relationship Management (CRM), mySAP eProcurement, mySAP Business Intelligence, and mySAP Human Resources. See Table 9-10 for a complete list of mySAP.com applications.

TABLE 9-10 SAP's mySAP.com

Solutions	*Purpose*
mySAP Workplace	Provides an enterprise portal with access to all internal and external applications
mySAP CRM	Supports sales prospecting, lead generation, sales tracking, contact management, order acquisition, Internet pricing and product configuration, and field sales
mySAP eProcurement	Supports electronic buying and purchase requisitions via the Internet
mySAP Business Intelligence (BI)	Provides a decision support system for managers
mySAP Supply Chain Management	Enables a company's supply chain to merge with eMarketplaces to integrate acquisitions directly into supply chain operations; enables the entire supply chain to react immediately to changing customer requirements
mySAP Human Resources (HR)	Provides on-line personnel administration functions
mySAP Financials	Provides external and internal accounting and control functions; integrates the various aspects of accounting with the logistics chain from procurement to sales
mySAP Marketplace	Provides the software to support virtual markets, allowing multiple organizations to buy, sell, and conduct collaborative trading opportunities

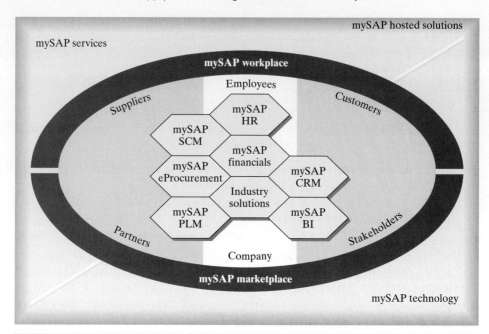

FIGURE 9-5   The mySAP.com Business Platform

Source: Copyright SAP AG.

SUPPLIER RELATIONSHIP MANAGEMENT: SAP'S ePROCUREMENT

The case of eProcurement is a good example of how eBusiness is creating opportunities to cut paperwork by providing electronic transactions among the buyer, the purchasing manager, the vendor, and accounting. The case of Charles Blake, an Administrative Manager at Wright Manufacturing, is an excellent example of how eProcurement facilitates the purchasing function by creating electronic linkages. This eliminates bottlenecks and diminishes the time and cost of paperwork in procurement.

At Wright Manufacturing, Charles Blake is the Administrative Manager. To purchase office supplies, he uses SAP's eProcurement to create a Shopping Cart with all the office supplies he needs from an on-line catalog. Before the Purchase Requisition can become a Purchase Order, he needs to obtain approval so he routes the Purchase Requisition to the Purchasing Manager electronically. The Purchasing Manager turns the electronic document into a Purchase Order, and it becomes a Sales Order on the vendor's system. The Administrative Manager can view the status of the Order on-line. When the order arrives, he confirms receipt of the goods and notifies Purchasing that everything has come in. The information is transferred to Accounting, which pays for the office supplies.

A summary of the roles of the administrative manager, purchasing manager, buyer, and accounting function in eProcurement is shown in Table 9-11.

TABLE 9-11 Roles in eProcurement	
Role	*Activity*
Administrative manager	Creates a shopping cart with needed supplies
Purchasing manager	Receives purchase requisition; creates purchase order;
Vendor	creates sales order; ships supplies enters invoice
Administrative manager	Confirms receipt of goods; notifies purchasing of
	receipt; checks invoice
Accounting	Pays for the supplies

◆ BUSINESS INTELLIGENCE WITH ERP

ERP systems generate much data, but the data are often not in the form managers can use to make decisions. Managers need timely access to data about customers, products, and competitors. These data can help them understand markets and spot trends to boost profitability. The solution to meeting these management information needs is using a data warehouse, a data mart, and data mining.

DATA WAREHOUSES

A data warehouse is a repository of known facts and related data used as a basis for making management decisions. Data for a data warehouse are gathered from operational systems (e.g., from POS cash registers) and from external data sources (e.g., economic data). A data warehouse will not work if information is missing, inconsistent, or inaccurate. To assure data integrity, the data must cleaned by resolving inconsistencies, filling in gaps, and developing consistent formats before being entered into the data warehouse.

DATA MART

A data mart is a subset of data warehouse information, usually designed for a specific set of users. Data marts are created for special data analysis. For example, a data mart can be created to answer specific questions, such as: What are the characteristics of customers who buy the company's product? What is their response to an email ad? What is the impact of advertising on increasing sales for certain products?

DATA MINING

Data mining involves the analysis of large quantities of data (e.g., bar-coded grocery sales data) as a basis for sales forecasting, inventory management, or other applications. Data mining includes identification of a problem, development of research questions (e.g., comparison of response rates to different types of advertising), data collection, and data analysis using statistical analysis. Sometimes, data mining is used

TABLE 9-12 Questions Answered through Data Mining

Business Unit	Data Source	Information Provided
Grocery stores	Cash register data	What are the characteristics of potential defectors?
Banking	Customer data	Who are the most profitable customers? What is the effectiveness of various marketing programs? Which customers are good prospects for a new service? Which customers can benefit by having a chance to lower their mortgage rates?
Credit card management	Customer prospect data	Which customers are the best prospects for credit card promotions? What credit limits should be established for various applicants? What services are customers most likely to be interested in? What is the long-term value of various customers?
Insurance	Customer data on claims	What would be the impact of lowering insurance rates for sports cars? How can we detect insurance fraud?
Telecommunications	Customer data on cell phone switching	How do we reduce churning (switching carriers) due to poor service? How can we detect and fix poor service before customers complain?
Telemarketing	Customer data	Which customers respond to travel packages? Which subset of customers responds to discounts?
Human Resource Management (HRM)	Employee data	Which employees will be likely to leave the company if they do not get additional compensation, benefits? Which employees use various services (e.g., training)?

to test a hypothesis, such as which banking customers, who are Internet users, are likely to take their business to a competitor in response to Internet advertising (see Table 9-12).

At other times, there is no preconceived relationship, and masses of data are analyzed to see what relationships might exist. For example, questions might be: What are the probabilities of response to alternative advertising strategies? Who are the most profitable customers in the casino business?

Many successful companies use data mining. For example, Wal-Mart buyers use a data warehouse processing 65 million transactions per week to predict product and market trends.

Name	Products	Web Site
Comshare	Analytical business applications for business performance analysis and improvement	www.comshare.com
CorVu	Balanced scorecard and business intelligence solutions	www.corvu.com
Cognos	Business intelligence tools and application development tools	www.cognos.com
Hyperion	Enterprise applications for budgeting, forecasting, consolidation, and analysis	www.hyperion.com
IQ	Enterprise reporting tools offering desktop and production reporting functionality for business and IT professionals	www.iqsc.com
Seagate	Business intelligence products, including Crystal and Holos	www.seagate.com

TABLE 9-13 Business Intelligence Vendors

Source: Adapted from "Support for the Strategists," *Accountancy International,* June 1998, pp. 50–53.

BUSINESS INTELLIGENCE VENDORS

Since some ERP systems do not have tools for satisfying management reporting requirements, a number of business intelligence vendors, such as Comshare, CorVu, Cognos, Hyperion, and IQ, offer applications for business analysis (see Table 9-13). These alliances between ERP vendors and business intelligence specialists extend the capabilities of ERP to meet managerial information needs.

Other tools for data mining and data warehousing are IBM's Intelligent Mining Toolkit, SAS Institute's System for Information Delivery, and Oracle's 9i Developer Reports toolkit, and SAP's Business Intelligence. SAP's Business Information Warehouse enables managers to make queries using existing databases and to generate reports via the web (see Figure 9-6).

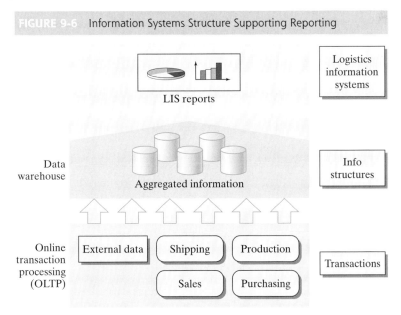

FIGURE 9-6 Information Systems Structure Supporting Reporting

Source: Copyright SAP AG.

◆ FUTURE DIRECTIONS FOR ERP

Future directions for ERP include increased integration through the supply chain, use of shared services and application service providers, and application software integration.

INCREASED INTEGRATION THROUGH THE SUPPLY CHAIN

Increased integration through SCM, using eMarketplaces and exchanges, will continue to evolve. ERP supports the backoffice functions, including financial, HR, manufacturing, and sales. Add-ons to ERP are CRM systems, which interface with the customer, and SCM systems, which interface with the supplier. ERP provides the core infrastructure for CRM and SCM (Shanks, Seddon, and Willcocks, 2003).

USE OF SHARED SERVICES AND APPLICATION SERVICE PROVIDERS

Application Service Providers (ASPs) offer cost efficiency, accelerated application development, and access to the latest technology and support (Ross, Lacity, Willcocks, 2002). Using an ASP provides services by simply "plugging in." Companies can obtain off-the-shelf ERP systems for a fixed monthly fee. Services can range from standardized off-the-shelf modules to fully customized ERP systems.

One of the strategies for acquiring external services is netsourcing, which provides ERP services, applications, and infrastructure over the web, on a rentable basis (Kern, Lacity, and Willcocks, 2002). Netsourcing arrangements pose certain risks, from the viewpoint of potential customers and from the viewpoint of existing customers (see Table 9-14) (Ross, Vitale, and Willcocks, 2003).

In a netsourcing ERP arrangement, small companies can gain access to ERP packages inexpensively. However, in any case of netsourcing ERP, risks may arise from contracts, risks may occur during migration to the ERP system, and risks may occur during post-contract operations.

In netsourcing ERP, it is important to recognize that the ERP system runs the business. This means that internal IT people should maintain responsibility for ERP

TABLE 9-14 Major Risks of a Netsourcing Venture

*From the Viewpoint of Potential Customers:**	*From the Viewpoint of Existing Customers**
1. Service and business stability	1. Netsourcing's longevity and existence
2. Security	2. Reliability
3. Reliability	3. Netsourcing provider's service and business stability
4. Netsourcing's longevity and existence	4. Security issues
5. Netsourcing's dependency on other parties	5. Integrating netsourcing solution with existing applications

*Numbers represent order of importance of these risks, from the standpoint of potential customers and existing customers.

development. In the process of migrating to the ERP system, retaining internal technical expertise and troubleshooting capability are important. In post-contract operations of the netsourcing contract, internal IT capability must be maintained (Ross et al., 2003).

In managing a netsourcing contract, it is important to work closely with the vendor and to take internal responsibility for ERP implementation. Internal technical expertise is critical. The ERP will drive changes in processes, and when companies add on new modules, even more process changes are likely to occur.

Through their Internet strategy, mySAP.com, SAP offers 22 industry templates, (e.g., aerospace and defense, automotive, banking, telecommunications), which provide business applications relevant to industry functions. Through application hosting, SAP offers this industry-specific ERP software, infrastructure, services, and support via the web. Large and small companies can take advantage of these applications. To minimize the risk factors associated with netsourcing contracts, companies need to include clauses that cover exit terms and to construct service performance measures before signing the outsourcing contract. Service guarantees need to be monitored to ensure the deal is working (Ross et al., 2003).

APPLICATION SOFTWARE INTEGRATION

A third future development is application software integration. This is a strategy for integrating legacy systems with ERP systems. Using Enterprise Application Integration (EAI) software from vendors (e.g., WebMethods and WebSphere) companies can take advantage of middleware to link legacy applications with ERP systems.

ERP systems will be built increasingly from plug and play modules (Latamore, 1999). Companies will be able to pick and choose modules which are best suited to their business. These flexible, modular systems will be built using standard interfaces, or middleware, which will enable integration among modules provided by different vendors. In addition, third-party bolt-on modules will be used to augment ERP software suites (Latamore, 1999).

◆ SUMMARY

The purpose of SCM is to link activities through the supply chain from the acquisition of raw materials to the selling of the product to the customer. In the new supply chain, close partnerships exist between the manufacturer and the retailer. For example, P&G links into Wal-Mart's POS system to determine inventory trends and to resupply Wal-Mart's inventory of P&G products whenever necessary. Linkages between manufacturers and retailers are based upon shared information about sales and inventory levels. The emergence of eBusiness creates a virtual value chain, which facilitates interactive relationships and information sharing between suppliers, manufacturers, retailers, and customers. ERP is a foundation for eBusiness, because it provides the data foundation for web-based transactions. ERP is also the foundation for business intelligence systems that provide managers with the information they need to make decisions.

Questions for Discussion •

1. How can an ERP system improve SCM by providing linkages among firms? Provide examples of the following:
   a. Linkages between suppliers and manufacturers
   b. Linkages between customers and manufacturers
   c. Linkages between manufacturers and retailers
2. Investigate the use of data warehouse and data mining strategies in these industries by conducting on-line research in trade publications to find relevant examples.
   a. Banking
   b. Brokerage firms
   c. Telecommunications service providers
3. How is the use of data warehousing and data mining facilitated by ERP?
4. How do ERP systems supporting SCM provide a foundation for eBusiness?
5. What are the major risks of a netsourcing arrangement for ERP? What strategies can minimize these risks?

◆◆◆ Cases

Data Solutions

Data Solutions is a company specializing in network implementation and management. It provides networking services to mid-sized companies, which do not have an internal networking analyst or IT manager. These organizations include real estate companies, law offices, medical practices, architectural/engineering firms, construction companies, business services providers, country clubs, community organizations, and churches.

Data Solutions uses a legacy accounting system to handle its financial accounting and financial management functions. It has added on a billing package for client services. The next step is to obtain a CRM capability to manage information about current and prospective customers more effectively.

CASE EXERCISES

You have been assigned to identify potential sources for a netsourcing arrangement with an ERP vendor, which provides CRM capability.

a. Identify potential sources of the software.
b. Identify three alternative providers.
c. Determine five criteria you will recommend be used to evaluate each of these alternative providers.
d. Evaluate each of the alternatives with respect to the criteria for evaluation.
e. Make a recommendation to management.

TechKnowledge

TechKnowledge is a start-up founded in 1997 by Robert Thyer. The company is a distributor of presentation technologies, including computer-based projection systems, video equipment, and display technologies. The firm has 25 employees and does $5 million in sales. It is growing rapidly. The owner, Robert Thyer, would like to netsource

the back-office functions of the firm because the company does not have an internal IT capability. The applications to be netsourced would include sales and distribution, financial accounting, and inventory management.

TechKnowledge would like to source SAP or another ERP vendor via a hosting arrangement.

It does not expect to do much customization, and it does not have any legacy systems.

CASE EXERCISE

Investigate at least three netsourcing hosts for TechKnowledge to consider.

1. What factors should it use to evaluate each of these potential hosts?

2. What agreements need to be in place in advance of implementing the hosting arrangement?

3. What controls should be in place to monitor the hosting arrangement?

4. What IT capabilities should be developed and maintained in-house?

Featured Article

Based upon this article, how is Dow Chemical leveraging the ERP backbone?

LEVERAGING THE ERP BACKBONE

Not only is Dow Corning following its implementation with SAP's Business Information Warehouse, it participated in the beta testing program.

IN 1995 DOW CORNING CORP. started its journey to integrate its global business processes and improve its business intelligence capabilities with a decision to begin implementation of a basic ERP backbone. Step one was R/3, the enterprise resource planning solution from SAP AG. By replacing a multiplicity of legacy systems running on mainframes, Dow Corning began the process of meeting a variety of phase-one objectives.

"Not only did we hope to gain efficiency in our transactional processes by being able to perform better, faster, and more cheaply, we also had global integration problems that we wanted to solve," says Cynthia A. Hartz, Dow Corning's manager of the SAP business-information framework in Midland, Mich. In addition to more fully automating and integrating business processes, the company wanted to share common data and practices across the entire global enterprise.

The company, a manufacturer of chemicals, produces more than 5,000 products in 32 manufacturing facilities. In 1997 it generated $2.6 billion in sales with more than 60% of its business originating outside the U.S. In September 1996 three manufacturing sites in the UK were the first to come on-line. Implementations at the other sites completed phase one by the end of 1998.

Phase two, Dow Corning's business-intelligence strategy, takes advantage of SAP's announcement last September of its Business Information Warehouse (BW). SAP's intent is to offer the ability to consolidate internal and external information and to make it possible to take advantage of its Strategic Enterprise Management tools and processes.

"It is a follow-up to a direction we started almost 20 years ago when we said our business customers needed integrated systems," says Michael Kiemen, SAP's corporate director of sales and marketing, Waldorf, Germany.

Last fall Dow Corning became a beta site for SAP's BW and began the evaluation process with other early adopters such as Colgate-Palmolive Co., Intel Corp., and Bay Networks Inc. "We met with them and SAP on a regular basis, sharing our visions for business intelligence," says Hartz. "We performed data modeling and walked through typical business-case scenarios."

Components of SAP's solution include the BW Server; automatic-extraction capability; InfoCubes for multidimensional reporting; Business Explorer, a new front-end reporting and online-analytical-processing solution; the Administrator Workbench; and Business Applications Programming Interfaces.

Hartz plans to launch a product-costing activity as the first production application for the SAP BW. In addition to pulling in data from R/3, Hartz is evaluating the data warehouse's potential for using data from other sources. Some of her examples include data from plant-floor data-collection software, patent information, and external benchmarking.

Hartz says Dow Corning hopes to be able to leverage some of the skills and technology developed in connection with the R/3 implementation to facilitate the rapid scale-up of the data-warehouse capability. "We'll have over 4,000 users associated with the SAP ERP, and the same look and feel can be applied to the data warehouse."

She says that an important lesson learned was the value of going into the software-evaluation phase with all the details decided about the specific business reports that would need to be created. She also values the chance for technology exploration the software-evaluation process afforded. "We had this wonderful opportunity to draw on the wisdom of the entire development team. . . . That helped us visualize future potential for business intelligence in the post-ERP implementation phase," Hartz adds.

From the SAP perspective, the data warehouse is seen as vital business-intelligence infrastructure. "It is an enabling step that can help businesses bridge the gap between operations and strategy," says SAP's Klemen.

———
Teresko, John, "Leveraging the ERP backbone," *Industry Week*, v. 248, n. 3, February 1, 1999, p. 25. Cleveland, Ohio: Penton Publishing 1999.

References

Alexander, Steve. "Printer manufacturer tracks your inventory." *Computerworld* November 16, 1998.

Copacino, William C. 1997. *Supply Chain Management, The Basics and Beyond*. Boca Raton, FL: St. Lucie Press.

Dahlen, C., and J. Elfsson. 1999. An analysis of the current and future ERP market—With a focus on Sweden." Master's Thesis. Stockholm, Sweden: The Royal Institute of Technology.

Evans, Philip, and Thomas Worster. 1999. "Getting real about virtual commerce." *Harvard Business Review* 77(6):84–94.

Ghosh, Shikhar. 1998. "Making business sense of the Internet." *Harvard Business Review* 76(2): 126–135.

Hamel, Gary, and C.K. Prahalad. 1993. "Strategy as stretch and leverage." *Harvard Business Review* 71(2):75–84.

Jacob, P. 1995. "Hallmark Replenishment Program Set." *Brand Marketing* September: 65.

Kaplan, Steven, and Mohahbir Sawhney. 2000. "e-Hubs: The new B2B marketplaces." *Harvard Business Review* 78(3):97–103.

Kern, T., M. Lacity, and L. Willcocks. 2002. *Netsourcing: Renting Business Applications and Services Over Networks*. New York: Prentice-Hall.

Latamore, B. 1999. "ERP in the new millennium." *APICS—The Performance Advantage* June:29–32.

Lummus, Rhonda R., and Robert J. Vokurka. 1999. "Managing the demand chain through managing the information flow: Capturing 'Moments of Information.' " *Production and Inventory Management Journal* First Quarter.

Margulis, Ron. 1999. "Reebok runs on a new ERP path." *Consumer Goods* March/April.

Mistry, Prafal. 1997. "Benchmarking study shows dramatic reduction in costs using best practices for supply chain management." *Insight* (Pittiglio, Rabin, Todd, and McGrath, Weston, MA), Winter.

Ross, Jeanne. Michael Vitale, and Leslie Willcocks. 2003. "The continuing ERP revolution: Sustainable lessons, new Modes of delivery," in *Second-Wave Enterprise Resource Planning Systems*. Graeme Shanks, Peter Seddon, and Leslie Willcocks (Eds.), Cambridge: Cambridge University Press, 2003. pp. 102–132.

Shanks, Graeme, Peter Seddon, and Leslie Willcocks. "Introduction: ERP—the quiet revolution," *Second-Wave Enterprise Resource Planning Systems*. Cambridge: Cambridge University Press, 2003. pp. 1–23.

Stalk, George, Philip Evans, and Lawrence E. Shulman. 1992. "Competing and Capabilities: The new rules of corporate strategy." *Harvard Business Review* 70(2):57–69.

"Support for the strategists." *Accountancy International* June 1998, 50–53.

Werbach, Kevin. 2000. "Syndication: The emerging model for business in the Internet era." *Harvard Business Review* 78(3):84–93.

Integrated Case Study: Bandon Group, Inc.

PART 1: BUSINESS BACKGROUND

Bandon Group is a family owned distributor of copiers, electronic printers, faxes, and other office equipment. The company was started by Bud Bandon, who bought a copier dealership in Phoenix in 1953. Through Bud's entrepreneurial skill, motivation, and commitment to customer service, Bandon Phoenix aggressively gained market share and grew to $10 million in sales in the Phoenix marketplace by 1972. One of Bud's greatest accomplishments was the creation of Bandon Leasing Company, which held leases on copiers and electronic printers and became a major source of positive cash flow.

Excellent customer service, technical support, and innovative products enabled the company to grow continuously through the 1970s, and profits enabled Bud to purchase another copier franchise in Salt Lake City. By 1980, the Salt Lake City dealership grew to $10 million in sales.

When Bud passed away in 1972, his two sons, Ed and Steve Bandon, continued the business. Their growth strategy was to acquire additional dealerships in growing markets. By 1995, Bandon had grown to four divisions, in four different markets in the western U.S. Portland, Oregon; Phoenix, Arizona; Salt Lake City, Utah; and Denver, Colorado. Each division president is responsible for developing sales and marketing strategies that will meet the customers' needs in the particular market segment. This decentralized sales strategy enables each division to meet the needs of their respective local markets.

The corporate headquarters in Phoenix, handles central administrative functions and information systems support for order processing, billing, accounts payable, and accounts receivable.

The divisions report to Ed and Steve Bandon, the co-owners of Bandon Group, Inc. The primary objective of senior management is to generate a 10% profit on sales, so profits can be used to re-invest in the overall enterprise and

to purchase new divisions in markets that are growing in importance.

The Mission, Values, Goals, and Objectives of Bandon Group, Inc., are expressed in the views of Ed Bandon, its co-owner: "Our objective is to provide office information systems supported by a networking infrastructure which facilitates information sharing and systems integration." In addition, notes Steve, its co-owner, "Bandon Divisions can offer value-added services and technology integration which meet the needs of customers in their respective marketplaces. Our responsiveness to customer needs is the key to our profitability and to our market success."

One of the important elements of the company's profitability is its excellent sales organization and professional service organization. Its salespeople receive extensive training from experienced sales managers. Its service technicians are among the best in the industry and maintain high levels of expertise in problem diagnosis, troubleshooting, and reconciliation.

The competitive environment includes large national manufacturers, such as IBM and Xerox, which are managed through branches in major metropolitan areas. Bandon Group and its divisions have effectively competed by serving the needs of mid-market companies (e.g., $25 million to $400 million in sales) and by offering mid-tier equipment (e.g., copiers, faxes, electronic printers) at cost-effective prices in regional markets. Their ability to offer quality-manufactured products (e.g., Canon, Minolta, Kyocera Mita, Sharp) has given their dealerships a reputation for quality and superior service at cost-effective prices.

Information Systems Environment

In the 1970s, Bandon Group contracted with a software development firm to develop custom software for its industry. Its administrative information systems were developed over a ten-year timeframe and handled major administrative and accounting functions, including order processing, inventory control, accounts receivable, accounts payable, general ledger, and meter click billing. Most of the information systems functions for applications supporting the business are generic, but the meter click billing software is unique to the industry. As a result, it made sense to contract for proprietary, or customized, software to support the business applications. The software was written in Business Basic, and the applications ran on an HP server in a Unix operating system environment.

Acquisition of OMD

By 1994, Bandon Group's business expansion meant the company had outgrown its legacy systems. At that time, it hired a full-time Director of Information Technology, Brian Manning. The Director of Information Technology reported to the Vice-President of Finance, William Bruen, within the Corporate Headquarters of Bandon Group, Inc. One of Brian's first responsibilities was to search for a commercial off-the-shelf package that supported the administrative information systems of Bandon Group, Inc. After a lengthy analysis, the company selected Office Machines Dealership (OMD), a package developed by a larger dealer.

The OMD System was being adopted by many dealers across the country because it included software supporting the meter-based billing application, unique to the copier industry. Meter-based billing in the copier industry is similar to meter-based billing in the utilities (e.g., gas) industry. In most cases, customers obtain a contract for a certain volume of copies per month, and their billing is based upon this contract. To monitor usage, customers report their meter reading, and any overage (above contract volume) is additionally billed. In some cases, customers contract for a cost per copy basis, and they are billed according to this volume. The meter-based billing software within OMD was written in COBOL. Enhancements to the core OMD system included many sales management and service management reporting systems, which the prior versions did not include. OMD uses a dealer advisory board to obtain recommendations for further enhancements and modifications to the package. One enhancement is a web-based interface for customer entry of meter readings. This enhancement is called I-Manager.

One of the limitations of OMD is that it was not built using a relational database. As a result, ad hoc query and reporting is difficult, and managers have to stick with periodic reports provided from the system. Most of the reports are obtained by requests to the systems group since generating these reports requires knowledge of the OMD report generator. Some managers complain about OMD's lack of flexibility, and attempts were made to transfer data extracts from the OMD database into microcomputer-based database files using Microsoft Access so that managers can make these queries and generate on-demand reports. However, the complexity of the OMD database makes it difficult to create these data extracts and to refresh them on a timely basis.

Connecting the Divisions

Another major responsibility of the Director of Information Technology is to serve the IT needs of the divisions. By 1995, the four divisions were connected to the central OMD system. Brian spends a major portion of his time designing and maintaining a telecommunications network with T-1 capability to connect each of the divisions to the central OMD administrative system in Phoenix.

Sales Prospecting

The office systems dealership industry depends upon effective sales prospecting. The typical sales representative uses a prospect database to make 25 calls each day. Of these 25 calls, five translate into an opportunity for an equipment demonstration. Of these five demonstrations, one or two might lead to an actual sale. Sales prospecting is critical to the success of the sales representatives throughout the industry.

In 1992, Bandon Salt Lake acquired *Pivotal,* a sales prospecting tool, which supported ad hoc queries in a relational database environment. Sales support analysts used external market databases, such as Dun & Bradstreet, Inc., to create prospect databases within *Pivotal,* and these were used to support the sales representatives. In addition, existing customer data was re-keyed into *Pivotal* from the OMD customer database because *Pivotal* and OMD were not integrated.

In 1993, Bandon Phoenix and Bandon Portland adopted *Pivotal* as their sales prospecting tool. In 1995, Bandon Denver adopted

Pivotal. These divisions adopted a similar strategy of importing prospect data from external market databases into the *Pivotal* database to create sales leads. As with Bandon Salt Lake, internal customer data had to be re-keyed from OMD into the *Pivotal* database because OMD and *Pivotal* were not integrated. Over time, this created inconsistency between the OMD and *Pivotal* databases and resulted in a duplication of effort in maintaining these two database environments.

Across the divisions, the *Pivotal* databases were used to varying degrees. At Bandon Salt Lake City, external market data and internal customer data were entered into the *Pivotal* databases to create sales leads. At Bandon Portland, these external market data and internal customer data were used for sales prospecting as well. At Bandon Denver, the *Pivotal* sales prospecting system was introduced, but the licenses fell out-of-date, and data were not entered periodically. As a result, sales representatives created their own local prospect databases, using the contact management tool within Microsoft Access and GoldMine, a popular microcomputer-based sales and contact management system.

At Bandon Phoenix, a number of Customer Relationship Management (CRM) applications were developed by an internal systems designer between 1993 and 2003, and these applications were quite sophisticated. For example, *Pivotal* applications developed at Bandon Phoenix generates service alerts when a particular customer calls in a service call more than three times in one month. Another *Pivotal* report, an excess volume report, generates a customer alert whenever copier volume on a particular unit runs 150% over its recommended volume. This information enables the sales representative assigned to this customer account to follow-up with the customer to determine if an upgrade is appropriate. To date, over 50 CRM applications run in the *Pivotal* environment at Bandon Phoenix. These applications support territory management, lead management, external market data integration, sales forecasting, customer retention, sales analysis, and sales compensation.

Evaluating CRM Solutions

The importance of sales prospecting to the divisions led the division presidents at Bandon Portland, Bandon Salt Lake, and Bandon Denver to seek alternative sales prospecting and CRM software solutions. Since each division tries to meet the needs of its respective marketplace, the division presidents sought software solutions that supported their application requirements. The division presidents in Portland, Salt Lake City, and Denver considered adopting the *Pivotal* CRM applications, which had been developed in Phoenix, but they felt these applications were too extensive and complex to meet their needs and did not meet their unique requirements. One important achievement in Phoenix was the creation of a data migration path between the OMD database and the *Pivotal* database in Phoenix. With the help of Brian Manning, the Director of Information Technology for Bandon Group, Inc., data from the OMD database are used to refresh and to update the *Pivotal* CRM database in Phoenix on a weekly basis.

Between November 2002 and August 2003, the other divisions analyzed and evaluated other sales prospecting and CRM applications. Robert North, the Division President at Bandon Portland, decided to pilot the new Microsoft CRM package and to customize it for their use. One of the advantages of the Microsoft CRM package was its integration with Microsoft Office applications, including Excel, Outlook, and Access. A limitation, however, was its lack of integration with the proprietary OMD database and proprietary OMD operating system. Robert hired a consulting firm to address the challenge of creating a data migration path between the existing OMD database and the Microsoft CRM database, so customer data from OMD could continuously refresh the CRM database.

Edmund Scott, the Division President of Bandon Salt Lake, decided to implement a sales prospecting package, which had been developed by another copier dealership in Pittsburgh. The *Soaring* package supported lead management and sales prospecting. In addition, the *Soaring* package used a Microsoft SQL Server database, permitting ad hoc queries and on-demand reports. One of the major advantages of the *Soaring* package was its integration with the OMD legacy system database, and this permitted the migration of customer data from OMD to *Soaring* for customer account follow-up and analysis purposes.

With Phoenix using *Pivotal,* Portland piloting the Microsoft CRM, and Salt Lake City implementing *Soaring,* John Werner, the Division President of Bandon Denver decided to rely upon local microcomputer-based sales prospecting software, including the contact management system within GoldMine, until such time as one of the solutions was proven to be most cost-effective. John did not want to spend a lot of money and time on an expensive CRM application, when other more cost-effective solutions existed.

The lack of integration among the four different sales prospecting/CRM environments and the central administrative information systems and customer databases posed a problem to Brian Manning, the Director of Information Technology at Bandon Group, Inc. It was difficult for him and his small staff to support numerous sales prospecting applications, each of which required data migration from the OMD database to the CRM environment on a periodic basis. While the *Soaring* software was integrated with the OMD database, it had limited functionality outside the traditional copier line of business, and the other division presidents felt strongly that their CRM tools needed to support new and emerging lines of business, including information systems consulting, document outsourcing, color graphics, and document management.

An Information Systems Study for ERP

Ed and Steve Bandon, the co-owners of Bandon Group, Inc., felt that it was time to do an information systems study to determine how Information Technology (IT) could best support the overall mission, goals, and objectives of the corporation over a three-year to five-year period of time. While they recognized that each division had the right to pursue autonomous CRM and sales prospecting applications, they saw that this approach created duplication of effort, suboptimized the outcome, and caused a great deal of extra expense. In addition, the central IT staff managed by Brian Manning, the Director of Information Technology, was small and had trouble providing data migration, network support, technical support, and training for four different local sales prospecting and CRM solutions.

Another factor motivated the information systems study. Other large copier dealerships were beginning to implement ERP solutions, including SAP and the administrative information systems of Oracle ERP. These ERP solutions provided administrative systems grounded in relational database technology that allowed cross-functional integration. This integration included support for front-end applications such as CRM, which were integrated with the ERP systems.

Many competitive dealerships were moving toward eBusiness solutions, which enabled web-based supply ordering, service call entry, and meter click reporting. In this competitive environment, Ed and Steve Bandon felt it was time to move toward eBusiness solutions. However, in the current fragmented environment in which the legacy OMD system had a proprietary database and was not integrated with the various CRM solutions adopted by the divisions, it was almost impossible to move toward eBusiness. eBusiness requires a foundation in administrative systems supporting order entry, service call management, customer service, and supply ordering, and the foundation ERP systems were not in place at Bandon Group, Inc.

Need for an Information Systems Study

With these pressing issues in hand, Ed and Steve Bandon decided to bring in an external information systems consulting firm to analyze the current information systems environment, to assess problems with the current environment, and to propose changes in systems to enable the company, including its respective divisions, to achieve the sales and service objectives.

In addition to assessing the feasibility of an ERP system, Ed and Steve wanted the consultant to address senior management concerns, such as the need for more information for tactical and strategic management, the need to standardize business processes, and the need for more targeted marketing. The centralized versus decentralized organization of IT was a dilemma. Over the last ten years, the sales prospecting and CRM applications had become totally decentralized and under the control of each autonomous division. Though this provided flexibility and control over data, it added considerable expense and made it difficult for centralized IT to support this environment.

In the current environment, addressing the issues of eBusiness and data integration was difficult. Managers within all the divisions were seeking better management information, but without a relational database environment supporting the legacy OMD applications, it was almost impossible to provide ad hoc queries and on-demand reporting. It seemed that each new IT issue was being addressed by a piecemeal or "fire-fighting" approach. It was time to create an integrated IT plan to spell out directions for central and decentralized IT and to enable each division to achieve its strategic marketing objectives.

The external consultant assigned to accomplish this study, Elizabeth Sudduth, of TechKnowledge, Inc., was one of the best in the business. She started by providing Ed and Steve with a detailed nine-step plan of action for the study.

ASSIGNMENT

Your assignment is to conduct the information systems study for Bandon Group, Inc., using the interviews, supplementary materials, and resources provided each part of the study. Your work will enable you to evaluate the feasibility of ERP systems for the organization, including CRM and eBusiness. You will follow the process outlined in the following table. The documentation you need is included in the attachments, which correspond to each of the steps in the study. Your part of the project is outlined in the "Things to Do" section associated with each step.

TABLE 1	Information Systems Study: Bandon Group, Inc. Activities, Documentation, Things to Do		

Strategy	*Activity*	*Documentation*	*Things to Do*
Purpose and scope of study (Step 1)	Define the purpose and scope of the MIS study.	Purpose and scope of the MIS study	
Document high-level business direction (Step 2)	Executive management interviews	Transcripts of executive management interviews	Write a summary of major problems and opportunities defined by management, focus on common problems/opportunities
Identify key information needs and measures (Step 3)	Executive management and team interviews	Matrix: goals, critical success factors, measures, IT needs	Write a summary of common or shared CSFs, measures, IT needs
Determine detailed business requirements (Step 4)	In-depth interviews with division presidents and teams	Interview findings: problems, goals and opportunities, IT needs, priorities	Write a summary of common or shared priorities
Document current IT situation—Internal (Step 5)	Data collection and interviews	IT infrastructure	
Document current IT situation—External (Step 6)	Marketing intelligence; collecting data on what competitors are doing with IT	Review competitive dealer web sites to determine what web-based services are offered (service call entry, meter reading submission, supply ordering)	
Determine gap between current IT situation and desired IT direction (Step 7)	Follow-up interviews with division presidents	List of IT priorities	Identify common IT priorities among divisions by completing the chart

(cont.)

TABLE 1 (cont.)			
Strategy	**Activity**	**Documentation**	**Things to Do**
Determine feasibility of an ERP system (Step 8)	Assessment of the feasibility of ERP and CRM	Web-based resources on ERP and CRM; articles in trade publications; vendor resources	Write a recommendation to address these questions: (1) Should Bandon Group pursue an ERP solution? (2) should they pursue a CRM solution? and (3) in what order should they plan to acquire ERP? CRM?
Determine ERP design issues (Step 9)	Assessment of alternative ERP and CRM packages	External research on ERP packages with integrated CRM capabilities (e.g., trade publications, vendor reports, web-based materials)	Evaluate alternative ERP and CRM packages for Bandon Group (e.g., Microsoft Great Plains, J.D. Edwards, SAP, etc.) and make a recommendation for a solution which will meet their needs

Integrated Case Study: Bandon Group, Inc.

STEP 1: PURPOSE AND SCOPE OF THE STUDY

Objectives of the Study

To determine the major initiatives that the MIS organization and business management must accomplish over time to move the company from the current situation to the development of an integrated information management strategy that will enable the organization to achieve its business objectives.

Benefits

a. *Assures that IT plans support business plans.*
b. *Provides a basis for linking IT expenditures to the business direction.*
c. *Provides a context within which functional area managers and MIS professionals can make decisions.*
d. *Communicates the overall direction of information use and management throughout the organization.*
e. *Provides tighter integration of common systems and networks while simultaneously decentralizing the technology and operational activities.*

f. *Provides guidance in selecting vendors for workstation-based, local area network-based, and web-based solutions to problems.*
g. *Provides a context for using IT to gain a strategic advantage.*

STEP 2: EXECUTIVE MANAGEMENT INTERVIEWS

The executive interviews with four Division Presidents and the Chief Financial Officer for Bandon, Inc., provide insight into business objectives, marketing strategies, and future opportunities. Based upon these five interviews, develop a list of major objectives to be achieved by an integrated information system.

Robert North, President Bandon, Inc., Portland Executive Management Interview

1. Charter, Mission, Vision, Values, Goals, Objectives:
   a. What is the mission and vision of the organization?
      Addressing the needs of 6,000 companies with >25 employees and specific technology-dependent targeted markets

b. Are there any other high-level business direction statements like values, credo?
Value-added marketing approach
Customer centric; understanding the customer
Experience the difference; differentiation of services
Integration of information-based network services
Providing strategic outsourcing services

c. What are the goals and objectives of the organization?
Revenue growth from $23 M to $30 M
Grow our network and imaging out-sourcing business
Only focus on our targeted markets/customers

d. Is there a goal in terms of market position?
Growth in market share in IT consulting business
Growth in service base
Network and document infrastructure consulting

2. Strategies, Business Priorities for the Year, Critical Issues for the Year:

a. What are the specific strategies or business priorities for the year, in order of priority?
Ability to focus on higher-margin accounts
Effective relationship building with customers
Effective contact management
Effective customer information gathering and utilization

b. What must we accomplish this year to remain competitive?
Technical expertise
Effective customer service
Product knowledge
Better defined targeted markets

c. What critical issues face the organization today?
Accurate and timely billing
Accurate and timely collections
Effective sales support
Inventory management
Retention and recruitment of quality people

d. What critical issues face the organization in the future?
Increasing integration of information/network services with traditional lines of business
Diversity of services and solutions offered to our targeted markets
Dealing with the limitations of OMD:
  Inability to bill for non-copier-related services
  Inability to handle on-line transactions (on-line meter collection)

3. Business Information:

a. Are any acquisitions or growth anticipated?
Expansion of the IT consulting business

b. Are there any changes in business markets in the future?
Trend to selling information services and network-based services (e.g., document management)

c. Who are our customers?
Mid-market companies (e.g., law firms, manufacturing, country clubs, professional services firms, construction-related companies, health care)

d. What makes customers buy from us versus the competition?
Value-added; service-based approach
Our knowledge of their industry

e. What are your basis product lines?
Copying, network services, information services, imaging, document and network infrastructure design and implementation

f. What has the growth rate been over the past several years?
Our growth in output related solutions has been steady but still single digit. In information systems consulting, the growth has been dynamic.

g. How many employees are at your location? Do you anticipate this to change?
We have between 90 and 100 people and this should remain steady for the next three years.

4. Industry:

a. What share of the market do you have?
Two percent in region.

b. What industry associations of affiliations do you participate in?
Copier Dealers Association (CDA)

c. What trends, developments or changes are taking place in your industry?
Evolution toward selling information services and network-based services.
Copy volumes are declining
More services are being outsourced

d. What are your customers requesting of you?
More knowledge of technology and its impact on business today
Easier ways to do business with us
Better return on investment
More accountability

e. What competitive advantage do you currently have?
Effective customer service and support
Our people and their tenure
Our vendor relationships (e.g., Canon, in particular)
Network infrastructure design and implementation team
Knowledge of industry-specific software applications

5. External Factors:
a. Are there any external environmental factors?
Fast pace of technology
Finding good people

b. What challenges do you face in the marketplace?
Increasing number of electronic prints and scans versus copies
Getting the customer to understand the complexity of some of the solutions today

c. What are the external opportunities or threats?
The shrinking cost per copy on our traditional business
Many companies are competing on price
High-volume print applications
Convergence of documents, networks, and data under the document management umbrella
Customers looking for one point of accountability for technology development

6. Internal Strengths and Weaknesses:
a. What are the internal strengths of your organization?
Our people
Network knowledge

Our ability to handle every aspect of document management, (e.g., creation, conversion, storage/retrieval, management/ security, distribution, output)

b. What are the internal weaknesses of your organization?
Our central information system's handling of other services outside of document output

c. What internal challenges, opportunities or threats exist in your organization?
Turnover of people
Missing opportunity based on not seeing the proper path to capitalize on technology
Wasting of resources

7. Information Technology (IT):
a. What areas must IT improve?
Account profitability report (margins/ customer)
Web-enabled customer support
Automated customer contact solution (e.g., e-mails)
Sales and marketing data and marketing analysis reports
Better resources for obtaining industry-specific information
Web-enabled access to information
PDA compatible solution for database access, contact management, and calendars
Customer feedback
Billing system for information consulting services
Web-based project tracking and reporting
Invoicing solution that utilizes fax, e-mail, Internet, and paper invoices
Service management reports (e.g., need response time reports)
Accurate cost tracking and reporting

b. What do you know about the IT of your competition?
They are working with Oracle and other ERP vendors

c. What IT related features or functionality can they offer that you currently cannot?
Their web applications are better
National account tracking and reporting

d. What business decisions are difficult or impossible to make given existing information available from IT?

We move our resources, not based on a plan but based on the "squeakiest wheel."

e. How are decisions being made currently?
By the management team

f. Who needs the information to make these decisions?
Division presidents
All managers

g. What boundaries or desires do you have with respect to this IT planning process?
It would be nice to understand what IT will provide, change, or develop in the next year.
What is our total cost of IT? Is it justifiable? Is it consistent with industry standards?

Richard Roberts, President
Bandon, Inc., Phoenix
Executive Management Interview

1. Charter, Mission, Vision, Values, Goals, Objectives:
   a. Are there any other high-level business direction statements like values, credo?
   Value-added approach to marketing
   b. What are the goals and objectives of the organization?
   Revenue growth
   Increase market share in document out-sourcing, digital imaging, color graphics, facilities management
   Growth in market share in IT consulting
   Growth in service base
   Administrative cost control; efficiency of administrative operations

2. Strategies, Business Priorities for the Year, Critical Issues for the Year:
   a. What are the specific strategies or business priorities for the year, in order of priority?
   Ability to attract new accounts
   Timely appointment setup
   Ability to identify new leads and emerging accounts
   Integration of sales leads with compensation processing
   Effective relationship building with customers
   Effective contact management
   Value-added approach to marketing

   b. What must we accomplish this year to remain competitive?
   Technical expertise
   Effective contact management
   Effective customer service
   Product knowledge
   Ability to anticipate service upgrades
   Accurate and timely billing
   Accurate and timely collections
   Ability to offer web-based information services (e.g., meter-reading submission, service call reporting)
   Ability to provide electronic bill presentment
   Effective sales support

   c. What critical issues face the organization today?
   Increase in laser (electronic) prints versus traditional copies
   Increasing emphasis on information services/network services

3. Business Information:
   a. What are your basic product lines?
   Document outsourcing, digital imaging, color graphics, facilities management
   b. What has the growth rate been over the past several years?
   Five percent growth per year in document outsourcing, color graphics
   c. How many employees are at your location? Do you anticipate this to change?
   Eighty to 90 employees; should remain constant

4. Information Technology (IT):
   a. What is IT currently doing well?
   We have developed a series of database applications using Pivotal software. Here are some of the successful applications developed in this environment:
   Integration of Dun & Bradstreet and iMarket data with Pivotal
   Pivotal forecast analysis
   Pivotal call/appointment setup
   Pivotal sales lead and compensation reports (e.g., automated e-mails, alerts triggered on completed appointments, commission payout)
   Pivotal sales and marketing data (account tracking)
   Service management reports (response time, meter-read alerts, excess service call alerts)

Customer service history reports
Pivotal lease expiration reports

b. What areas must IT improve?
Integration between sales prospecting and administrative systems
Migration of OMD data into a relational database
Migration of OMD data into a data warehouse
Upgrade to the GUI version of OMD
Extending the use of external industry databases for sales prospecting (e.g., Dun & Bradstreet, I-Market)
eBusiness front-end to OMD for meter-reading submission (I-Manager)
eBusiness front-end for service call reporting, toner fulfillment, service history
Global Positioning Satellite (GPS) for service tech tracking
Bar code scanners for car stock inventory
Creation of "suspect" activity report (e.g., machines running high on service calls)
Integration of I-Manager with the Bandon Phoenix web site
Accounting system for IT business consulting services
Better invoices
Increase in collections
Web-based information services
Electronic bill presentment

c. What IT-related features or functionality can they offer that you currently cannot?
Web-based information services (e.g., meter reads, service calls, supply orders)

Edmund Scott, President
Bandon, Inc., Salt Lake City
Executive Management Interview

1. Charter, Mission, Vision, Values, Goals, Objectives:
   a. Goals and objectives
   To grow our business at a profitable rate
   b. Market position goal
   To be known as the premier service provider in the Salt Lake City market
2. Strategies, Business Priorities for the Year, Critical Issues for the Year:
   a. Specific strategies or business priorities
   Grow our business at a rate of 5%

Increase profitability to 7% pre-tax
Improve quality of service to our customers
Eliminate multiple operating systems and utilize one system for all aspects of our business
Bring each aspect of our business closer to the customer level by eliminating departments and cross-training all individuals
Make it easier for our customers to do business with us (on-line billing and improved invoicing)

b. Critical issues facing our organization:
Maintaining profitable growth
Recruitment and retention of people
Increased market competitiveness
Internal process improvements
Implementation of new technologies
Technological training (staying ahead of the curve)
Communications
Information sharing
Generating a better product for our customer outside of equipment

3. Business Information:
   a. Future business market changes
   There is constant change in our market due to manufacturers' product development.
   b. Customers
   The ideal customer for us, based around our success, is identified as having 20 cpm to 85 cpm machines. Broken down further, it is the customer with a range of units between 1 and 10 where we are most successful.
   c. What makes customers buy from us versus the competition?
   Longevity of the sales department
   They want what we offer in a value-added package
   Independent local dealer
   We carry our own leases
   Average 4-hour response time
   Guaranteed 8-hour up time
   3-year fixed service and supply piecing
   3-year or 5-year unconditional replacement guarantee
   All of this at a 10% to 12% premium
   Accurate billing

d. Basic product lines

Minolta	*Digital and color copiers/printers; faxes*
Kyocera Mita	*Low-end digital & color copiers/printers; faxes*
Hitachi	*Mainframe printers*
IBM	*Mainframe printers*
T/R Systems	*Print on demand*
EFI & IBM	*Front-end controllers*

e. Growth rate

	Sales	*Service*
1998	*− 4.3%*	*+ 5.3%*
1999	*+ 16.2%*	*− 7.3%*
2000	*+ 15.5%*	*+ 1.3%*
2001	*+ 1.1%*	*+ 3.2%*

f. Number of employees
   Service: 30
   Sales: 26
   Admin: 15
   Total: 71

4. Industry:
   a. Market share
      1% of copier market in the region
   b. Industry associations
      Copier Dealers Association (CDA)
      Midwest Minolta Dealer Association
   c. Trends, developments or changes
      The obvious change is to digital Purchasing is no longer the go-to for all decisions. IT is becoming an integral part of the decision-making process
      Staying ahead of the technological curve is now a key element in differentiating our company
      With scanning capabilities, the next obvious move is storage and retrieval
   d. Customer requests
      Better reporting, e.g., downtime, response time, population reports
      Readable and understandable invoices
      On-line ordering
      On-line billing

5. External Factors:
   a. External environmental factors
      Economy
      Competition
      Recruitment
      Technology
   b. Challenges in the market place
      Maturity of our market regarding the industry, which is not growing

c. External opportunities
   Our product line is still weak in the high end (65 cpm and higher), compared to our two largest competitors, Canon and Xerox. This forces us to focus on the mid-tier of our market and forces us to provide a better product regarding service and support, e.g., price versus value. Thus, one opportunity is high end but not until our manufacturers provide us with a competitive product.
   Color has high potential to grow our business. With a quality line from Minolta and Kyocera Mita, this will have great impact.
   High print volume is a big opportunity, but we have failed in penetrating accounts and providing solutions.
   Storage and retrieval is another growth opportunity for our business.

6. Internal Strengths and Weaknesses:
   a. Internal strengths
      Quality service
      Customer friendly and driven
      Accuracy
      Longevity of people
      Strong people development
   b. Internal weaknesses
      Too much paperwork; we make it difficult for people to do business with us and our reps are required to be paperwork geniuses.
      Archiving and retrieval of documents

7. Information Technology (IT):
   a. What is IT currently doing well?
      Basically maintaining current systems: OMD, phone, e-mail, network backbone
      Generating routine reports
   b. Areas IT must improve
      I don't think IT is paying attention to how we can integrate information services to better improve our companies' responsiveness to customer needs
      Responsiveness
      We seem to be left to support ourselves with new technology
   c. IT of competition
      They seem to be bringing solutions to their companies that help them provide a better product, e.g., Ikon/Xerox with on-line ordering and EDI services

d. Current decisions
Decisions are being made currently at the Operating Division level because there is no central IT plan in place.

John Werner, President
Bandon, Inc., Denver
Executive Management Interview

1. Charter, Mission, Vision, Values, Goals, Objectives:
   a. What is the mission and vision of the organization?
   Provide outstanding customer service
   b. What are the goals and objectives of the organization?
   To promote enthusiastic internal and external support
   c. Is there a goal in terms of market position?
   No
2. Strategies, Business Priorities for the Year, Critical Issues for the Year:
   a. What are the specific strategies or business priorities for the year, in order of priority?
   Double-digit growth in sales and profit
   b. What must we accomplish this year to remain competitive?
   Increase use and knowledge of technology
   c. What critical issues face the organization today?
   Better utilization of technology to increase productivity without additional headcount
   d. What critical issues face the organization in the future?
   Successful integration of systems consulting team into organization; make sure we have the right vendor; controlling costs
3. Business Information:
   a. Are any acquisitions or growth anticipated?
   Always keeping an eye open for a good growth opportunity. Possible increases in personnel relating to systems consulting
   b. Are there any changes in business markets in the future?
   Networked products
   c. Who are our customers?
   For systems consulting, they are small to medium size businesses that have no dedicated IT staff

d. What makes customers buy from us versus the competition?
Better service and training resulting in better utilization of products purchased; taking care of customer needs at a fair price; accurate billing; making them loyal customers

e. What are your basis product lines?
Canon for copiers and fax; systems consulting offers multiple choices on computer products

f. What has the growth rate been over the past several years?
13.4% last year

g. How many employees are at your location?
77

4. Industry:
   a. What share of the market do you have?
   Not sure
   b. What industry associations of affiliations do you participate in?
   Copier Dealers Association (CDA), Young Presidents Organization (YPO), Chamber of Commerce, Rotary. All managers maintain some type of affiliation
   c. What trends, developments or changes are taking place in your industry?
   Transition to digital technology, connectivity. Customers are increasingly technical, which requires higher degree of technical skills in sales and service. Purchasing wanting price versus IT wanting functionality/technology
   d. What competitive advantages do you currently have?
   We offer value, knowledge and integrity; well-trained staff
5. External Factors:
   a. Are there any external environmental factors?
   The economy; job market
   b. What challenges do you face in the marketplace?
   Price versus value
6. Internal Strengths and Weaknesses:
   a. What are the internal strengths of your organization?
   We have a planning process in place and it is communicated throughout the organization; corporate buying power

b. What internal challenges, opportunities or threats exist in your organization?
Integrating systems consulting data into OMD systems

7. Information Technology (IT):

a. What is IT currently doing well?
Listening to concerns and helping people understand why things are the way they are. Training is going well.

b. What areas must IT improve?
Taking time out to communicate and not just wait for a problem to develop

c. What do you know about the IT of your competition?
Aside from Ikon and Xerox, we are well ahead of our local competition.

William Bruen, President
Bandon, Inc., Phoenix
(Corporate Headquarters)
Executive Management Interview

1. Charter, Mission:
Overall, the company has 495 employees. The mission for the corporate administration group is to "provide the operating divisions with centralized services that are cost effective, while assisting them in achieving their goals."

The guiding mission statement was published by Bandon executive management in 1993, but this philosophy has taken a back seat to the specific goals of each operating division.

The goals, objectives, and marketplace targets are a function of each operating division and are never rolled up into an overall target, but rather a "sum of the parts" rather than "the parts achieving the overall goal."

2. Strategic Business Priorities for current year:
From a corporate administrative viewpoint, there are a few priorities; but here,

too, these priorities are in support of the operating divisions:
Install the "e-mail" invoice/payment package
Continue the process improvement program regarding administrative procedures
Continue review of operating processes to control costs

3. Internal strengths/weakness:
The most significant strengths we have are our financial stability and our approach to the marketplace using a decentralized approach which allows us to address the market, with the centralized corporate back-office to minimize redundancy.

The largest weakness is we do not have a formal structure for doing administrative tasks, allowing each operating division to "do it its way," which creates redundancy and a higher cost structure.

The challenge, opportunity, and threat within the organization are to address the business as a whole and not a consolidation of several silos.

4. Information Technology (IT):
Based on our structure, IT has an ongoing challenge to keep the various operating divisions functioning within corporate guidelines.

The comparison of Bandon, Inc. versus the competitions' IT must be made by the operating divisions as they are closer to the customer and the market; based on what I know, we are with them or even ahead of them in some instances. I feel we have to address the IT process as a company-wide process to allow us to address the marketplace on a broad, cost-effective basis and not to develop programs specific to each division. We must keep our costs in line, or we will not remain competitive.

STEP 3: GOALS, CRITICAL SUCCESS FACTORS, MEASURES, IT NEEDS
Bandon Portland
Robert North, President

Goals	Critical Success Factors	Measures	IT Needs
Revenue growth from $23 M to $30 M	Ability to focus on higher-margin accounts; ability to merge critical account information with usage and industry-specific data	Account, profitability analysis; account potential versus actual reporting; customers using web-based services; customer contacts	Account profitability report (margins/customer); ability to track and measure potential; web-enabled customer support; improved invoicing; automated customer contact solution
Addressing the needs of 6,000 companies with > 25 employees in specifically targeted markets	Effective relationship building with customers; effective contact management; effective customer information gathering and utilization; strategic information added to database	New accounts, net adds, replacements; growth of information about accounts and industries; detailed information about non-customers	Sales and marketing data and marketing analysis reports; Better industry-specific information; Web-enabled access to information; PDA compatible solution for database, contacts, and calendars
Growth in market share in IT consulting business	Technical expertise; effective contact management	Growth of knowledge; growth of IT market share	Customer feedback; billing system for services; web-based tracking and reporting; invoicing solution that utilizes fax, e-mail, Internet, and paper invoices
Growth in services base	Effective customer service, product knowledge; need the ability to track prints, scans, and copies separately	Response time; efficient dispatching of service calls out to techs	Service management reports (response time); accurate cost tracking and reporting
Cost control	Accurate and timely billing; accurate and timely collections; effective sales support	Lack of customer complaints; less internal verification of reports	Better invoices; increase in collections; better tracking of accrual accounts

Bandon Phoenix
Richard Roberts, President
Goals, Critical Success Factors, Measures, IT Needs

Goals	*Critical Success Factors*	*Measures*	*IT Needs*
Revenue growth	Ability to attract new accounts; timely appointment setup; ability to identify new leads and emerging accounts; integration of sales leads with compensation processing	First Time Account (FTA) analysis; integration of D&B and iMarket industry database for targeted prospecting; sales forecasting; sales call/appointment setup; automated sales lead routing, and compensation processing	FTA Report: Integration of D&B and iMarket data with *Pivotal* database; call/appointment set-up; *Pivotal* Sales lead and compensation reports (e.g., automated e-mails, alerts triggered on completed appointments, close, payout)
Increase market share in document outsourcing, digital imaging, color graphics, facilities management	Effective relationship building with customers; effective contact management; value-added approach to marketing	New accounts, net adds, replacements	Sales and marketing data (e.g., account tracking)
Growth in market share in IT consulting	Technical expertise; effective contact management	Growth of knowledge; growth of IT services by service type	Customer feedback; accounting system for IT business consulting services
Growth in service base	Effective customer service; product knowledge; ability to anticipate service upgrades	Response time: efficient dispatching of service calls out to techs; service call tracking; service history analysis; automatic competitive and Bandon lease expiration information	Service management reports (e.g., response time, meter read alerts, excess service call alerts); customer service history reports; lease expiration reports
Administrative cost control; efficiency of administrative operations	Accurate and timely billing; accurate and timely collections; ability to offer web-based information services (e.g., meter reading submission, service call reporting); ability to provide electronic bill presentment; effective sales support	Lack of customer complaints; customer satisfaction	Better invoices; Increase in collections; web-based information services; electronic bill presentment

Bandon Salt Lake City
Edmund Scott, President
Goals, Critical Success Factors, Measures, IT Needs

Goals	Critical Success Factors	Measures	IT Needs
Grow business at the rate of 5%	Value-added package	Customer feedback	Customer feedback questionnaire
Increase profitability to 7% pre-tax	Accurate billing	Invoices that are easy to read and to understand	Redesign invoices
Improve service quality to customers	Average 4-hour response time; guaranteed 8-hour up-time	Better reporting (Mean Copies Between Failures); downtime; response time	Service management reports for customers
Cost reduction	Paperwork reduction	Efficiency of business processes	Cost study
Effective use of technology to support business processes	Integrated planning process	Cost savings	Cost study
Strong people development	Retention and development of key people	Turnover and retention data	HR study

Bandon Denver
John Werner, President
Goals, Critical Success Factors, Measures, IT Needs

Goals	Critical Success Factors	Measures	IT Needs
Double digit growth: $15 million by 2003	Value, knowledge, and integrity	Customer feedback	Customer feedback survey
Creating loyal customers	Accurate billing; better service	Customer feedback Response time	Redesign of invoices Service management reporting system (e.g., response time)
Effective relationship marketing	Better customer training resulting in better utilization of products purchased	Reduction of service calls per customer	Service management reports (e.g., #calls/copier)
Cost control	Effective use of technology to increase productivity without additional headcount; controlling costs	Administrative cost reduction	Cost study

Bandon Group (Corporate Headquarters)
William Bruen, Chief Financial Officer
Goals, Critical Success Factors, Measures, IT Needs

Goals	Critical Success Factors	Measures	IT Needs
Increase sales and revenue	Effective use of sales prospecting systems at the division level	Growth in high-margin accounts	Effective use of sales prospecting systems
Administrative cost control	Maintenance and continuous upgrades of back-office systems; standardization of business processes	Cost control	Upgrades to OMD
Increased customer service	Ability to provide web-based information services; ability to provide electronic invoicing	Customer satisfaction; timely receipt of accounts receivable	I-Manager (web-based information services), electronic invoicing system with electronic funds transfer
Increased market share	Ability to service accounts on a timely basis	Customer service history reports; service alerts	Service management reports (e.g., reports on excess copy volume, reports on excess service calls)
Increased use of information for strategic advantage	Timely reports for tactical and strategic management	Sales forecasting; marketing analysis; targeted marketing	Management information systems for sales, service, and new market development

STEP 4: IN-DEPTH INTERVIEWS: PROBLEMS, GOALS/OPPORTUNITIES, IT NEEDS, PRIORITIES
Bandon Portland
Interview with Robert North, Division President
and Management Team

	Problems	Goals/Opportunities	IT Needs
Sales	Lack of ability to generate needed information from OMD, which results in re-keying data into Excel spreadsheets in order to create reports	Design a sales management reporting system providing ad hoc queries and reports	A sales management reporting system (i.e., a front-end to OMD); a data warehousing solution for OMD data access and reporting
	Lack of access to signed leases for easy reference	Design a document imaging system for leases	A document imaging system for leases (.pdf)

(cont.)

	Problems	*Goals/Opportunities*	*IT Needs*
	Insufficient training in OMD	Improve OMD training	OMD training
	Insufficient training on sales prospecting and sales management reports	Improve training in sales prospecting	Provide training in making queries and generating reports for sales prospecting
	Lack of web-based services		Implement I-Manager, which provides web-based services
Service	Need ability to manipulate OMD data for useful reporting	Design a service management reporting system providing ad hoc queries and reports	A service management information system (a front-end to OMD)
	ADS (i.e., a phone-based system for recording completion of service calls) makes it necessary for technicians to close calls using the phone at the customer's site	Consider the feasibility of e-mailing service call reports	Evaluate the feasibility of providing service techs with laptops
	Technicians lack access to technical manuals in electronic format	Provide technical documentation in electronic format	Use laptops for access to technical manuals
Administration	Customers do not understand invoices; often, these invoices must be accompanied with spreadsheets with duplicate data in user-friendly format	Improve the readability of invoices	Reformat invoice data to provide customized invoices
	Would like to be able to query OMD to obtain data on a timely basis	Improve real-time access to OMD data for ad hoc queries and reporting	
	Lack of integration between on-line ordering to Canon and OMD	Improve interface between supplier ordering (e.g., Canon) and OMD	Create an interface between on-line ordering to Canon and OMD purchase order entry
IT-internal	Need to address desktop workstation issues: upgrades, virus protection, version control	Create a standardized desktop workstation environment	Standardize e-mail client software, operating systems, and desktop workstations
IT-external	Need a better systems to support IT consulting business (e.g., infrastructure development, document management, electronic document distribution, workflow automation)	Develop systems capabilities for new lines of business	Continuous evaluation of accounting tools for IT consulting business

Bandon Phoenix
Interview with Richard Roberts, Division President and Management Team

	Problems	*Goals/Opportunities*	*IT Needs*
Sales	Lack of an integrated system for sales prospecting (sales prospecting data are not integrated with back-office administrative information systems)	Increase sales to high-potential accounts	Integration between sales prospecting and administrative systems; extending the use of external industry databases for sales prospecting (e.g., Dun & Bradstreet, I-Market)
	Incompatible data between OMD and *Pivotal*		Migration of OMD data into a relational database
	Lack of effective account management reporting (e.g., thorough account review, analysis of how equipment is used)		Migration of OMD data into a data warehouse
Service	Lack of web-based process for meter reading		eBusiness front-end to OMD for meter reading submission (I-Manager)
	Lack of web-based customer interface for service-call reporting, service history	Provide web-based interfaces for Meter reading, service-call reporting, service history	eBusiness front-end for service-call reporting, service history
	Lack of service tech auditing and call tracking		GPS for service tech tracking
	Lack of real-time inventory		Bar code scanners for car stock inventory
	Lack of automatic alerts on meter increase/decrease data; lack of automatic alerts for service supervisors based upon excessive service calls (3 or more calls in 30 days)	Provide sales reps with real-time data on customer alerts (e.g., excess copier volume)	Creation of "suspect" activity report (e.g., machines running high on service calls)
Administration	Customers cannot easily understand invoices (e.g., lack of customized invoices)	Improve invoicing	Creation of an invoicing subsystem that provides effective invoices
	Some customers need electronic bill presentment		Electronic bill presentment
IT	Invoices do not serve the needs of the IT consulting business	Improve invoicing system for IT consulting	Creation of accounting system for IT consulting

Bandon Salt Lake City
Interview with Edmund Scott, Division President
and Management Team

	Problems	*Goals/Opportunities*	*IT Needs*
Sales	Lack of an integrated system for sales prospecting (current sales prospecting database is not integrated with OMD)	Increase sales to high-potential accounts	A sales and marketing analysis add-on to OMD
	Need sales analysis tools to identify customers where costs of sales and service are lower; need sales analysis tools to identify customers where costs of sales and service are higher		
Service	Lack of an automated process for meter reading (e.g., use fax server currently)	Increase efficiency of the meter reading process	eBusiness front-end to OMD for meter reading (I-Manager)
	Inability to flag copiers with excess copy volume	Provide sales reps with real-time data on customer alerts (e.g., excess copier volume)	
	Service dispatching does not have access to accounts receivable records	Provide service with real-time information on A/R (so, we do not provide service to accounts which have not paid)	
Administration	Customers cannot easily understand invoices (e.g., cannot get information such as number of copies/month/machine)	Improve invoicing	Creation of an invoicing subsystem that provides better information
	Inventory reports are difficult to understand (e.g., cannot associate parts with corresponding machines because there is no relationship in the database between parts and corresponding machines)	Improve inventory information	
IT	Difficulty in obtaining customer service data in an efficient manner	Need more timely customer service feedback	Create a web-based customer service questionnaire

Bandon Denver
Interview with John Werner, Division President and Management Team

	Problems	*Goals/Opportunities*	*IT Needs*
Sales	Need a user-friendly database that enables queries and reports (e.g., reports on high-potential accounts, customers with over-or-under target copy volume, other account information)	Provide access to account information	Development of sales prospecting database with ad hoc query and reporting capability
	Need access to leases via document imaging for timely access (.pdf files)	Provide access to leases via .pdf files	Access to leases via .pdf files, or access to lease invoices via the Bandon Group intranet site
	Customers need easy-to-read reports on meter reading	Provide customers with reports on meter reading	Implement OMD interface to retrieve meter readings for networked machines
	Need to update the Dun & Bradstreet database		Update the D and B database for sales prospecting
	Need to improve sales prospecting systems and software	Improve sales prospecting software	
	Lack of web-based information services (e.g., supply ordering, meter reading, service call reporting)	Evaluate the feasibility of web-based information services	Provide web-based information services (e.g., for web-based service calls, meter readings, supply ordering)
Service	Need a way to share vendor's technical updates	Provide service techs with access to vendor's technical updates	Create a CD repository of vendor's technical updates
	Lack of bar coding for parts inventory	Use bar coding for parts inventory	
	We can submit orders to vendors on-line, but then we need to re-key a duplicate purchase order into OMD	Create an interface between vendor's ordering system and OMD	Evaluate the feasibility of creating an interface between OMD to submit purchase orders electronically to suppliers directly from OMD
Administration	Invoices are difficult to understand	Provide customized invoices	Creation of a new invoicing system

(cont.)

	Problems	Goals/Opportunities	IT Needs
	Customers are requesting electronic bill presentment	Provide electronic bill presentment	Implement electronic bill presentment system, using a Forms package, which captures the invoice image and generates a .pdf or .tif file for print, fax, e-mail, or archiving
IT	Lack of coordination between information systems consulting and OMD data	Provide an accounting and invoicing system for IS consulting	Evaluate accounting software for IS consulting

Bandon Group
Interview with William Bruen, Chief Financial Officer and Management Team

	Problems	Goals/Opportunities	IT Needs
Sales	Need better sales prospecting capability	Strategic advantage can be gained through sales prospecting and marketing systems, mostly at the division level	Continuously update sales prospecting systems and software at the division level
	Back-office functions need to be continuously streamlined, consolidated	Back-office systems should be centralized to avoid redundancy	Continuously maintain and upgrade operational systems (OMD) at the corporate level
	Current accounting systems do not support IT consulting line of business	Develop a secondary accounting system for IT consulting line of business	Acquire an off-the-shelf accounting package for the IT consulting line of business (e.g., integrate summary level data with the main system)
	Lack of web-based information services	Evaluate a web-based meter reading tool	Acquire a product for web-based meter reading
Service	Need better information on copier volume versus electronic/laser printer volume on multi-function devices	OMD has a volume flag, by type of equipment (connected versus non-connected), by model, for multi-function devices, which provides information on copier volume versus laser print volume	Create a management reporting system to continuously assess copier volume versus laser print volume on multi-function devices

(cont.)

	Problems	*Goals/Opportunities*	*IT Needs*
	Need more effective service management reporting systems (e.g., excessive volume, excessive service calls)	Design service management reports that deal with these issues consistently (e.g., excess copier volume, excess service calls)	A service management reporting system using OMD data that provides timely alerts on excess copier volume, excess service calls
Administration	Invoices need to be improved	Electronic invoicing	Design an electronic invoicing system which supports payment processing via electronic funds transfer
IT external	IT consulting is in early phase of development (5% of overall sales)	Develop sales prospecting capabilities for IT line of business	Sales prospecting system; add-on an accounting system for IT consulting
IT internal	Lack of centralized licensing of desktop software (MS Office)	Standardization	Provide central licenses and upgrades for desktop software

Integrated Case Study: Bandon Group, Inc.

STEP 5: IT INFRASTRUCTURE, BANDON GROUP, INC.
Bandon Portland

- Desktop O/S Windows 98, 2K, and XP
- Server O/S NT4 and 2K
- Network is switched 10/100 (143 ports) and 100/1000 (19 ports)
- Internet access via DSL
- Domain, BANDON_PORTLAND

Bandon Denver

- Desktop O/S Windows 98, NT, 2K, and Apple 9, X
- Server O/S NT4, 2K, Netware 5.1, 6.0, and Mac X
- Network is switched Ethernet
- Internet access via DSL
- Domain BANDON_DENVER

Bandon Group, Inc. (Phoenix—Corporate Headquarters)

- Desktop O/S Windows NT4 and 2K
- Server O/S NT4 and HP-UX v10.20
- Network is switched 10/100 Ethernet
- Internet access T-1 w/ Symantec Raptor firewall
- Domain BGI
- Backup
  - Servers complete Mon, Tue, Wed, Thu, Fri (data safe)
  - Servers complete end of period (offsite)

Bandon Phoenix

- Desktop O/S W2K
- Server O/S NT4/2K
- Network Switched 10/100 Ethernet
- Internet access T-1 w/Cisco 2600 Router, firewall
- Domain BANDON_PHOENIX

Bandon Salt Lake City

- Desktop O/S W98, and W2K
- Server O/S NT4
- Network Switched 10/100 Ethernet
- Internet access via T-1
- Domain BANDON_SALTLAKE

Integrated Case Study: Bandon Group, Inc.

STEP 7: LIST OF IT PRIORITIES, BANDON GROUP AND DIVISIONS AND SOFTWARE SYSTEMS SUPPORT

TABLE 1	List of IT Priorities				
IT Need	*Bandon Portland*	*Bandon Salt Lake City*	*Bandon Group Corporate*	*Bandon Denver*	*Bandon Phoenix*
Sales					
Ad hoc query ability					
Relational database					
Lease documents in Adobe format					
Lease invoices in Adobe format					
Electronic meter-reading capture					
Desktop application software					
Import D&B data					
Customer web access (I-Manager)					
Remote access					
User-defined fields					
Sales prospecting tools					

(cont.)

IT Need	Bandon Portland	Bandon Salt Lake City	Bandon Group Corporate	Bandon Denver	Bandon Phoenix
Service					
Remote access via laptop					
Technical updates via CD					
Electronic purchase order interface					
GPS tracking for service technicians					
Suspect service activity reporting					
Management reporting for service (e.g., excess volume)					
Administration					
Customize invoice format					
Electronic invoicing capabilities					
Billing for technology services					
Central licensing of desktop software					

Index